From Archetype
to Zeitgeist

From Archetype to Zeitgeist

Powerful Ideas for Powerful Thinking

by Herbert Kohl

with the assistance of Erica Kohl
and Dee Garner, Antonia Kohl, Joshua Kohl, and Megan Marsnik

illustrated by Deborah Hohenberg, Madeline Kibbe, Antonia Kohl,
Joshua Kohl, Haruko Nishimura, and William Zindel

Little, Brown and Company
Boston Toronto London

For Judy with love

First Edition

Art credits: Deborah Hohenberg, pages 59, 125, 191, 200; Madeline Kibbe, pages 6, 36, 42, 51, 88, 127, 155 (bottom), 159, 172, 182, 187, 209; Antonia Kohl, pages 13, 82, 155 (top), 195; Joshua Kohl, pages 14, 113, 116, 126, 132, 134, 160, 198, 212, 225; Haruko Nishimura, pages 184, 203; William Zindel, pages 7, 11, 29, 35, 52, 92, 137, 197.

Library of Congress Cataloging-in-Publication Data

Kohl, Herbert.
    From archetype to zeitgeist: powerful ideas for powerful thinking / by Herbert Kohl ; with the assistance of Erica Kohl and Dee Garner . . . [et al.]. — 1st ed.
        p.   cm.
    Includes bibliographical references (p.   ) and index.
    ISBN 0-316-50138-7
    1. Encyclopedias and dictionaries.   I. Kohl, Erica.   II. Title.
AG105.K64   1992
031 — dc20   91-37658

10 9 8 7 6 5 4 3 2 1

RRD-VA

Printed in the United States of America

It is the fate of those who toil at the lower employments of life, to be rather driven by the fear of evil, than attracted by the prospect of good; to be exposed to censure, without hope of praise; to be disgraced by miscarriage, or punished for neglect, where success would have been without applause, and diligence without reward.

Among these unhappy mortals is the writer of dictionaries; whom mankind have considered, not as the pupil, but the slave of science, the pioneer of literature, doomed only to remove rubbish and clear obstructions for the paths through which Learning and Genius press forward to conquest and glory, without bestowing a smile on the humble drudge that facilitates their progress. Every other author may aspire to praise; the lexicographer can only hope to escape reproach; and even this negative recompense has been yet granted to very few.

Dr. Samuel Johnson
Preface to *The English Dictionary*

Contents

Acknowledgments

I would like to thank Antonia Kohl, Erica Kohl, and Joshua Kohl who helped me research many of the entries in this book and who helped with all the tedious details of keeping track of the hundreds of definitions, word lists, and references that went into the making of this guide. Their extensive written research reports provided the basic material used in many definitions.

I particularly want to thank Erica for how much I learned in the hours of conversations we had on the nuances of meaning involved in many of the words included here. She provided insight into current academic debates in sociology and critical thinking that was very helpful in showing me how to shape the entries. She also wrote preliminary versions of a number of the definitions, though she bears no blame for the inadequacies that I might have added in the final revisions.

I also want to thank Dee Garner and Megan Marsnik, two students of mine at Hamline University in St. Paul, Minnesota, who helped research some of the words listed in the guide. In addition, a number of other students and faculty at Hamline helped me shape the list of words. The university, through the Gordon B. Sanders Chair in Education, generously provided me with research support and time to work on this book.

I taught a freshman seminar at Hamline that focused on the language of intellectual discourse and the students in that seminar helped me test ideas that I've worked into the book. I thank them for the opportunity we had to spend a delightful semester exploring the meaning of words.

Tracy MacDonald also helped me out toward the end of the work on this book and was very helpful at just the right time.

Finally, Judy Kohl shared the making of this book with me as she has with all of my work, and was always there to push it to conclusion when I was ready to throw up my hands and give in to the comments of many people who had told me that individuals shouldn't embark on writing this kind of book.

Introduction

Why a Guide to the Language of Ideas?

I began thinking about writing this guide to the language of ideas because high school and college students I taught did not have a vocabulary adequate to express their ideas. They stumbled over describing a style, criticizing a political position, discussing a social problem, or analyzing their own values. It was clear to me that the problem was not intelligence so much as lack of vocabulary and inexperience with using language well. At first I tried having my students use dictionaries, but that didn't work. Dictionary definitions were too brief and didn't provide enough information on how words work in context to help them speak and write well. I began writing short essays on words such as *race, culture,* and *ideology* and sharing them with my students. These essays became the basis for class discussions and for the broadening of my students' thinking and writing.

At that stage I began to think about my own vocabulary and that of my friends. Words such as *postmodern, deconstruction, paradigm,* and *irony* appeared in journals and magazines, and slipped into our vocabularies, sometimes uncritically. I began to investigate the history and uses of these words and to write mini-essays about them as well. As I shared them with friends it became clear that the guide to the language of ideas that I had begun to work on could be as useful to well-educated readers seeking to improve their understanding of ideas and concepts as to students who needed to master these concepts for the first time. In this time of the frequent abasement of language and careless disregard for ideas, it became clear to me that a guide to the language of ideas can contribute to the persistence of intelligence and the encouragement of intelligent discourse.

This language consists of core concepts that are used in analyzing, writing, and talking about ideas. Each academic area of study has its own key words and special vocabulary, which often have meanings that either differ from the ones they have in conversational usage or are not part of ordinary language. For example, in philosophy words and phrases such as *epistemological, falsification, ontological,* and *logical truth* are particular to the field and it's assumed that everyone who speaks within that field understands their meanings. The same holds true in literary criticism (e.g., *genre, deconstruction,* and *canon*), sociology (e.g., *anomie, hegemony,* and *stratification*), anthropology (e.g., *acculturation, assimilation,* and *diffusion*), and all the other subject areas that have been separated out as independent areas of study in Western European and U.S. universities.

In addition to concepts and ideas closely linked to different subject areas, there is also a more general language of ideas that crosses over subject areas and that is assumed to be understood as part of the intellectual apparatus of educated people. It contains words such as *deduction, induction, style, inference, geist, reductionist,* and *parameter*.

The language of ideas is not static. New words are constantly being created to represent new ways of organizing experience and new ideas. Over the past forty years, for example, cybernetics, ergonomics, and ecology have become major areas of speculation and study, and whole new vocabularies have been created in order to facilitate communication within these fields.

There is, however, a major problem even well-educated people confront in mastering the language of ideas, a problem that has led to the creation of this book: The language of ideas and the language of ordinary discourse are not the same. The language of ideas is not learned informally through casual conversation. Nor is it learned from listening to the media. Somehow it is expected that the complex and sophisticated language of ideas will be absorbed through reading, listening, and perhaps some mystical forms of osmosis. As soon as one gets to college, however, knowledge of the language of ideas is assumed. Few professors spell out the key concepts and ideas that are presupposed for understanding their fields, and many freshmen get lost in a sea of strange words during their first few months of college. Some never get their linguistic and conceptual bearings and fake it throughout their college careers and beyond. They use words they hear their professors using, but without a clear sense of the nuances of meaning and the correctness of usage that are needed to speak and write well. In effect, students imitate the language of ideas as best they can to pass tests without ever developing the fluent use of complex ideas and concepts that can lead to clear and sensitive thinking.

It is not the fault of students that so many of them do not learn to speak about ideas easily and well when they are not adequately prepared to think and be articulate about their thoughts. This book is an attempt to be explicit about the language of ideas, to provide definitions of concepts that are needed in order to be articulate both within the humanities and social sciences, both at college and later in life when thinking about important issues such as race, gender, power, pain, and politics. The definitions provided here attempt to demystify ideas and concepts and explain them in ordinary language whenever possible. Examples drawn from everyday life are often provided in order clarify particularly complex ideas.

The inspirations for this guide are twofold. One is my love of dictionaries. Language has always been alive and magical for me and I actually enjoy reading and collecting dictionaries. My first dictionary was read to me by my aunt Addie when I was almost three and I remember feeling that each new word I learned was like growing an inch. I could understand adult conversations better, make sense out of the words that came over the radio, and think wider thoughts because of what I learned from the dictionary. The idea of writing a dictionary always seemed presumptuous and slightly wicked to me, though when I discovered and fell in love with Eric Partridge's *Origins* many years ago, I realized it was possible for a person to write a dictionary. *Origins* is one of the ten books I would take with me to a desert island.

In 1985 when our family spent a year in London I was a reader at the British Library where many great scholars and thinkers studied and wrote. There were a number of desks used by these people at the library which are places of homage. Karl Marx's desk, for example, was reverently visited by people from all over the world. When I learned that Eric Partridge had a desk at the library and did research and writing on his dictionaries there, that desk, or rather the place where it was, became a thinking place for me. That's when I first thought that someday I might write a modest, useful dictionary that filled a need not filled by other dictionaries.

The second inspiration was a class I taught in 1987 on civics, sociology, and economics. What I discovered was that my students did not have the language to communicate their thoughts, feelings, and opinions to me or to each other. They had not acquired, with some exceptions, ease and fluency discussing ideas. They did not, for example, have a way to discuss differences in style, political orientation, or philosophical belief. They had little sense of comparative political and economic structures, and had not acquired a critical vocabulary that was useful for analyzing what they read. In fact they were not accustomed to analyzing different positions on issues that affected their lives even though they were concerned about them. They wanted to think and speak about environmental issues, about war and peace, race and gender, and the feelings they had of alienation and fear about the future. In conversation they often seemed inarticulate, but I saw them as silenced. In their school there was little discussion of ideas; they were merely expected to get through the textbooks. Few of their classes gave them a sense that there were ways to think and talk about important issues, or that there were thinkers who attempted to provide structures and language for the intelligent analysis of experience.

During the course of the year we were together, I found it very useful to teach ideas and words directly. I believe the students found it useful and know that by the end of our time together they could speak specifically of what was on their minds rather than just express general approval or disapproval. Terms like *cool* and *far out* began to be replaced with more measured and thoughtful language. I remember, for example, introducing the concept of a double bind to the group and listening as they put words to painful situations they had merely suffered before and began to speculate on ways of undoing neurotic knots. The same thing happened when I introduced the concept of fallacious reasoning and gave examples of a number of classical fallacies. These ideas were immediately applicable to analyzing contemporary political speeches and enabled the students to be precise in countering glib and deceptive arguments.

The Organization and Use of This Book

Most dictionaries are organized alphabetically. That is because dictionaries are commonly used when problems with word meaning or spelling arise. People don't read dictionaries through, or study them as texts. Rather, they wait until an unfamiliar word or questionable spelling arises in the course of reading or writing and then look up the appropriate meaning or the correct spelling. In order to accommodate that use, a list of all the words defined in this book is provided at the end of the book. *The list gives the page number of the definition,* so that the book can be used, like most dictionaries, to look up unfamiliar words that are encountered in reading or conversation. However, a guide to ideas cannot be used in exactly the same way that a comprehensive dictionary of English is used. First of all, the number of words is limited. Second, the listings are longer and more detailed than the ones you'll find in an ordinary dictionary. If you just want to check spelling, or get a quick take on a meaning, it's better to use one of the more common comprehensive dictionaries such as the *American Heritage Dictionary of American English, Webster's Collegiate Dictionary, The Random House Dictionary of American English,* or the *Shorter Oxford English Dictionary.*

This book will be particularly useful when you read material in a new field of study, or encounter words that represent ideas or philosophical concepts that you want to understand in order to read and speak intelligently in that field. Skipping over such words, or settling for abbreviated impressions of their meaning, can lead to misunderstanding. This book is meant to be a positive learning tool and help you understand the concepts and vocabularies used to discuss ideas in the humanities, literature and the arts, and the social sciences. Because of that, the definitions themselves have been organized according to major areas of human inquiry and the book can be studied as an introduction to ways of thinking about ideas and concepts. Here is an overview of the organizational structure of the book:

The Arts
Literature
Religion
Philosophy
Logic and Reasoning
Critical Thinking
Anthropology and Linguistics
Sociology
Psychology
Economics
Political Science

Because of this structure, the book can be used in the following ways:

to prepare yourself to do research on a specific subject or read a text in a given academic field

The book can help you get a grasp on the vocabulary of a field that you intend to read in. For example, if you are going to read a book of contemporary literary criticism, it makes sense to read the entries on literature and perhaps also on critical thinking; if you're going to do research on racial conflict, it makes sense to read the entries on political science and sociology. This should help familiarize you with the basic concepts in the field you are interested in, and give you a sense of the kinds of questions and explanations that characterize it.

to serve as a companion to accompany reading of magazines and books

The vocabulary of ideas shifts as new issues, philosophies, and values emerge. Magazines and journals often adapt themselves to these linguistic shifts without explicitly preparing readers. Thus, the vocabularies of ergonomics, ecology, postmodernism, critical theory, feminism, etc. all have surfaced fairly recently in books and journals. People not directly involved in these debates on an academic level and yet who feel a need to be knowledgeable about them can use the guide to the language of ideas to acquaint themselves with the contexts in which these clusters of words and ideas arose and are used. The book can be used concurrently with reading magazines and journals as diverse as *The New York Review of Books, The Nation, The New Republic, The National Review,* and *The Atlantic.* All of these publications, for example, have recently published articles discussing multiculturalism, affirmative action, and literary and academic canons. This guide to the language of ideas has sections on all of these issues and can help you make a more informed assessment of these disagreements.

to learn new vocabulary and new concepts

This book can be used to add to your vocabulary and introduce you to unfamiliar concepts. One way to do this is to pick a category and try to learn a new word or concept a day, or refresh yourself on words and concepts you are familiar with but haven't thought much about. Take fifteen or twenty minutes a day to study ideas and words. Get a notebook. When you settle on a word to learn, read the dictionary definition and then write your own definition of the word in the notebook. Then write a sentence using the word or draw a picture that embodies the meaning of the word. Don't try to memorize the dictionary definition. Instead, try to internalize that definition and make it your own.

Start each word on a new page. If, in the course of your reading, you come upon a particularly interesting usage of a word in your notebook, copy that sentence on the page where the word appears. This is a good way to internalize the use of idea words and should have a beneficial effect on your own writing. I have done this for years and found it time well spent. It makes a wider range of literature accessible and develops critical reading and thinking habits.

Finally, this book can be used as a text for high school or college classes on the language of ideas, or as a supplementary text in introductory humanities, literature, and social sciences classes. It can also be used as a text for ideas discussion groups and high school seminars on how to take control of the language of college learning.

I taught a freshman seminar at Hamline University which consisted of studying the words in this book, category by category. The class was meant to prepare students for the language they would encounter in the course of their studies at the university. Even more important, it was meant to help them develop ideas and concepts that could aid them in analyzing their experiences and understanding events that were affecting their lives. It was an attempt to provide them with tools to become intelligent citizens and thoughtful people.

According to students I've talked to during the years after the course, they felt that knowing how to speak about ideas was useful across the curriculum and even more useful in understanding some of the happenings of these turbulent and unpredictable times. They also indicated that they were surprised at how pervasive the language of ideas is, and how there is a core vocabulary that is used throughout the humanities and social sciences that, once mastered, gives you a way in to understanding texts, arguments, and even events.

I believe that the intelligent and sensitive use of language is a necessary survival skill and an indispensable part of responsible democratic living. I hope this book will contribute a bit to helping people think and speak carefully and sensitively about ideas, and help them articulate intelligent solutions to the serious long-range problems we all must confront if our planet is to remain habitable.

Providing a vocabulary that will help one get by in college and in later life is only one part of what I hope this book will achieve. My main goal for this book is to make words available that will help people describe, analyze, and understand the complexities and nuances of their experience.

Having words to express what one feels and thinks is a way of stepping outside of one's experience and reflecting on it in order to manage it sensibly. Learning a word for a new idea is not just a matter of being able to answer a vocabulary test or sound intelligent on a term paper. It is a way of expanding one's ways of thinking and becoming liberated from other people's ideas and other people's judgments and, most crucially, other people's language. It is a way of learning to speak fully in one's own voice about the world as it is and as it might be.

Pronunciation Guide

ə   about, column, balloon

'ə, ˌə   someone, rebut

ə   before l, n, m, n: settle, them, rotten, fish and chips

ər   hamburger, third

'ər   worry, furry

a   hat, sad, rag, nap, catch

ā   grape, tray, ade, sedate, atheist

ä   rot, dart, bother, father

au̇   out, sauerkraut

b   bone, crib

ch   church, teacher

d   die, dad, sadder

e   fetch, wreck, federal

'ē, ˌē   seed, read, emotion

ē   truly, sleazy

f   fine, enough, fluff

g   go, hug

h   hum, ahead

hw   while, as pronounced by speakers who do not pronounce *while* the same as *wile* or *whale* the same as *wail*

i   if, vanish, trivial

ī   fight, ride, try, buy

j   juicy, genius, joy, hedge

k   kiss, candy, school, ache

k̲   rare sound in English, German **Ich** leibe dich, Scottish lo**ch**

l   lovely, cruel

m   memory, symphony, trim

n   new, nonagenarian, know

ŋ   ring, singer, finger, sink

ō   alone, crow, bureau

ȯ   draw, fall, bought, taught

ȯi   loin, convoy

p   pretend, up, supper

r   rare, around, arrest, for

s   sauce, sassy, mess

sh   she, tissue, artificial, machine

t   to, attitude, bet, date

th   theory, both

t̲h̲   the, bother

ü   union, youth, sensual, few

u̇   full, wood, look, durable, fury

v   voice, survive

w   war, aware

y   yesterday, you, cute

z   zip, ozone, praise

zh   television

'word   marks a syllable with primary stress:

word,   marks a syllable with secondary stress

-   indicates syllable division

The Arts

The distinction between *abstract* and *representational* applies primarily to twentieth-century painting and sculpture. Ever since Wassily Kandinsky (1866–1944), Sonia Delaunay (1885–1979), Kazimir Malevich (1878–1935), Piet Mondrian (1872–1944), and other painters began experimenting with "subjectless" painting around 1910, a continuing tradition of paintings that represent nothing other than themselves has developed. In this tradition, the work of abstract art is a self-contained object whose effect upon the viewer depends solely on the work and has no reference to objects or events or people in the world beyond the surface of the work. Though originating with painting, the idea of abstract (or nonrepresentational as it is sometimes called) art has spread to sculpture, collage, and even film and video.

Some abstract art consists of formal studies in color or form. Other abstract art attempts to express emotion through the use of color and form and has therefore been called abstract expressionism. Kandinsky's later paintings were explicit attempts to express emotions through the use of color and form. He had been influenced by the **expressionists,** who used color and the exaggeration of shape and form to put extreme emotion into the landscapes and people they represented in their paintings. Kandinsky used their techniques, but in a way that eliminated explicit representation and tried to get at abstract emotion divorced of content.

Just after the Second World War, a number of American and European painters, including Lee Krasner (1908–1984), Jackson Pollock (1912–1956), Mark Rothko (1903–1970), Franz Kline (1910–1962), Robert Motherwell (1915–1991), Willem de Kooning (1904–), Clyfford Still (1904–1980), Hans Hofmann (1880–1966), and Philip Guston (1913–1980) began experimenting with the abstract expression of emotion and, though their work differs considerably, have been grouped together by art historians as abstract expressionists. They have also been called the New York School. Pollack, in particular, has been called an action painter because in his later work he moved around and flung paint on the canvas, getting the action of the painting into the rhythm of the painted canvas to come closer to expressing the desired emotion.

Representational art is art with a subject, art with reference to things and people in the world beyond the work itself. Nonrepresentational art has no subject other than the canvas itself or the emotion it is sometimes intended to convey. With the exception of decorative art, whose purpose is to embellish a surface, such as a wall or the exterior of a building, without any representational function,

abstract

'ab-,strakt,'ab,

adj [from Latin *abstractus,* drawn off, from *ab,* away + *trahere,* to draw]

representational

,rep-ri-,zen-'tā-shnəl,-shən-ᵊl

adj [from Latin *repraesent,* from *re,* again + *praesentare,* to present] most of the art of the world up to the twentieth century had been representational.

baroque

bə-'rōk, ba-, -'räk, 'rȯk

adj, n [French, from Italian *barocco*; from Portuguese *barrôco*]

There are at least two contrasting accounts of the derivation of the word *baroque*: one claims that the word comes from the Portuguese word *barrôco*, which is used to describe an irregularly shaped pearl; the second, that it comes from the Italian word *barocco*, which is the name of an elaborate and complex form of logical argument. *Baroque* refers to a style of visual arts that flourished in Europe and in Spanish- and Portuguese-dominated Latin America from roughly 1600 to 1750. The word is also used to refer to the music composed during that period, which has some of the same **stylistic** characteristics.

The baroque style is characterized by intricate ornamentation, realistic detail, the elaboration of simple forms into more complex involuted ones, and the portrayal of people and animals in motion: twisted, curving, and slightly distorted. This type of painting and sculpture can be seen either as a reaction against the proportion and balance found in much of **Renaissance** art or an extension of it into the realm of exaggeration.

The sculptures and architecture of Gian Lorenzo Bernini (1598–1680) were dominant influences in the period. The sculptures, such as his *Ecstasy of St. Theresa* in Rome and his bust of Louis XIV in Versailles, were characterized by realistic detailing and exaggerated posing that portrayed intense emotion as well as the subject's inner life. The architecture, which used light in dramatic ways and was often monumental in scale, influenced buildings, fountains, and public squares in Europe and Latin America throughout the seventeenth century.

The paintings of Peter Paul Rubens (1577–1640) were also influential and are examples of the baroque at its most powerful. Rubens's figures are often portrayed in the midst of dramatic activity. Facial expressions reveal intense emotion, and bodies are twisted and shaped to express physical exertion and motion.

Compared with the preceding **mannerist** and Renaissance styles of the fifteenth and sixteenth centuries, baroque style is more open and emotional. Though it combines naturalistic, classical, and decorative elements, it does so within the framework of unbounded space and often frenzied activity. It is a busy world, not a calm one.

Some baroque art displays a sensitive feeling for the wonders of nature. This is perhaps an artistic reflection of the scientific explorations and discoveries of the seventeenth century. During the baroque period the development of the telescope opened up the skies and the microscope opened up the world of the minuscule. Landscape became a separate subject of the artist's concern for the first time. Natural space was portrayed and the details of light and shade were emphasized, as were the mysteriousness and the spiritual aspects of nature. This mysteriousness and the power of shadows and nuances of light characterized the paintings of the Dutch baroque master Rembrandt van Rijn (1606–1669).

In the eighteenth century, baroque style became exaggerated. Details were elaborated ever more finely and a decorative style of art called **rococo** evolved.

One distinctive characteristic of music in the baroque period was the conscious separation of different **genres** of music for different performance contexts. The three most usual genres were church, chamber, and theater music. The baroque period also saw the development of complex patterned music with many different harmonized instrumental voices held together rhythmically by an accompanying bass line. Composers such as Johann Sebastian Bach (1685–1750) and George Frideric Handel (1685–1759) were active during the baroque period.

When the word *baroque* is used as an adjective to refer to a style independent of reference to a historical period, the word means elaborate, flowing, and full of flourishes and curves. Baroque thinking is full of elaborate arguments, historical references, and polysyllabic words.

classical

'klas-i-kəl

adj [from Latin *classicus,* of the highest class of Roman citizens, of the first rank]

The word *classical* is used to refer to a style of art and a way of thinking. More specifically, it refers to the historical periods in Greece from approximately 400 to 350 B.C., when that style was developed, and in Rome from approximately 50 B.C. to A.D. 50, when it was imitated and elaborated on. Classical thought and art are characterized by rationality, logic, balance, idealized beauty, perfected form, and clarity. In Western Europe from the renaissance of the fifteenth century on, many scholars considered the classical style to embody universal principles of beauty and eternal truths. All other styles were measured by how they compared to the classical works of Greece and Rome.

Classicism is contrasted with romanticism, and the classical style with the **romantic** style, which emphasizes inspiration, imagination, spontaneity, naturalness, and passion.

People who work in the classical style proceed by analyzing a subject into its constituent parts and then abstracting the essential elements in order to formulate universal laws of form and structure. These laws are then used to create a work which is seen as an instance of a perfect universal form. Thus a person in a classical sculpture or painting is to be seen not as the image of a particular individual or god, but as a purified and abstracted ideal type of person or god; the shape of a particular building will be an instance of an idealized perfect building.

The ideal model of classical art is the temple of the Parthenon, which was constructed from 447 to 432 B.C. Some of the main characteristics of that work are an idealized conception of the human form and its proportions, and a serene, godlike, and detached bearing.

The elevation of Greek style to universal status has led to the development of the concept of "classic" human creations ranging all the way from sculpture and painting to wines and cars. Claiming that a car or wine is classic, for example, is to attribute to it beauty and perfection that transcends time. It is also to claim that this beauty emerges from elegant simplicity, fine design, and balance that creates a form that does not diminish with time.

The classical styles of Greece and Rome have often been cited in Western European history as the inspiration for contemporary work that emphasizes balance, proportion, rationality, and claims to universality. This work is said to be neoclassical. There have been a number of neoclassical periods in European history. The **Renaissance** claimed inspiration from the nature of Greek and Roman art and from the secular and humanistic ideas of Greek philosophy. Two other such periods in European history were the mid-seventeenth and mid-eighteenth centuries. The neoclassical painter Nicolas Poussin (1594–1665) was active during the first period and Jean Auguste Domique Ingres (1780–1867) was active during the second period. Both consciously elaborated on the balance and clarity of classical Greek art in their canvases.

In late eighteenth- and early nineteenth-century Germany, the classical ideal was developed into an ideology that claimed Western European culture was rooted in Greek culture. The writings of Wilhelm von Humboldt (1767–1835), who was the Prussian minister of education, were particularly influential in placing the idea that classical Greece was the starting point of European culture in school curriculums. Greece was portrayed as a miraculous fount of creativity that was not influenced at all by Asiatic and African sources, and was superior to all other prior human expressions. This assumption has played a very strong role in defining European consciousness and has been used in arguments that have attempted to justify **imperialism, colonialism,** and **racism** over the last two centuries.

Only recently has the idea of a classical Greece without African and Asian influence been questioned, and many scholarly (though heated) debates rage over the degree to which Greece was influenced by other cultures.

Part of the ideology of classical Greek superiority is the belief that works of art from different cultures and historical periods can be ranked in order of superiority and value. A work that is judged by European (and more recently American) experts to be of the highest nature (approximating the perfection of the classical Greeks) becomes a classic of Western civilization. Knowledge of these classics is considered, by some, to be a necessity for an educated person, and their inclusion in educational curriculums is standard.

The question of who judges what is and is not a classic is a difficult and cantankerous one. There is no explicit agreement on who qualifies to define high culture, and many scholars and other educated people question the justification for such ranking of writings and works of art. The criteria used to include or exclude works from the body, or **canon**, of works considered to be classic is also being challenged. (For a more detailed discussion of choosing the classics, see the entry **canon**.)

A collage is a picture created by gluing a combination of materials such as cloth, newspaper, magazine cutouts, wood veneer, string, and colored paper to a canvas or board. Often these fragments are combined with painting. Collages are also called *pâpiers collés*, though *pâpiers collés* implies that only paper is used, while a collage may utilize a wider range of materials. Georges Braque (1882–1963) is credited with making the first collage. Pablo Picasso (1881–1973), who collaborated with Braque at this time, soon began creating collages also.

Since the early work of Braque and Picasso, collage has become a widely used technique and is even in the repertoire of kindergarten arts and crafts.

The idea of collage, of bringing together bits and fragments of ordinary materials that contrast with each other to create a single work of art, has taken on a more generalized meaning. There are collaged poems utilizing bits and fragments of scraps from various kinds of printed matter and overheard conversations, as well as collaged videos, films, and pieces of music.

The word *assemblage* was used by the French painter Jean Dubuffet (1901–1985) in the late 1940s to distinguish his own works, in which pieces of paper and other objects are glued together and

collage

kə-'läzh, kȯ, kō-

n [from French *coller,* to glue]

painted to build thick three-dimensional surfaces on top of a canvas, from collages. The word *assemblage* has since taken on an expanded meaning, referring to an artistic movement in the United States and Europe of the 1950s and 1960s, in which everyday objects are assembled on canvas or in three-dimensional structures. These assemblages often satirize or display the horrors of modern urban, mechanized society.

Examples of such works are the machines of Jean Tinguely (1925–1991), which self-destruct; the constructions of Louise Nevelson (1900–1988), which have mysterious interiors; and the painting-constructions of Robert Rauschenberg (1925–) and Jasper Johns (1930–), which use images and photos from popular culture.

cubism

'kyü-,biz-əm

n [from Latin *cubus,* from Greek *kybos,* cube]

Cubism is the name given to the form of painting developed by Georges Braque (1882–1963) and Pablo Picasso (1881–1973) in France during the years 1908 through 1911. It is characterized by the reduction of landscapes, still lifes, and people to basic geometric forms, especially the cylinder, cone, and pyramid; the simultaneous representation of many different views of the same person or object; the use of intersecting planes rather than traditional perspective; and, beginning around 1908, the pasting of newsprint, wallpaper, string, and paper painted to look like wood, brick, and stone on to the canvas. This latter characteristic led to the development of collage as an art form.

A 1907 exhibit of the last works of the French painter Paul Cézanne (1839–1906), which consisted of landscapes reduced to the essential geometric forms that constituted them, is said to have been a strong influence on both Braque and Picasso. For Picasso, there was the additional influence of the African masks and statuary he was studying around the turn of the century. These works of art used techniques of simplification and of unfolding surfaces to reconstruct them to show simultaneous views of the same object.

Another influencing factor in the development of cubism was a rejection of painting that created the illusion of reality by selecting out a single view of a scene and subjecting it to the strict rules of perspective. For Picasso and Braque these rules, created in the **Renaissance,** provided the illusion of three-dimensional reality while only showing a single view of a three-dimensional object. They wanted to encompass more of reality in their work through showing the insides, outsides, fronts, and backs of things all at the same time.

During 1912 and 1913 the techniques of representation developed by Braque and Picasso were taken up by the Spanish painter Juan Gris (1887–1927) and the French painter Fernand Léger (1881–1955), who elaborated on them in distinct styles of their own. By the 1920s there was an international cubist movement and a distinctly cubist style.

*D*ada is the French word for hobbyhorse. It became the name of an irreverent movement in the arts which began in February 1916 in Zurich, Switzerland, when a group of young artists and cabaret performers picked that word at random out of a French dictionary. The individual who actually made the random choice was Tristan Tzara (1896–1963), a Romanian artist who along with the French artist Jean Arp (1887–1966) and others made up the original Dada group. Later on the work of the French painters Marcel Duchamp (1887–1968) and Francis Picabia (1879–1953), and the United States artist Man Ray (1890–1976) became associated with Dada.

Dada was antirational and revolted against prettiness and polite upper-class arts. It also rejected **cubism** and other forms of serious experimentation in the arts.

Dada was resolutely antiserious and mocked the arrogance of many artists and intellectuals. Its central driving force was a rejection of pretension of all sorts.

There were Dada exhibits held in public toilets and Dadaists were known to specialize in antilogical behavior such as staging mock fighting and fainting and vomiting in public places, and parading around in outrageous clothes chanting meaningless syllables. During World War I Dada was also antiwar, and Dada performances and art works ridiculed war.

Dada

'däd-(ˌ)ä

n [French, hobbyhorse]

*E*xpressionism was a movement in painting, music, literature, and theater that began in Germany at the turn of the twentieth century and reached its height in the 1920s. Two groups of German painters, the Bridge (die Bruche), founded in 1911, and the Blue Rider (der Blaue Reiter), founded in 1905, are credited with developing the tone and styles of the movement.

Ernst Ludwig Kirchner (1880–1938) and Emil Nolde (1867–1956) were prominent members of the Bridge. Their work was characterized by a use of bright, almost shocking color and distorted perspective and proportion. Its content was characterized by emotional intensity, sometimes verging on madness. The Bridge group

expressionism

ik-'spresh-ə-ˌniz-əm

n [from Latin *exprimere,* to press out, express, from *ex-,* out + *premere,* to press] considered that it was representing **modern** emotions that showed a world in spiritual turmoil and economic and industrial crisis.

The central figure in the Blue Rider group was Wassily Kandinsky (1866–1944), whose work was also intensely emotional. Kandinsky is usually credited with beginning experiments with abstract painting in 1910. He began painting in a realistic style and moved from studies of landscapes and figures into more and more experimentation with form and shape, systematically eliminating the realistic subject from his work. His work influenced a number of U.S. painters who embraced abstract painting and began the **abstract** expressionist movement. These U.S. painters included Jackson Pollack (1912–1956) and Franz Kline (1910–1962) and were known as the New York School.

In theater, one of the prime movers of expressionism was the Swedish dramatist and novelist August Strindberg (1849–1912), whose plays such as *Miss Julie* and *The Father,* and novels such as *The Red Room,* portrayed people who were alienated from work and family, and experienced anxiety and feelings of meaninglessness that originated in the dehumanizing conditions of life resulting from the industrialization of society. Strindberg's work, and the work of other expressionists, went beyond realism to portray the emotional stress underlying the surface of appearances.

Expressionist theater made use of masks, stylized and ritualistic language and gesture, and disrupted time sequences. Special lighting effects and stage sets were also used to produce overall emotional tonalities in performances of works by American playwright Eugene O'Neill (1888–1953). Plays such as *Mourning Becomes Electra, The Great God Brown, Strange Interlude,* and *Marco Millions* used all of the techniques of expressionism and are good examples of expressionist style.

There was also a strong expressionist movement in film, particularly in Germany after World War I and through the 1920s. One of the pioneering films in the history of cinema, *The Cabinet of Dr. Caligari* (Austria, 1920), utilized film techniques such as sharp camera angles and distortions of perspective to show the twisted perceptions and fantasies of distressed and disturbed characters living in a hostile and menacing world.

*I*conography and *iconology* are terms in art history and criticism. Both words are derived from the Greek root *eikon,* which means representation, image, or likeness. Iconography is concerned with the subject matter and symbols in works of art. It deals primarily with the identification, history, and classification of visual representations. Iconology adds to iconography a study of the psychological, social, and cultural meaning of these symbols and their interrelationships. Thus, iconology attempts to understand works of art in terms of particular cultures.

Iconology is a fairly new field that was developed by the German-born art historian Erwin Panofsky (1892–1968). Panofsky moved beyond the more traditional study of the subject matter of a work of art to its underlying meaning. In his studies of North European and Italian painting in the fifteenth and sixteenth centuries, he elaborated on the meanings these paintings had for the societies from which they grew. For example, in his *The Life and Art of Albrecht Dürer,* Panofsky studies Dürer's paintings, drawings, and prints in the context of Europe's transition from medieval to Renaissance society.

Iconology has become a very important branch of cultural studies as well as of art history. It studies popular cultural icons, advertising, and other forms of popular art as well as the so-called fine arts. It is, as a field, not immune from criticism itself. Some argue that iconological meanings can be manufactured by ingenious scholars where none actually exists. This is especially true when hidden meanings begin to emerge in analysis and it becomes unclear whether they were intended by the artists or simply created by the critics.

Another criticism of iconological method is that it promotes a tendency to view a work of art as the embodiment of ideas rather than as visual form with aesthetic dimensions that should be evaluated aesthetically and not intellectually.

*I*mpressionism is a style of painting that originated in the 1860s and '70s in France. The word *impressionism* was derived from a painting exhibited in 1872 by Claude Monet (1840–1926) entitled *Impression, Sunrise.* That painting, along with Monet's other works, portrays a scene caught at a particular time, in a certain light, in a specific season. Monet conveys the impression of the moment, and molds the sensual surface of the scene on canvas, using colors to show how a scene's lighting shapes objects. Impressionism, as a style, is concerned with the study and representation of light and color. People and objects are revealed through the way they are illuminated and

iconography

ˌī-kə-'näg-rə-fē

n [from Greek *eikonographia,* sketch, description, from *eikon,* an image + *graphein,* to write]

iconology

ˌī-kə-'näl-ə-jē

n [from Greek *eikon-,* an image + *-logy,* study]

impressionism

im-'presh-ə-ˌniz-əm

n [from Latin *impremere,* from *in-,* in + *premere,* to press]

are built not out of lines but of overlaid and juxtaposed colors. A close look at Impressionist canvases will reveal a jumble of colors with no shapes of objects or outlines of people. When one steps away from the canvas, however, shapes and forms emerge, composed by our brains out of the relationships among these colors.

Pierre Auguste Renoir (1841–1919), Edgar Degas (1834–1917), Camille Pissarro (1830–1903), Alfred Sisley (1839–1899), and Berthe Morisot (1841–1895) were also part of the French Impressionist movement. The American painter Mary Cassatt (1845–1926), who lived in France, was also considered an Impressionist.

One of the main subjects of Impressionist paintings is landscape. Many Impressionist landscapes contained a body of water. The sea coast, riverbanks, and lakes all fascinated Impressionist painters, who worked magic with colors to portray how surfaces reflect light, and how light from an object colors nearby objects. Clouds, fog, mist, and light rain also appear in many Impressionist works. The Impressionists each had their own personal styles and subject matters, however. Monet, Pissarro, and Sisley preferred landscape; Degas concentrated on the human figure and interior scenes; while Renoir painted figures, interiors, and landscapes.

mannerism

'man-ə-,riz-əm

n [from Latin *manuarius*, of the hand]

Mannerism is a style of painting, sculpture, and architecture that developed in Italy from 1520 to 1580 as a reaction against the classical art of the Renaissance. Mannerism rejected the balanced proportions and idealized characterizations of Renaissance art. Instead it portrayed extreme emotions and the distortion of movement and proportion. In painting and sculpture, the natural proportions of the human figure were twisted and stretched, and gestures were exaggerated to dramatize emotion. Scenes were imbued with sensational lighting, as in the paintings of El Greco, whose work is characterized as mannerist.

The origins of mannerism can be traced to the work of Michelangelo (1475–1564) and Albrecht Dürer (1471–1528). Two of the leading mannerist painters are the Florentine Jacopo Pontormo (1494–1556/57) and the Roman Francesco Parmigianino (1503–1540).

In general, a style can be referred to as mannerist if it is highly emotional, exaggerated, and heavily dramatic.

The medieval period or the Middle Ages are the years between the end of the **classical** periods of Greek and Roman culture and the beginning of the Italian **Renaissance**, beginning in the seventh century A.D. and ending in the fifteenth century. The dominant force in Europe during this time was the Roman Catholic Church. Philosophy and art were created within the context of Catholic doctrine. The period of the Middle Ages from the seventh to the eleventh centuries has sometimes been called the Dark Ages because of the Church's control of thought and artistic expression and the lack of development of nonreligious intellectual or artistic traditions.

Medieval style set severe restraints upon artistic expression. Medieval painting, for example, used no perspective and little shading. The themes represented were taken from the Bible, with a particular emphasis on the New Testament. Innovation was discouraged, and the arts of ancient Greece and Rome were suppressed. Representations of the naked human body were forbidden, except in the case of the partially naked body of Christ on the Cross.

There was a great burst of innovation and creativity toward the end of the medieval period, beginning in the twelfth century and continuing through the late fourteenth century. The art from this period is called Gothic. The Gothic period was driven by the worship of Mary, Jesus' mother, as the central figure in Christianity. As part of this worship, enormous and majestic cathedrals dedicated to Mary were built, first in France and then throughout Europe and even in parts of the Middle East. These Gothic cathedrals were designed in the shape of the cross, and were oriented in an east/west direction. This orientation was highlighted by large, beautifully crafted stained-glass windows set in the east and west facades of the cathedrals. These windows gave the interior light in the cathedrals a mysterious and sanctified quality.

Stone sculpture and architecture also flourished in the Gothic era. Most Gothic building projects were enormous and many were worked on for over a hundred years. The artists of the Gothic period are not known to us as individuals, and the cathedrals themselves were modified and reconstructed over generations and most were never completed.

medieval

,mēd-ē-'ē-vəl, ,med-, ,mid-, mē-'dē-vəl, mid-'ē, med-'ē-

adj [from Latin *medius*, middle + *aevum*, age]

modern

'mäd-ərn

adj [from Latin *modo,* just now]

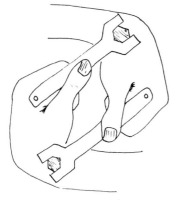

The historical period dating from the end of the nineteenth to the mid-twentieth century is known in Europe and the United States as the modern era. It is identified with dreams of the perfectability of human society through rational management and the development of technology. Modernity was manifested in politics by the development of the national state and in economics by the development of large-scale corporate capitalist culture and the intensification of the struggle between centralized communism and centralized capitalism.

Modernity is characterized by both sanctioned uniformity and by the development of cultural and social forms of revolt against uniformity and rationality. While some artists and musicians tried to build rational and mechanical systems to analyze the visual and aural worlds (such as **cubism**, twelve-tone serial composition, and futurism), others took the opposite tack and celebrated irrational eruptions of the unconscious in the midst of rationality. This led to movements such as **surrealism**, **Dada**, and atonal music.

Modernism thus has two faces, one rational, orderly, and planned, the other alienated, rule breaking, and defiant. Both tend toward the abstract, breaking down objects into component shapes and forms and unfolding the surface of reality to reveal underlying structures and forces. Thus modern architecture's elimination of ornamentation and reduction of buildings to their functional elements symbolize the triumph of rationality and planning, while **abstract expressionism** and surrealism's breakdown of representational form and their revelations of the passionate and the irrational symbolize the breakdown of humanity under the pressure of too much structure.

Modern styles in the arts and design can be characterized by this duality. Fernand Léger's (1881–1955) paintings endow people with the same structure, color, and form as the machines and buildings they create. Léger was a communist, and many of his paintings celebrated his belief in the perfectability of humanity through the rational control of technology. Pablo Picasso (1881–1973), in his *Guernica* period, also broke down forms and showed people and animals transformed into objects. But Picasso's work, a response to the fascist bombing of the town of Guernica during the Spanish Civil War in the mid 1930s, was full of the anguish and agony created by mechanization and the machinery of modern warfare, which kills indiscriminately with planned and rational application of force.

Of course, there are works of art and social and political attitudes that can be dated from the modern period that don't manifest the characteristics of modernity. It is important to be careful when using a stylistic term like *modern* and to be aware that the term is a shorthand for a predominant character of a historical period that does not necessarily apply to everything that happened then. In the case of modernity, it is also important to realize that it applies to Europe and the United States. Thus while "modernism" is a concept useful in characterizing a period in "Western" history, it is only one of many different historical experiences of humanity during the late nineteenth to the mid-twentieth century.

There are different ideas about the breakdown of modernity in Europe and the United States, which has been placed anywhere from after World War I to the 1960s and '70s. This breakdown has been characterized by a loss of the belief in the rational perfectability of human society, an abandonment of faith in centralized planning in both communist and capitalist societies, greater planetary consciousness, and a sensitivity to issues of cultural pluralism, gender discrimination, and racism. Some scholars believe that modernism has been replaced by **postmodernism**.

motif

mō-'tēf

n [French, motive, motif]

A motif is a recognizable repeating unit in a work of art. It may be a geometric pattern, an icon, or a visual sign or symbol that recurs throughout a painting or a series of paintings. It may also be an image, metaphor, phrase, or even scene or character that recurs in a poem, novel, play, or film. For example, in the comic-book world, Clark Kent is always seen at the end of a Superman adventure looking bewildered and regretting that he missed all of the action. And Superman appears shedding his Clark Kent clothes, stepping out of a phone booth or some other public yet hidden place. Without these motifs, a Superman adventure would be incomplete.

Leitmotif is a word that can be used interchangeably with *motif*. However, *leitmotif* is usually reserved for special musical motifs or themes that are associated with and announce the presence of particular characters, emotions, or situations. These leitmotifs, which are short melodies, occur throughout the operas of Richard Wagner (1813–1883), for example, and an experienced listener can read much of the plot from them.

In modern jazz there are a number of standard tunes (most of which are published in a "fake book") that every jazz musician is expected to know. These tunes appear woven in and out of performances, and a lot of improvisation centers around the ingenious and imaginative weaving and transforming of these standard jazz leitmotifs.

pointillism

'pwaⁿ(n)-tē-,(y)iz-əm,
'pȯint-ᵊl-,iz-əm

n [from French *pointillisme,*
from *pointiller,* to stipple, from
point, spot]

Pointillism is a technique of painting developed by Georges Seurat (1859–1891) in the late 1870s and 1880s. It consists of applying small dots of carefully selected pure prismatic colors on the canvas in such a manner that, when viewed by the human eye, these dots would merge to produce other colors. For example, the intermingling of dots of blue and red would appear, at a distance from the canvas, as purple. Seurat discovered that this process achieved a radiance not possible with mixed colors.

Seurat was very interested in the physics of color and optics and developed pointillism by paying careful attention to the scientific study of color vision. In this he differed from the **Impressionist** painters who were his contemporaries. The Impressionists chose their colors intuitively and depended upon sensibility and trial and error. Seurat chose subject matter that was similar to that portrayed by the Impressionists, however. The subject of his masterpiece, *Sunday on the Island of La Grande Jatte,* was an outing in the park, peopled by respectable members of the French middle class. Similar subjects appear in Impressionist paintings. What distinguishes Seurat from the Impressionists are the elaborate theoretical underpinnings of his work and the carefully worked out plan he followed while painting.

renaissance

,ren-ə-'sän(t)s, 'zän(t)s

n [from French, rebirth, from
Latin *renasci,* from *re-,*
again + *nasci,* to be born]

The word *renaissance* means rebirth in French. A renaissance is a cultural, social, or political rebirth, one that usually occurs after a war or some other major change in power structure in a society. Such changes, when accompanied by a reference to an idealized past, and the reconceptualization of older forms in the arts, are often thought to be part of the coming of a new golden age of personal and social perfection. The "renaissance" of mural painting in twentieth-century Mexico began during the Mexican revolution and drew upon the inspiration of pre-Columbian art; the renaissance of African-American literature in the 1960s during and after the civil rights movement utilized African themes; and the renaissance of feminist literature in the 1970s was both part of current feminist struggles and was influenced by newly discovered women's writing of the eighteenth and nineteenth centuries.

The word *Renaissance* with a capital *R* was first used in 1840 by the French historian Jules Michelet (1798–1874) to refer to the historical period in Europe comprising the fifteenth and sixteenth centuries that followed the period known as the Middle Ages (600 to approximately 1250). During that time there was a break with the dominance of the Roman Catholic Church and the rebirth of interest in classical Greek and Roman art forms. This rebirth originated in central Italy and was marked by a flowering in the arts of painting, sculpture, architecture, and literature. In the visual arts, Renaissance style was characterized by the idealization of the human body in imitation of Roman and Greek styles, the development of perspective in drawing and painting, and the use of mathematical formulas to determine proportion and balance in the portrayal of the human body. The art represented a **paradigm** shift from a God-centered universe to a human-centered one. The works of Michelangelo (1475–1564), Leonardo da Vinci (1452–1519), Raphael (1483–1520), Titian (1477–1556), Jan van Eyck (1370–1440), and Albrecht Dürer (1471–1528) among others, were products of this period.

During the Renaissance, developments in the arts were accompanied by the beginnings of modern science, the invention of movable type and the printing press, and the spread of literacy beyond the Church into the commercial middle class. Changes in European society, which centered around the development of international trading, the exploration and exploitation of the resources of North and Central America, and the replacement of Church dominance by monarchies, princedoms, and a few small trading republics, also occurred during this period.

A philosophy that developed during this period of European history was called humanism. Included in this worldview were support for the idea of the central role and dignity of the individual; the development of all of the human faculties, especially the artistic ones, and not merely the intellectual ones; the teaching of **classical** grammar, history, rhetoric, poetry, and moral philosophy derived from Greek and Roman models (what is now called the humanities); and the elevation of rationality to the highest place among human faculties.

The Protestant religion also developed during this period. Led by the German theologian and activist Martin Luther (1483–1546), this revolt against the centralized control of religious thinking and practice by the Roman Catholic Church based faith on the individual's inner experience of spiritual struggle and salvation and was called the Reformation.

rococo

rə-'kō-(ˌ)kō, rō-kə-'kō

adj [French, alteration of *ro-caille,* rockwork]

Rococo is a flamboyant eighteenth-century decorative style of painting, sculpture, architecture, and music. It is an extension of the **baroque** style and is characterized by frills and elaboration, often derived from natural forms such as seashells and patterned rock and earth formations.

Rococo style was developed in France. Two of the major painters who worked in this style were Jean Antoine Watteau (1684–1721) and Jean Honoré Fragonard (1732–1806). Many of Watteau's works present elaborate scenes of courtiers and merchants clothed in flowing silken dress, gesturing and posing theatrically. His portraits and sketches showed similar lavish and decorated lives. Fragonard's work was even more elaborate and showed love scenes of coy and contented couples in carefully cultured parks and woods. Much of his work was done for the private chambers of the nobility and rich merchants, and shows an amazing mastery of elaborate decorative techniques combined with the energetic portrayal of lives of leisure and pleasure.

French music of the eighteenth century has also been called rococo. It too is full of frills and elaborations on the music of the baroque, and was often composed and performed for rich merchants and nobility. The work of composer Françoise Couperin (1668–1733) is associated with the French rococo style.

More generally, rococo refers to work that is overly elaborate, decorative, and sensually self-indulgent.

romantic

rō-mant-ik, rə-

adj [from French *romantique,* from Old French *romans,* romance]

The words *romantic* and *romanticism* refer to a style of art and a way of thinking, and to the historical period during which the style developed in Europe, the mid-eighteenth to the mid-nineteenth centuries. Romantic thought and art is characterized by an emphasis on inspiration, imagination, spontaneity, naturalness, originality, unconscious intuitiveness, passion, and, in some of its manifestations, sublimity, frenzy, and mystery. Romanticism is contrasted with **classicism,** which emphasizes rationality, balance, idealized beauty, perfected form, clarity, and adherence to so-called universal rules and eternal truths.

Many romantic ideas were derived from the works of the Swiss-born French philosopher Jean Jacques Rousseau (1712–1778). Rousseau contrasted nature, which he believed to be pure, innocent, and virtuous, with society, which he felt encouraged deceit, hypocrisy, and the reign of self-interest needed to maintain an unequal distribution of wealth. In the state of nature, a person's genius can flower and his or her childlike innocence reveals the creative self free of hypocrisy. For romantics, the state of nature and the innocence of childhood are all part of a lost Garden of Eden that society has corrupted. In much romantic writing one finds a longing for this idealized, purer time. The American writer Henry David Thoreau (1817–1862), who can be considered a romantic writer and thinker, even went so far as to retreat from society and live alone at Walden Pond as part of his search for a pure, nonviolent, and uncorrupted way of living.

In the world of the romantics, pure and ecstatic love is a common goal of personal relationships. This romantic love, which involves complete immersion in the loved one to achieve ecstasy, is often portrayed in romantic literature as unrequited and impossible in vile society. One of the most famous tales of unrequited love is Johann Wolfgang van Goethe's (1749–1832) *The Sorrows of Young Werther,* which is claimed to have caused dozens of young German men to commit suicide when it was published.

Romanticism idealizes the tragic and heroic life of genius that strives for perfection and ends in early death. German romantic and idealist philosophers such as Friedrich von Schlegel (1772–1829), Johann Gottleib Fichte (1762–1814), and Georg Wilhelm Friedrich Hegel (1770–1831) wrote about the struggle for freedom, the role of genius and inspiration, the nature of ego and self-awareness, and the transcendent reality that lies beneath the surface of impure nature. Hegel, for example, considers romantic art as the highest form of expression of the free creator, higher than **classical**, **Renaissance**, **medieval** and all of the other art forms and styles that preceded it.

The writings of these philosophers, as well as those of Romantic poets such as George Gordon, Lord Byron (1788–1824), Percy Bysshe Shelley (1792–1822), John Keats (1795–1821), and Samuel Taylor Coleridge (1772–1834) centered around perfecting human life, finding pure love, creating social and spiritual revolution, searching for innocence, beauty, and purity, coming into contact with the sources of imagination, and mourning the pain and imperfection of everyday life. They had **utopian** visions of possible worlds and wrote of quests to find lost paradise and perfect love.

The German Romantics used the phrase **Sturm und Drang** (meaning storm and stress) to characterize the pain and struggle for unattainable perfection that was central to Romantic sentiment. The British Romantic poets Byron, Shelley, and Keats as well as the musicians Schumann, Schubert, and Chopin all lived romantic lives and died young. In addition to producing extraordinary poetry and music, they became exemplars of the romantic hero.

In music, the works and performances of Robert Schumann

(1810–1856), Clara Wieck Schumann (1819–1896), Franz Schubert (1797–1828), Frédéric Chopin (1810–1849), and Johannes Brahms (1833–1897) are also considered Romantic. These works are passionate and full of what William Wordsworth (1770–1850), another British Romantic poet, called "the spontaneous overflow of powerful feelings." The composers were more concerned with expressing the flow of emotion and the evocation of romantic images than with traditional forms of musical composition.

In painting, French Romantics developed a spontaneous, open style that blurred boundaries, molded light, and in other ways illuminated the spiritual behind the natural environment. Romantic landscape painting portrayed nature according to Rousseau, and historical romantic paintings, such as those of Eugène Delacroix (1798–1863) portrayed humans struggling and suffering for liberation.

Throughout the late nineteenth and twentieth centuries, the so-called **modern** and **postmodern** eras, there have been artists and thinkers whose work has been inspired by Romantic ideas. Such work is often called neoromantic.

There is a negative use of the word *romantic* that is common among some critics these days. They call people who believe in the perfectability of human society on earth "romantics," implying that they are unrealistic and do not acknowledge that self-interest is the central factor governing human life. Romantics are accused of foolishly proposing schemes for the perfection of human society and personality and not being sufficiently realistic. Some modern romantics do not take that accusation as an insult, but believe that one must dream of perfection and work toward it even if the result is only to make life a little bit better.

Sturm und Drang

,s(h)tùr-mùnt-'drä η

In German, *Sturm* means storm and *Drang* means stress. Sturm und Drang is storm and stress in one's personal life or in confronting a corrupt and cruel world. The phrase was originally the title of a play by the German eighteenth-century writer Friedrich von Klinger (1752–1831). It was adopted by German Romantic poets and philosophers (see **romantic**) during the late eighteenth and early nineteenth centuries to characterize the struggle for unattainable perfection that they felt was characteristic of creative genius. There were many romantic novels and poems written at this time that portrayed people in revolt against the intolerable stress created by early industrialization.

Sturm und Drang is both a metaphysical and emotional response to spiritual and material crisis. When a person loses hold of traditional moral values, finds social and political life dehumanizing, and tries to oppose all of the horror of an indifferent society while struggling to create a newer, better world, or return to an older, better world, they experience Sturm und Drang.

The word *style* comes from the Latin *stylus,* which means both a pointed instrument for writing and, by extension, a manner or particular way of speaking or writing. A style is a constellation of attributes or qualities that together distinguish an individual, group, historical period, or work of music, art, or literature from other individuals, groups, historical periods, or works of music, art, or literature. Different styles can be attributed to the same object depending upon one's focus. For example, Michelangelo's sculpture *David* can be studied as an example of the individual style of Michelangelo, as an example of **Renaissance** Italian period style, of fifteenth-century high Renaissance style, as a **neoclassical** work that has echoes of early Greek and Roman styles, or as a unique work that is stylistically distinct from all other sculpted portrayals of David.

Style is not absolute. Different stylistic categories are somewhat roughly drawn in order to help in understanding the uniqueness of different forms of human expression or historical periods. For this reason, there are many disagreements about where one style ends and another begins, and about how to classify particular works according to style. It is best to look upon style as a conceptual shorthand created for analytic convenience. There is no absolute definition of style, just as there are no exact cutoff dates in history where one period begins and another ends. If used to understand the ways in which changes in forms of expression take place over time, style can be a helpful concept.

style

'sti(ə)l

n [from Latin *stilus,* stake, stylus, style of writing]

The surrealist movement was launched in 1924 in France by the writer André Breton (1896–1966), who published the *Manifesto of Surrealism.* It was a movement in the arts whose goal was to release all inhibitions and restraints on the mind. It rejected logical reason, realism, and the social and cultural conventions that European society accepted as normal at the turn of the twentieth century. For a surrealist, any objects or beings could be merged, shaped, proportioned, or distorted. Time periods and landscapes could be juxtaposed and transformed in ways that made the resulting work seem like a dreamscape or an expression of the logic of the unconscious.

surrealism

sə-'rē-ə-ˌliz-əm, -'ri-, -'rā-

n [from French *surréalisme,* from *sur-,* over + *réalisme,* realism]

Surrealist writers wrote down whatever came into consciousness. They used this automatic writing to free the mind of the constraints of habit. Other techniques used by surrealists in the different arts were drug-induced hallucinations and recordings of actual dreams and daydreams. Surreal works often portrayed a detailed super-reality, which was full of sexual innuendo and random violence. The paintings of Salvador Dali (1904–1989) provide examples of such surrealist work.

Surrealism introduced techniques such as free association, the use of nongrammatical word order and nonsequential time order, the creation of dreamlike atmospheres and environments, and the juxtaposition of shocking and seemingly unrelated images into the artist's repertoire.

Literature

An allusion is an implied reference to a work of literature, art, or music to a historic event or personage, or to some element of popular culture. The following sentences provide examples of allusions:

- She thinks she's going to achieve power but she's just tilting at windmills.
- They started out wild and happy but their yellow submarine universe sank slowly to the bottom of the pond.
- She refused to let her job be taken by a man; no one was going to send her to the back of the bus.

The first sentence alludes to the main character in *Don Quixote,* who battled windmills; the second, to the Beatles' song "Yellow Submarine"; and the third to Rosa Parks's refusal to move to the "colored" section of the bus, one incident that sparked the U.S. civil rights movement of the 1950s and 1960s.

Allusions can be used to illuminate an idea or make a statement more dramatic or complex. For example, the first sentence brings up the image of Don Quixote and all of his battles against illusory enemies, implying that the person referred to is embarking on a career of illusions and failure, with a touch of romanticism nevertheless. The second sentence brings up images of the world of the Beatles and the utopian and somewhat innocent dreams they represented at the time they wrote "Yellow Submarine." The third gives the impression of a determined and courageous woman.

When an allusion is used there is an underlying assumption that the speaker or writer and the audience have a common culture in which the things alluded to are mutually understood. It is common to miss allusions in works that assume the reader is aware of literary or historical traditions that are no longer part of common knowledge. This lack of a common tradition makes some older literature difficult for the contemporary reader. If you find some poetic imagery or literary allusions obscure, it makes sense to find some critical glosses on the text that will fill you in on the world the writer assumes her or his reader will know about.

Allusions have to be used and read very carefully. At best, allusions clarify and strengthen a text. Sometimes, however, they are used to show off the author's knowledge and can actually distract from the meaning.

allusion

ə-'lü-zhən

n [from Latin *allusus,* pp of *alludere,* to play with]

bowdlerize

'bōd-lə-ˌrīz, 'baud-

v [after Thomas *Bowdler,* English editor]

To bowdlerize a text is to cut out parts of it (especially sexual references) that are considered offensive. In 1818 Thomas Bowdler published *Family Shakespeare,* in which he cut and censored Shakespeare's plays in order to make them fit for "the perusal of our virtuous females." He eliminated those parts of the plays he considered immoral, obscene, indelicate, or sexually suggestive. In memory of his work, any text that is "cleaned up" and expunged of sexual reference or other sensitive material is said to be bowdlerized.

canon

'kan-ən

n [from Latin *canon,* rule, ruler, standard, from Greek *kanōn*]

The word *canon* comes from the Greek *kanōn,* which is a word for a straight stick or bundle of sticks that was carried as a sign of authority, power, or office. In an extended sense, the *canon* became a standard, rule, or principle by which excellence or superiority is measured. In the Catholic Church, for example, the canon is the list of books of the Bible formally accepted by the Church as genuine and inspired.

A good example of the use of a canon in the arts is the list of six canons of Chinese painting formulated by the Chinese painter and aesthetician Hsieh Ho (479–501). These canonical rules, which describe ways of observing nature and of using the brush, have been followed (with variations and changes) for about fifteen hundred years, and are still part of the working knowledge of Chinese painters.

In the world of European, European-American, Indian, Arabic, Chinese, and many other classical music traditions, there is a repertory of most-performed pieces that constitutes a canon. Classical performers are expected to master a good part of the classical canon of music for their instruments, and new pieces enter the canon with great difficulty.

The way in which canons are chosen is subject to speculation. Great performers have made their contributions as have music critics and patrons of the arts. At the core of the European canon one finds composers like Beethoven, Bach, Mozart, Brahms, Schumann, and Schubert. More recent composers like Anton von Webern (1883–1945) and Béla Bartók (1881–1945) are considered part of the canon by some and not by others. Supposedly the canon separates "major" composers from "minor" composers. The strongest defenders of the canon are the people who control the programs of concerts. However, there is no single definition of excellence in musical composition upon which all musicians, critics, and serious listeners agree. It is interesting to note that all of the musicians included in the core of the Western classical music canon are white male Europeans.

Until recently the same has been true of painters included in the canon of works of Western European painting and sculpture. The classical canon in painting is established for the most part by scholars, museum trustees and directors, and private collectors. The canon of works of contemporary art is more fluid than that of earlier work but is also established by a combination of scholars, critics, and people and institutions who can afford to buy paintings. In both these canons some effort is being made to include works by women and African-American and other minority artists.

Similarly, the literary canon is the body of literature that is supposed to consist of the most superior works. Authors within the canon are considered to have major status while others are minor. There are no set rules for what belongs in the canon and what is outside it, though inclusion in the Norton anthologies of literature, which are required readings for many college students, is one criterion many university professors accept.

In literature, as in music and the arts, scholars, critics, and people who control access to the works (publishers in the case of literature) control the making of the canon. Almost all of the works that have been traditionally included in the canon of European and United States literature have been written by white European males. Almost all of the critics and managers of access are also white European males. No canon has yet been established in Latin American or African literature, though there are traditional Asian canons. However, with the increasing interest in cultural diversity in the United States it would not be surprising to see a rush to new types of canon formation on the part of publishers and critics. In fact, a Norton anthology of African-American literature is currently being compiled and is expected to constitute a canon of writing by African-Americans.

Recently literary canons, and to a lesser degree those in the visual arts and music, have come under major attack from feminist, African-American, Latin, Native and Asian-American, and gay and lesbian critics. Controversies over canon formation, that is, the making of a canon, are part of larger struggles in contemporary United States society over valuing cultural diversity and eliminating gender bias throughout society.

The major thrust of the attack on traditional canons has been to point to excluded literature and show how a white male European and United States canon has been established by white European and American males based on self-interest. A multiplicity of voices has been called for and many so-called minor and neglected works have been discovered or reevaluated. Canon reformation has been called for and has begun. In addition to separate canons, women and

African-American writers have been added to the general canon of major works. One can also expect new canons in other culturally defined areas.

There are also some radical critics who call for the abandonment of canons all together.

The struggle over literary and artistic canons shows how self-interest, bias, and commercial interests can creep into any attempt at inclusion and exclusion, and illustrates how difficult it is to make any absolute judgments in matters of culture, personal preference, and taste.

criticism

'krit-ə-ˌsiz-əm

n [from Greek *kritikos,* able to discern or judge]

$\mathbf{A}$ critic is a person whose business it is to analyze, interpret, and evaluate the nature and quality of an attitude, opinion, theory, work of art or literature, or social, political, or historical situation or any form of activity and behavior. In cultures throughout the world where public media have developed, critics play the role of experts qualified to judge events and activities or arts and literature and make their pronouncements public. Some are very influential in affecting the economic success or failure of a work, or the public attitude toward an event or social policy.

Attitudes toward criticism as an activity are divided. Some people consider critics to be indispensable to the intellectual life of a culture. Critics are seen as revealing hidden meanings, seeking the logic of arguments, comparing works with works defined as classic, and providing measured and intelligent judgments on truth and quality. But criticism is also often thought of as negative, and critics have often been compared to parasites living off other people's work or serving the powerful. For example, the French novelist Gustave Flaubert (1821–1880) said, "One becomes a critic when one cannot be an artist, just as a man becomes a stool pigeon when he cannot be a soldier."

Criticism can assume a number of different forms, depending upon the system the critic uses to conduct analysis and make judgments. Some of the most common systems of criticism are:

- criticism based on so-called universal principles such as balance, harmony, and the imitation of **classical** models;
- criticism based on the idea that a work or an event has to be understood in isolation from other works and events and must be analyzed solely on its own terms;
- criticism that sets its subject in the economic, social, or historical context of its production;
- criticism that seeks contradictions, inconsistencies, con-

tradictory claims, and other forms of weakness and imperfection;

- criticism that concentrates on how its subject affects the critic, and that bases itself on the critic's credentials as an expert;
- criticism based on principles of **aesthetics**, and other theories of value.

These are only a few of the systems used by critics. When you read a critical work, it is important to make an effort to uncover the theory or system used by the critic that underlies her or his judgment.

The literal meaning of *deconstruction* is the undoing, piece by piece, of a building or other construction such as a bridge or a monument, until there is nothing left. However, the word is not often used in ordinary language but refers to a theory in the field of criticism (art, music, film, philosophy, and so forth). According to Jacques Derrida, who is one of the developers of deconstructionist criticism, all texts and works of art say something other than what they are appearing to say, regardless of the artist's intention. There is no single meaning to be extracted from a text. Every text, through interpretation, can be shown to contain a multiplicity of meanings, and the job of the critic is to deconstruct the artist's intended meaning and expose the multiple meanings contained within the work.

The techniques deconstructionist critics use to expose the inconsistencies within a work are:

- comparing that work to other works by the same artist;
- analyzing internal contradictions in the work;
- using the artist's life history and social, political, and class background to contradict claims of the work;
- using statements made by the artist in interviews, reviews, and so on to expose inconsistencies between the artist's claims and statements in the work;
- analyzing the actual language used and its relationship to the attitudes, emotions, ideas, and so forth that the artist is communicating in the work

An example of the third technique can be found in some recent critiques of the works of Shakespeare. Attempts have been made to discredit and challenge the claims made for Shakespeare's works and his literary authority. This is done through an examination of Shakespeare's political alliances and social status during the time he

deconstruction

dē-kən-'strək-shən

n [from Latin *de-* + *constructus,* to build]

was writing. In the opinion of some critics, Shakespeare was committed to the Elizabethan political hierarchy and held a privileged position within that social structure that is reflected in the attitudes toward royalty expressed in his plays. The commonly held opinion that Shakespeare speaks with a "universal voice" is deconstructed, and he is shown to write with the bias of his class and historical time.

An example of critical deconstruction that uses several of the above techniques is found in the essay written by Nigerian novelist Chinua Achebe (1930–) titled "An Image of Africa: Racism in Joseph Conrad's (1857–1924) *Heart of Darkness*." Achebe deals with the question of whether a work can be considered great when the inherent racism in the piece has been exposed. In order to show the depth of Conrad's racism, Achebe analyzes not only the attitude with which the story's narrator speaks of Africa and African people, but also looks to other writings in which Conrad's own racist attitudes are apparent. For example, Achebe uses the following excerpts, one Conrad's account of his first encounter with a black man, the second his first encounter with an Englishman, to expose his racism:

> A certain enormous buck nigger encountered in Haiti fixed my conception of blind, furious, unreasoning rage, as manifested in the human animal to the end of my days. Of the nigger I used to dream for years afterwards.

> [His] calves exposed to the public gaze . . . dazzled the beholder by the splendour of their marble-like condition and their rich tone of young ivory. . . . The light of a headlong, exalted satisfaction with the world of men . . . illumined his face . . . and triumphant eyes. In passing he cast a glance of kindly curiosity and a friendly gleam of big, sound, shiny teeth . . . his white calves twinkled sturdily.

Knowledge of attitudes such as these gives Achebe grounds upon which to deconstruct Conrad's authority, expose racism in the text, and question its value altogether.

Deconstruction has played a positive role in debunking many claims to universality in art and in showing how complex the implications and structure of works of art can be. It has shown how the claim to uncover "the meaning" of a text is naïve and full of contradictions and inconsistencies. Deconstruction has illuminated the complex relationship between the author, the audience, and the text, and shown how many unexpected nuances and unintended implications can insinuate themselves into a work. However, when taken to extremes, deconstructionist positions border on the absurd, claiming as they do that no meaning can be found in a text, that authors' intentions can never govern a work, and that at bottom all and no truth can be found in every work of art. This disempowering of the author and the work goes against the fact that authors and artists do have intentions, and readers and viewers often are moved in precisely the ways that the authors and artists intended.

deus ex machina

ˌdā-ə-ˌsek-ˈsmäk-i-nə, -nä, -ˈsmak-ə-nə

n [Latin, god from a machine, translation of Greek *theos ek mēkhanēs*]

In some ancient Greek and Roman dramas, at the end of the tale an actor playing the role of a god was lowered onto the stage by a machine. That god/actor's role was to decide the final outcome of the plot. This device was criticized by a number of fifth-century-B.C. Greek writers, including Aristotle (384–322 B.C.), as being arbitrary and destroying the integrity of the play. The phrase *deus ex machina* has come to mean some device or character that is used in fiction, film, video, or theater that is introduced arbitrarily to solve an otherwise insoluble problem. For example, when rich relatives show up unexpectedly, long-lost brothers and sisters suddenly appear with crucial information, or objects fall and break open revealing vital documents, the deus ex machina is at work.

genre

ˈzhän-rə, ˈzhäⁿ-, ˈzhaⁿr, ˈjän-rə

n [French, from Middle French *genre,* kind, from Latin *genus,* race]

The French word *genre* means "a kind of," "a type of," or more generally a category. The word is used in literary criticism to signify a form or type of writing. There are many different ways of identifying genres, and the line between genres is not always precise. The earliest literary genres specified in Western culture were tragedy, comedy, epic, satire, and lyric. Tragedy had to do with the fall of heroic individuals; comedy with foolishness of the heroes and institutions of society. The epic dealt at length with heroic figures involved in important events upon which the fates of nations depended. Satire attacked individuals and institutions with scorn and invective and is much more hard-edged than comedy. Finally, the lyric was originally a song accompanied on a lyre which expressed personal and deep-felt emotions.

There are also poetic genres such as epitaph, ballad, elegy, and parody. Epitaphs are short poems in memory of someone recently dead; ballads are story poems (originally meant to be sung) dealing with themes such as love, courage, and encounters with the supernatural. Elegies are extended epitaphs, which are forms of mourning for the dead; parodies are humorous imitations of other writers' styles. These are not the only genres of poetry. In contemporary verse, the creation and exploration of new genres is not uncommon.

Pop poems, concrete poems, and found poems, for example, though they have historical precedents, have been explored and defined as forms only over the past twenty-five years. Pop poems are poems that take phrases and selections from the popular media or advertising and reposition or juxtapose them; concrete poems are shaped so that their meaning can be found in a combination of their words and their physical placement on the page; and found poems are selections found in almost any kind of written matter, from dictionaries to instruction manuals, and reorganized into poetic lines that transform their meanings in interesting ways.

Over the past two hundred years prose genres such as novels, essays, and biographies have developed. Within these genres many subgenres can also be selected for discussion and study. For example, within the genre of novels there are subgenres such as mystery, adventure, romance, and horror fiction.

There is no set number of genres, and many works fall across genre boundaries. The use of genres in discussions of literature is a matter of convenience. However, because of this looseness, it is important to discover exactly how critics define genre in order to evaluate their claims about the works they are studying.

Finally, the distinction between genres has been extended to films, painting, sculpture, and other media. There is no consensus on how to define these genres and so, in those areas, too, it's important to find out the criteria a particular critic uses to distinguish genres.

hermeneutics

ˌhər-mə-'n(y)üt-iks

n [from Greek *hermēneutikos,* interpret]

Hermeneutics is the art and craft of interpretation. The word *hermeneutics* is derived from the name of the Greek god Hermes, who was the messenger of the other gods on Olympus and, by extension, a bearer of secrets. Hermeneutics concerns itself with secret and hidden meanings in texts, music, works of art, and even speech and gesture.

Historically, the Hermetic writings consisted of a series of texts written in Greek during the early centuries after Christ (between A.D. 100 and A.D. 300) on the subjects of philosophy, astrology, and alchemy. These texts, collectively attributed to an Egyptian, "Hermes Trismegistmus," were claimed to hold the secrets of ancient Egypt. The search for hidden meanings in them gave rise to the notion of hermeneutical readings of texts.

Most scholars believe that there were a number of different authors of the Hermetic texts and that the texts were unified by a common religious sentiment that involved experiences of ecstasy and the renewal of life. During the Italian Renaissance (the 1400s) these texts were believed to contain magical formulas and to predate and predict the works of Plato and the birth of Christ. This would have them written before 500 B.C., at least six hundred years earlier than our current dating.

The meaning of the word *hermeneutics* has been broadened to include the discovery of supposed secret meaning in any text or cultural expression. Thus the attempt to uncover Freudian sexual meanings hidden in texts and works of art would be a hermeneutic exercise, as would the attempt to find political meanings in nursery rhymes or Satanic meanings in heavy metal records played backwards.

Hermeneutic thinking often involves a very close reading of a text, one that pays attention to recurrent themes in the work, to parallels between the text and events and ideas beyond the text, and to traditional symbol systems. The study of hermeneutics therefore often calls upon knowledge of psychology, anthropology, theology, and philosophy. Historical knowledge can also provide keys to unlocking texts.

In an extended sense, an understanding of the secrets of nature, of the reality beyond appearances can also be said to be a hermeneutic activity. Finding hermeneutic meanings in nature or in texts and works of art, however, can be little more than an act of the creative imagination that has more to do with the intent of the interpreter than what is interpreted. It is sensible to look upon hermeneutic interpretations as tentative guesses. For any interpretation, it is important to try to discover confirming evidence either in the words of the author or her or his contemporaries, or in current knowledge.

Hyperbole is a **trope** or figure of speech that consists of deliberate and bold exaggeration and overstatement. It can be used seriously or for comic effect. Cyrano de Bergerac (1619–1655) was a master of hyperbole. In the first act of Edmond Rostand's (1868–1918) play of the same name, Cyrano describes his rather large nose in the following ways:

> *Descriptive:* 'Tis a rock — a crag — a cape —
>   A cape? say rather a peninsula!
> *Kindly:* Do you love the little birds
>   so much that when they come and sing to you,
>   you give them this to perch on?
> *Eloquent:* When it blows, the typhoon howls
>   And the clouds darken.

hyperbole

hī-'pər-bə-(ˌ)lē

n [from Greek *hyperbolē*, excess, from *hyper-,* beyond + *ballein,* to throw]

Dramatic: When it bleeds —
The Red Sea!

On a more serious note, in *Richard II* Shakespeare has the king say:

Not all the waters in the rude rough sea
Can wash the balm from an anointed King.

incunabula

,in-kyə-'nab-yə-lə

n [from Latin *incunabula,*
swaddling clothes, cradle,
from *in-* + *cunae,* cradle]

The word *incunabula* refers to the books produced when the printing press was developed in Europe, around 1500. These printed works are extremely rare and are valued for their scarcity as well as for the fine quality with which they were printed. An example of an especially prized incunabulum is Sebastian Brandt's (1457–1521) *Ship of Fools* with woodcuts by Albrecht Dürer (1471–1528). This volume was printed in 1494.

Incunabula is derived from the Latin meaning cradle or a baby's swaddling clothes. More generally, the word can refer to works produced in an early period of the development of an art or craft.

By metaphoric extension, there can be incunabula in fields of the arts that are not very old, such as steel sculpture and computer-generated graphics. However, the word is usually reserved for arts that have a history dating back hundreds of years.

irony

'i-rə-nē, 'i(-ə)r-nē

n [from Latin *ironia,* from
Greek *eirōn,* dissembler]

The word *irony* comes from the Greek *eirōn,* meaning someone who hides under a false appearance or conceals facts or feelings by using some kind of pretense. There was a character in Greek comedy named Eiron who, through cleverness and deception, triumphed over the bully Alazon, who did not understand the trickery in Eiron's assertions.

Irony is a form of speech in which a person states one thing but intends another. Eiron's tone of voice was similar to the one that characterizes ironic statements. This tone is slightly mocking and a bit playful, and conveys the idea that all is not straight and aboveboard, that what the speaker says is not to be taken at face value. Ironic assertions often contradict the reality of a situation in a way that can be taken as insulting. For example, if someone sees a person slip on an icy path and comments wryly about the fall being a graceful pirouette, the irony might not be well received.

There are three major types of irony that are distinguished in literary criticism:

- Irony created by an author through a contradiction between what a character says and what he or she intends it to mean. An example of this is Mark Antony's statement in Shakespeare's *Julius Caesar,* when describing Caesar's murderers, "For Brutus is an honorable man; so are they all honorable men."

• Irony created by the disparity between appearance and reality. There are examples of this type of irony in Shakespeare's *King Lear.* Lear's attempts to assert the kingly power he once had are ignored by other characters, who know that the king is powerless. This makes for the bitter irony that pervades the play.

• Irony created by the difference between what a character says and what she or he does. An example of this is the behavior of Mrs. Jellyby, in Charles Dickens's *Bleak House,* who devotes all of her energies and conversations to the poor natives of various faraway places but fails to notice that her own children and husband are in a horrible state right under her nose.

A special form of irony, **Socratic irony,** is named after Socrates (469–399 B.C.), the Greek philosopher who pretended to be ignorant and questioned others in order to bring out the errors in their positions and lead them to see the truth as he saw it. Socratic irony consists of piling question upon question until the foundations of people's thinking collapse, or until every premise of their thought has been thoroughly examined.

Irony has been called the most characteristic mode of **postmodern** thought, which is characterized by a mockery of all established styles and a disbelief in the claims of established authority. Postmodern commentators are ironic, for example, when they assert, with tongue in cheek, that advertising is high art and that the rarest forms of beauty are to be found in the slickest manufactured consumer products.

Speech or writing is literal if it uses the ordinary common meanings of words and is free of elaborations and extended meanings such as **metaphors, similes,** or other **tropes** (nonliteral uses of language). For example, the following statements are literal:

> Julie's new car is red.
> I feel sad.
> Next week will be James's forty-fifth birthday.
> We will have a vegetarian dinner tonight.

literal

'lit-ə-rəl, 'li-trəl

adj [from Latin *litteralis,* of a letter, from *littera,* letter]

Here are some elaborations on them using nonliteral linguistic forms:

Julie's new car drips crimson.
I feel sweet sadness overcoming me.
Next week James enters into the midpassage of his life's voyage.
Tonight, dinner will be free of sacrifice of innocent lives.

The word *literal* is often misused in an attempt to provide emphasis in a nonliteral statement. For example, in the statement "I literally jumped out of my skin," the word *literally* is misused. Jumping out of one's skin cannot be done literally.

magic realism

Magic realism is the name given to a **style** of writing that has emerged in fiction written over the past twenty-five years in Central and South America. The style is characterized by a jarring juxtaposition of magical and strange occurrences described in ordinary and detailed descriptive language. Magic realism does not try to make the strange seem special or mystical, but rather matter-of-fact and part of everyday reality. The Columbian Gabriel García Márquez (1928–), one of the leading creators of this style, once said in an interview that attention to the concrete details of the magical event created the belief in magic as ordinary and within the world that is essential to this style. He gave an example of elephants flying through the sky, and said that one wrote that there were twenty-two elephants flying by instead of merely that there were elephants flying by, because that detail infused the magic with enough reality to draw the reader in.

Other writers whose work has been associated with magic realism are the Columbians Elena Garro and Antonio Torres, the Argentinian Luisa Valenzuela, and the American novelist Steve Erickson.

meiosis

mī-'ō-səs

n [from Greek *meiōsis*, diminution]

Meiosis, which is also known as understatement, is a **trope** or figure of speech that states something is less significant than it really is as a way of pointing out its actual importance.

Here are some examples of meiosis:

- Joe Montana had a fairly decent arm.
- I'll hand it to Einstein, he knew a bit about thinking.
- Whoopi Goldberg occasionally likes to tell a joke or two.

The word *metaphor* has two central meanings. In ordinary language a metaphor is a figurative or nonliteral use of words. Thus "She waved to me" is a literal use of language and "The grass waved to me" is a metaphoric use. However, there is a more precise use of the word metaphor. In this usage, metaphor is an implied rather than explicit comparison. The difference between metaphor and **simile** is, on a superficial level, the absence or presence of the words *as* and *like* to indicate the existence of a comparison. Thus, "Her hand is like a slender ivory sculpture" is a simile, and "Her hand is a slender ivory sculpture" is a metaphor. However, there are many instances in which metaphor goes beyond being simply a comparison. For example, "He has bloody hands": The metaphor *bloody hands* has a meaning not implicit in *bloody* or *hands*. Basically it means that he is guilty of some crime, probably involving violence, even though he did not necessarily administer the violence. Thus a dictator who orders someone executed may not have hands dripping with blood, but he is guilty of murder even though he didn't pull the trigger or wield the knife. The blood represents the act of murder, and the hands the person who performed it. The metaphor is a complex whole that draws on comparisons, identities, bold images, and complex ideas. Through complex juxtapositions, metaphors fuse feeling, thought, and images in ways that expand the expressiveness of the language.

As a form of thinking as well as a way of speaking, metaphor opens up the possibility of combining almost any two words and imagining a context in which they enhance meaning.

Here are some metaphors to consider:

a steely gaze
purple prose
an ironclad attitude
a frigid disposition
a hot temper

metaphor

'met-ə-,fȯ(ə)r, -fər

n [from Greek, from *meta-pherein,* to transfer]

metonymy

mə-'tän-ə-mē

n [from Greek *metōnymia,*
from *meta-,* beside + *ōnymon,*
name]

Metonymy is a **trope** or figure of speech in which a thing, concept, person, or group is represented by something closely associated to it. Referring to a baseball player as the glove, referring to the presidency as the Oval Office, or referring to a person who bets on horse races as the Horse are examples of metonymy.

The proverb "The pen is mightier than the sword" is an example of a double metonymy, the pen representing writing and the sword violence or warfare.

Synecdoche is a form of metonymy in which a part (for example of the body or of a machine) is used to represent the whole. Thus a car is referred to as wheels, and a singer as the voice, the throat, or the cords.

Metonymy is often contrasted with metaphor. Metonymy is characterized by association, whereas metaphor establishes a relationship of similarity. Thus referring to a king as the throne is an instance of metonymy. Referring to a king as a lion is an instance of metaphor.

négritude

'neg-rə-,tüd, 'nē-grə-, -,tyüd

n [French *négritude,* from
nègre, Negro + *itude,* state of
being]

Négritude is a term coined in the 1930s to express the sense of a common African heritage and destiny of black intellectuals and artists. It originated in French-occupied Africa and was developed by artists and writers in exile as well as in Africa and in the formerly French islands of the Caribbean. Négritude embraced the rejection of colonialist values and called for revolt against colonialism. It celebrated a common African past, and a desire to recreate the values of traditional pre-colonial Africa and to restore its beauty and harmony. In doing so, the writers of the négritude movement extended the French language to express complex African rhythm patterns and storytelling modes.

The ideas of négritude were articulated and developed most explicitly by the poet, writer, and president of Senegal Léopold Sédar Senghor (1906–) in *Chants d'ombre, Nocturnes, The Foundations of "africanite," "négritude" and "arabite"* and other works. In these two lines from *Chants d'ombre,* Senghor addresses the dry winds of a tornado and asks for inspiration to sing, in his poems, with the music and instruments of Africa, not with the guitars of Europe:

> Fire my lips with blood, Spirit, breathe on the strings
> of my kora
> Let my song rise up, as pure as the gold of Galam.

(A kora is a harplike instrument made from a gourd, with sixteen to thirty-two strings. Galam is a region in northeastern Senegal where the French used slave labor to extract gold for the French coffers. Senghor's poetry is resonant with reference to his people's experience.)

Other leading exponents and practitioners of négritude are the Martiniquean poet Aimé Césaire (1913–), whose works *A Season in the Congo, The Tragedy of King Christophe,* and *Discourse on Colonialism* are expressions of négritude, and the Algerian psychiatrist and political writer Frantz Fanon (1925–1961), who articulated revolutionary and postrevolutionary strategies for the decolonization of Africa and the celebration of négritude in his influential books *The Wretched of the Earth, Black Skin, White Masks,* and *A Dying Colonialism.*

objective correlative
əb-'jek-tiv kə-'rel-ət-iv

The term *objective correlative* was first defined by the poet T. S. Eliot (1888–1965) in 1919 in his essay "Hamlet and His Problems." In a discussion of the relationship between external events and emotions, Eliot writes that the objective correlative of an emotion is such that, "When the external facts, which must terminate in sensory experience, are given, the emotion is immediately evoked."

An objective correlative is usually thought of as a description of a place, action, scene, or of some physical details that is presented objectively and yet creates, for the reader, emotions the author intends to evoke. For example, an objective description of an impending storm might evoke fear, while a description of a room in which everything was out of place might bring forth anxiety.

Some critics claim that the conscious attempt by writers to use objective correlatives leads to mechanical work that is unemotional. Others contend that it is impossible to separate emotions from so-called objective description in writing and therefore objective correlatives are no different from other descriptive writing.

personification

pər-,sän-ə-fə-'kā-shən

n [from Latin *persona,* mask]

In this **trope** (nonliteral way of speaking), an inanimate object, an abstract concept, or a nonhuman living creature is represented as if it is alive and is endowed with human qualities or abilities. Here are some examples of personification:

- The car handled the curves well.
- The moon handed the sky over to the sun at dawn.

Here are two poetic examples:

> Mark how the bashful morn in vain
> Courts the amorous marigold
> With sighing blasts and weeping rain
> Yet she refuses to unfold.
> — Thomas Carew (1595–1645)

> Hey diddle diddle
> The cat and the fiddle
> The cow jumped over the moon
> The little dog laughed
> to see such sport
> And the dish ran away with the spoon.

simile

'sim-ə-(,)lē

n [from Latin *similis,* like]

A simile is a **trope** or figure of speech in which an explicit comparison is made using the words *as* or *like.* Here are some examples of similes:

- They fought hand-to-hand like two wounded wolverines.
- His hands moved like lead weights sinking to the bottom of the ocean.
- She was as swift as a cheetah chasing after a gazelle.

Below is a classic extended simile from the *Iliad* of Homer, perhaps the greatest master of this figure in written history:

> As when a goatherd looks out from a watchtower
> of a hill
> over the sea and sees a cloud coming afar off over the
> sea, carrying with it much tempest, showing to him
> blacker than pitch, coming on driven by the west wind,
> and he shudders to see it and drives his flock into a
> cave,
> so appeared the march of the Greek warriors. [4.275]

Here is another poetic simile from William Butler Yeats (1865–1939):

turn away
And like a laughing string
Whereon mad fingers play
Amid a place of stone,
Be secret and exult.
— *"To a Friend Whose Work Has Come to
Nothing"*

Stylistics is the study of style in literature and the arts. One of the earliest attempts to systematize the study of style was made by Italian Renaissance critics in the fifteenth and sixteenth centuries. They distinguished, in literature, between three levels of style, high or grand style, middle or mean style, and low, base or plain style. High style is supposed to be appropriate for portraying tragic and dramatic themes with heroic figures involved in important events; middle style for love stories and for portraying the trials and tribulations present in the lives of merchants, lawyers, and other ordinary and respectable lives; and low style for satire and tales of working people and the underworld.

High style is usually associated with formal language full of abstract adjectives and overlaid with **allusion** and extended **metaphor.** Middle style is much simpler and more informal, and utilizes the language and imagery of commerce and everyday life. Low style is more colloquial, and the imagery is more earthy and full of rough humor. Characters in works of art should be appropriately matched with the conventions of their social levels. Nobles should look and speak nobly, and base characters should be rough and ready in language and appearance.

This separation of stylistic levels came at a time where societies were rigidly hierarchical and class distinctions finely drawn; consequently, stylistic distinctions were class bound. In our contemporary, more democratic society, style is more widely distributed across class. People with money can style in any way they choose to and the three levels of style are blurred. In his book *The Well-Tempered Critic* (1963), the literary critic Northrop Frye (1912–) introduced a variant of the three-level theory of style, making the distinction between demotic style and hieratic style. Demotic style is modeled on the language of ordinary informal everyday speech, while hieratic style is more self-consciously literary and theatrical. Frye also distinguishes a high, middle, and low style within these two divisions.

The study of stylistics has developed in an attempt to understand what makes particular pieces or groups of writing or works of art

stylistics
stī-'lis-tiks

n [from Latin *stilus,* stake, stylus, style of writing]

distinct from others. It is part of the critical enterprise of trying to understand literary and artistic traditions and relate them to the cultures that nurtured them.

symbol

'sim-bəl

n [from Greek *symbolon,* literally, token of identity verified by comparing its other half, from *syn-,* together + *ballein,* to throw]

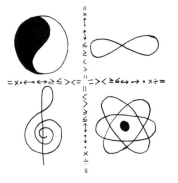

A symbol is something that stands for something else by reason of relationship, association, convention, or accidental resemblance. The following examples indicate the range of possible symbols:

- A red light can be a symbol for the command "Stop!"
- An x in an algebra equation can be a symbol for the as yet unknown solution to an equation.
- A cross can be a symbol for Christ.
- A flag can be a symbol for a nation.
- A coat of arms can be a symbol for a clan or lineage.
- A car or piece of jewelry can be a symbol for social status, sexual desirability, or wealth.
- A melody can be a symbol for a character in an opera (see **motif**).

Symbols can be created in a number of different ways: through resemblances between the symbol and what is symbolized, as in a picture of a hamburger symbolizing a fast food restaurant that specializes in hamburgers; through some relationship between the symbol and the symbolized, such as the relationship between twelve tolls of a bell and the number twelve on a clock indicating noon or midnight; through association between the symbol and the thing symbolized, such as a handkerchief and a cold, where the handkerchief symbolizes the cold; through a convention created and agreed upon by people, such as the use of the letter *m* to stand for the beginning sound in the word *mud;* or through association of personality characteristics and information like warnings or directions, such as an association of a picture of a German shepherd guard dog with a warning that it might attack.

Synecdoche is a **trope** or figure of speech in which a part (for example of the body or of a machine) is used to represent the whole. Here are some examples of synecdoche:

- They fought hand-to-hand.
- He has some cool new wheels.
- We need a new head of state.
- They are the eyes and ears of the authorities.
- His boom box hurts my ears.

Here are some poetic examples of synecdoche:

Farewell thou child of my right hand and joy;
My sin was too much hope of thee loved boy.
— Ben Jonson (1573–1637),
"On My First Son"

Faces along the bar
cling to their average day.
— W. H. Auden (1907–1973),
"September 1, 1939"

Synecdoche is a particular form of the trope **metonymy.** In metonymy, a thing, concept, person or group is represented by something closely associated to it. Referring to journalism as the press is an instance of metonymy.

synecdoche

sə-'nək-də-(ˌ)kē

n [from Greek *synekdochē,*
from *syn-,* together with +
ekdochē, sense, interpretation]

The word *text* is derived from the Latin *textus,* which means the texture of a woven fabric. That texture consists of threads that are woven together to create a single, coherent fabric that holds together. By analogy, a text is a piece of writing that consists of words and ideas woven together to make a coherent whole. Over the years the use of the word *text* has been extended to cover several meanings, including: an original printed or written form of a work that has been released for publication as opposed to a draft of a work that has not been offered to readers and is not considered complete or official; that part of a published work that contains the content and excludes the index, table of contents, references, and appendixes, sometimes referred to as the body of the text; a selection from the Bible or some other work used as the subject of a speech or sermon; and a written work chosen by a literary critic or reviewer for analysis.

Textual analysis has been one of the main roles of literary critics. There is no general agreement on the nature or function of criticism

text

'tekst

n [from Latin *textus,* texture,
context, from *textus,* pp of
textere, to weave]

or on the way texts are to be understood. Some critics try to set a work in its social, political, historical, or cultural context, that is, in the conditions under which it was created and published. Others analyze texts in the context of the writers' biographies or psychological histories. Illuminating a text by relating it to the circumstances of its creation is called contextualizing it.

Some critics take the opposite stance and decontextualize literary works. This is particularly true of a group of critics who worked primarily at Vanderbilt University in the 1940s and developed what was called the New Criticism. Some prominent New Critics were Allen Tate (1899–1979), Kenneth Burke (1897–), William Empson (1906–1984), and John Crowe Ransom (1888–1974). The New Critics disregarded biographical, social, historical, political, and cultural conditions in analyzing texts and analyzed texts with no reference to the external conditions of their creation. They decontextualized literary works and concentrated on a close reading of texts that explicated or spelled out and described the interrelations of different parts of a work and the ambiguities it contains. They also analyzed the imagery in a text and the intimate relationship between the language of the work and the content it expresses. Their theories held that the particular linguistic character of a work is inseparable from the meaning it conveys. They tried, in their critical writings, to establish the unity and internal coherence of great literary works.

In current criticism, the meaning of the word *text* has been extended considerably. For some critics, it designates every written message: from directions in a model airplane kit, graffiti, and menus to fiction and poetry. For others, such as the French critic Jacques Derrida (1930–), it goes beyond books and writing and extends to any subject, event, idea, discourse, or issue that can be critically analyzed. As he says, "I found it necessary to recast the concept of text by generalizing it almost without limit, in any case without present or perceptible limit, without any limit that *is*." The literary work is part of a larger social, political, and cultural context, and not separable from its position in human action, speech, and thought. The connectedness of a literary work with other works, and with culture, society, and the unconscious processes in the author's mind is called its **intertextuality**. The intertextual relations revealed by the critic, according to Derrida and other deconstructionists, discover things about texts that their authors might be totally unaware of and might even repudiate. Some critics even claim that there is no inner meaning of literary works and that meaning emerges only intertextually. An analysis of a text might reveal racism and sexism that the author had not intended and that most uncritical readers do not see.

The critic, having a deeper understanding, supposedly has a more correct view of the text. For Derrida and many other contemporary critics, the role of the critic is frequently to expose the text through an open reading that includes many things beyond the text and reveals the shallowness and deceitfulness of texts that are considered elevated and **classic**. The critic also takes on society and culture and all of their texts, and thus plays the role of philosopher, partisan, and even power broker.

Some thinkers criticize the fabrication of these extended meanings of text and feel that this broadening of the definition of text sets the critic up as a mediator between the reader and what is being read. As a consequence it is said to devalue the process of reading, while inflating the role and power of the critic. Questions have been raised about whether this form of criticism leads to overinterpretation and self-aggrandizement. Whether this is true or not, it has led academic textual criticism into the context of social and cultural debates about the future of society and has created some of the liveliest intellectual debates in years.

trope
'trōp

n [from Greek *tropos,* manner, style]

The word *trope* is derived from the Greek *trepein,* which means a turning away from something, and has been traced further back to the Hittite *teripp,* which also means turning but has the sense of turning over the soil, plowing it up. A trope is a turning away from the ordinary usages of language, a digging into linguistic soil to make the language more rich and fertile. Tropes are nonliteral forms of word usage and do not directly describe things, feelings, or events. Instead they use, among other techniques, comparison, exaggeration, the identification of a part with a whole, and the ascription of life to inanimate things, to build more complex portraits of the world than can be done with literal description alone.

Some of the most common tropes are **metaphor, simile, meiosis, hyperbole, personification,** and **metonymy** (with its related trope, **synecdoche**). For more about these tropes, see their separate entries.

The use of trope is quite common in language and many clichés are tropes that have been overused to the extent that their nonliteralness is no longer striking to us. Statements such as "We live a stone's throw from the theater," "She is the brains of the group," and "He is a horse's behind" are part of ordinary language. People often use tropes without giving the matter much thought. In much poetry, however, readers become more sensitive to the poet's conscious crafting of nonliteral language.

Religion

The word *agnosticism* was coined by T. H. Huxley (1825–1895) to represent his belief that nothing can be known about the existence of God, spirits, or the supernatural. Huxley believed that nothing can be known unless it is scientifically and logically proven, and therefore theological statements about the ultimate nature of reality can neither be established nor denied. He said:

> It is wrong for man to say that he is certain of the objective truth of any proposition unless he can produce evidence which logically justifies that certainty. This is what agnosticism is about.

Agnosticism is found in much twentieth-century writing concerning the supernatural. It is usually contrasted with theism, which is the belief in some sort of god, and **atheisim**, which is the belief there is no God or spiritual reality.

agnosticism

ag-'näs-tə-,siz-əm

n [from Greek *agnōstos,* unknown, unknowable, from *a-,* not, negative + *gnōstos,* known]

Atheism is the belief or opinion that no God or gods exist. This view differs from agnosticism, which claims that one cannot know whether there is or isn't a God. Atheism involves a positive and unambiguous assertion that God does not exist in any shape or form.

Atheism is most prevalent among people who believe that it is impossible to know anything that cannot be proven scientifically. This view asserts that since the existence of God cannot be proven scientifically, there is no God.

Other people hold atheistic beliefs because of personal experiences with disorder, chance, or injustice in the world. They claim that no good or just God could possibly create a world with so many problems.

atheism

'ā-thē-,iz-əm

n [from Greek *atheos,* godless, from *a-,* not, negative + *theos,* god]

Deism is the belief that God exists but can be understood only by studying the normal course of nature and history. Deists do not believe in divine revelation such as contained in the Old and New Testaments and the Koran. They deny that God can be revealed through a divine or supernatural agency. Deism was developed in England in the seventeenth century by anti-Christian rationalists influenced by the works of John Locke (1632–1704). It had many adherents in France, England, and the United States in the eighteenth century during the **Enlightenment.**

A deist is described by the poet Alexander Pope (1688–1744) as a "Slave to no sect, who takes no private road, but looks through nature up to God."

deism

'dē-,iz-əm, 'dā-

n [from French *déisme,* from Latin *deus,* god]

dogma

'dȯg-mə, 'däg

n [from Latin *dogma*, opinion, belief]

A set of beliefs is considered to be dogma if it is held as absolute, beyond question, and, usually, sanctioned by some authority. The word *dogmatic* refers to a person who treats his or her opinions as if they were facts and proclaims them arrogantly.

Dogma is intended to be followed without question. Dogmatic beliefs are not confined to religion but are held by some people in almost every form of human endeavor. For example, in economics there are dogmatic Marxists and dogmatic free-market advocates who simply do not communicate with each other.

When people adhere dogmatically to different belief systems, compromise is impossible and conflict is inevitable.

dualism

'd(y)ü-ə-‚liz-əm

n [from Latin *dualis*, from *duo*, two]

A dualistic approach to a subject divides it into two irreducible principles of opposition. For example, Manichaean thought supposes that there are two principles that work in the universe, good and evil. The dualism between good and evil then takes on a life of its own and all beings are seen as composed of different percentages of good and evil. The history of the world is seen as the history of the struggle between the two poles of the dualism.

Other dualisms are those between mind and matter, chance and necessity, will and intellect, natural and supernatural, and positive and negative.

Dualistic theories use either/or arguments. Everything fits under one or another of the poles of dualism or is composed of some combination of the two opposing principles. They do not allow for continuums. Thus a dualistic theory would reduce all degrees of hot and cold to some combination of hotness and coldness. A non-dualistic theory might instead posit a continuum such as freezing, frigid, cold, cool, tepid, warm, hot, and scalding. This could lead to a theory of heat in which there are many degrees of one underlying physical principle of heat.

A theory that posits one underlying principle to explain a phenomenon is called **monist**, and **monism** is the philosophical position that there is one principle or substance underlying all things.

When studying dualistic theories and trying to elevate them critically, a good strategy is to imagine whether the dualism can be replaced by some continuum or if the underlying phenomena can be explained by some principles that are not dualistic.

Enlightenment is a spiritual state that is the goal of a number of religions, including Hinduism and Buddhism. In that state the person or self is dissolved and a merging with the godhead is experienced. In that selfless state people are said to experience a removal from immediate spatial and temporal demands as well as a compassionate and peaceful distancing from the present. This state is achieved through diet, meditation, and engagement with a teacher who is already enlightened.

In Buddhism this state, which takes one beyond the cycles of birth, death, and rebirth that Buddhists claim characterize the existence of all creatures, is called nirvana.

In Hinduism this enlightenment consists of being absorbed into the *Brahman* or World Spirit.

enlightenment

in-'lit-ᵊn-ment

n [from middle English *en,* to put in, + *lightenen,* light, to put light into, to illuminate]

nirvana

ni(ə)r-vän-ə, (ˌ)nər-

n [from Sanskrit *nirvāna,* literally, act of extinguishing, from *nis-,* out + *vāti,* it blows]

Eschatology is the study of the ultimate fate of the human race and the universe. The word is usually used in the context of religious speculation and, within Christianity, in the context of studying the Last Judgment. To paraphase a poem by Robert Frost (1874–1963), some people speculate the world will end in fire and others that it will end in ice. No one will survive to be able to verify which guess is correct.

eschatology

ˌes-kə-'täl-ə-jē

n [from Greek *eschatos,* last, farthest]

A mandala is a Hindu or Buddhist painting enclosed in a circle. In Buddhism the circle of the mandala represents the outside borders of the universe and the painting within the mandala represents a spiritual map of the universe. In Hinduism the painting within the mandala consists of an arrangement of Hindu deities.

Some mandalas are painted on cloth, on temple walls, or on pavements with colored chalk powder. Mandalas have been used as the design plans for monuments such as the Barabudur Buddhist temple complex in Java.

mandala

'mən-də-lə

n [from Sanskrit *mandala,* circle]

The psychologist C. J. Jung interpreted mandalas as spiritual maps of the relationships among the **archetypes** of the collective unconscious for particular cultures and during particular historical epochs. As a technique, he had some of his patients paint mandalas to express the particular constellation of archetypes in their own unconscious.

millennium

mə-'len-ē-əm

n [from Latin *mille,* thousand + *annus,* year]

A millennium is a thousand-year period.

In the Bible (Revelations), the millennium is the thousand-year period during which holiness is to prevail and Christ is to reign on earth. Derived from this biblical prediction of a time of justice and peace, the word *millenarian* has come to refer to a person who believes that special things happen at the end of thousand-year periods. People who believed that the world would be saved (or damned) in the year 1000 were millenarians, as are people who believe that the year 2000 will bring a day of judgment. By extension, the word *millenarian* has come to mean a person who believes that there will be a major change in the way things happen within some finite, though distant, period of time. "Come the millennium, all things will be different," is a millenarian statement.

mysticism

'mis-tə-ˌsiz-əm

n [from Greek *mystikos,* from (assumed) *mystos,* keeping silence]

Mysticism is a doctrine that holds that the ultimate nature of reality lies beyond the experiences of the senses and outside the realm of reason. For mystics, reality cannot be described in terms of ordinary consciousness and can be reached only through a special state of ecstasy or divine inspiration. That state is qualitatively different from every form and activity of normal human experience. When one reaches this ecstatic state, all sense of separateness, apartness, and difference of the self from the nature of the Real disappears. Self-consciousness is obliterated, and the individual becomes one with the deepest level of reality. All oppositions disappear in that state, which merges subject and object, the self and others, finiteness and infinity, and even life and death.

Many religions and cultures throughout the world honor such mystical states and believe they can produce wisdom and the power of prophecy. Rationalists, **materialists,** and **naturalists,** however, deny the reality of ecstatic states and mystical reality, and explain them away as forms of psychological aberration.

The term *orthodox* refers to officially sanctioned beliefs, theories, opinions, and attitudes. There are orthodox, conservative, liberal, and radical views. There are religious orthodoxies, free-market orthodoxies, and communist orthodoxies. The word itself is derived from the Greek *orth,* meaning right or correct, and *doxa,* opinion. An orthodox view is a correct opinion according to some authority.

There is also a specific Orthodox church and religion. In the ninth century, the Eastern and Greek Christian churches separated from the Western (Roman) church over doctrinal differences and refused to accept the supremacy of the pope in Rome. These Orthodox churches accepted the patriarch of Constantinople as their head. There are approximately 170 million Orthodox Christians in the world today.

In Judaism, the word *orthodox* refers to those Jews who practice the dietary laws, use Hebrew as the language of prayer, observe the Sabbath, and in other ways adhere to the strict practice of the rituals of traditional Judaism. There are two other large groups of Jews who are not Orthodox. Reform Jews do not use Hebrew for prayers or observe Orthodox dietary laws. In general, Reform Judaism does not adhere to the rituals of traditional Judaism but does revere the books, ideas, and values of Judaism. A third group of Jews, the Conservatives, falls between Orthodox and the Reform Judaism. Conservative Jews use Hebrew and English in prayer, observe some dietary rules, and, in general, try to develop a compromise between the other two groups.

orthodox

'ȯr-thə-,däks

adj [from Greek *orthodoxos,* from *ortho-,* straight, right + *doxa,* opinion]

Philosophy

Aesthetics is the branch of philosophy that studies the nature of the beautiful in both art and nature and those aspects of experience (called aesthetic experience) induced by observing or participating in works of art. By extension, aesthetics studies the grounds and justification for judgments about beauty and ugliness. It tries to answer questions such as: Are judgments about beauty absolute or relative? What is the relationship between the feelings raised by a work of art and its aesthetic value? Is everybody's judgment about a work of art equally valid? What features make an object beautiful? Are there irreconcilable differences that can arise in the course of judging beauty? Is there truth in works of art? What is the relationship of art to nature? What do works of art mean? What are aesthetic standards, and what is the relationship between beauty and human welfare, the soul and money?

aesthetics
es-'thet-iks

n [from Greek *aisthētikos*, of sense perception]

*A*ngst is a German word that is most closely approximated in English by the word *anxiety*. It has taken on a special philosophical meaning from the works of the philosophers Martin Heidegger (1889–1976) and Jean-Paul Sartre (1905–1980) as well as other **existentialists** and **phenomenologists**. The concept was first described by the Danish philosopher Sören Kierkegaard (1813–1855), who described it as "the dizziness of freedom." What he meant was that the ability to choose values and actions is frightening as well as exhilarating. This is especially true when one considers such choices in the context of a finite life. Angst develops when one contemplates choice in the face of mortality and accepts the possibility of the world going on after one is dead; that is, the possibility of not being. It is not a personal response to a specific situation so much as an overriding dread of death and nothingness, which sets the context for major decisions in life.

Angst can be particularly intense when one has to make moral decisions that determine the nature of one's character and existence. Some people become paralyzed by angst and live in "fear and trembling" (another phrase from Kierkegaard) until they are forced to make decisions and exercise their freedom and accept the responsibility that it entails.

angst
'äη(k)st, 'aη(k)st

n [German, akin to Latin *angere,* to cause pain]

atomism

'at-ə-,miz-əm

n [from Greek *atomos,* indivisible, from *a-,* not + *temnein,* to cut]

The word *atom* derives from the Greek compound of *a,* which means *not,* and *tomos,* which means divided or cut up. Until the "splitting of the atom" began in the 1940s, the atom was believed to be an ultimate particle of matter that could not be cut up or divided in any way. There have been theories about the nature of matter dating back at least to the fifth century B.C. that claim that all matter in the universe is made up of combinations of indivisible and irreducible units called atoms. Democritus (circa 440 B.C.) and Leucippus (circa 475 B.C.) were early Greek atomists. In their theories, the universe consisted of atoms, combinations of atoms, and the void which contained the atoms.

In every type of atomic theory, atoms are considered to be the basic units from which all more complex structures are built. In contemporary physics, however, simple atomism has been abandoned and matter is seen to consist of many basic elements (the total number is not yet known) that are part **wave**, and part particle or **quantum**. The notion that reality at bottom is solid and consists of identical irreducible parts has been abandoned.

In sociology, atomism refers to the view that all social phenomena — groups, institutions, social classes, political parties, clans, etc. — must be regarded as the sum of the acts of individuals. Thus, the acts of individual people are regarded as the basic conceptual units for the analysis of all social phenomena. Atomistic theories are contrasted with **holistic** ones, which claim that the whole has characteristics that cannot be derived from any combination of the parts.

A theory in any intellectual or academic field is said to be atomistic if it has basic and indivisible units to which all other groupings can be reduced.

Buridan's ass

'ber-ē-dəns ,as

The French philosopher and scientist Jean Buridan (c. 1295–1358) posed the following philosophical question: Given two equally desirable alternatives, how is a choice to be made between them?

This problem is dramatized by the story of Buridan's ass, which found itself standing between two equally tempting bales of hay, unable to decide which to eat until it starved to death. Another version of this story tells of a person who found himself standing between two tables laden with equally attractive food and drink, and, having no basis upon which to choose between them, became paralyzed and starved to death.

The problem Buridan described is called *the problem of reasoned choice in the absence of any preferential factors.* This problem is based on the assumption that if there is no rational or emotional basis for preferential choice, a paralysis of will results and no choice can be made.

Jean Paul Sartre (1905–1980), one of the major **existentialist** thinkers, claims that decisions of this sort indeed have no grounds and therefore determine who one is as a person. They are what he calls existential choices, that is, choices that determine a person's character and fate, and the nature of his or her existence. For Sartre the question is not so much how we make these existential choices as whether we take responsibility for the choices we do make.

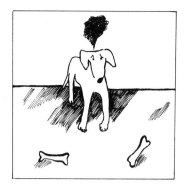

Diogenes (404–323 B.C.) was a member of a group of Greek philosophers called the Cynics. The name Cynics was derived either from the place where the group met, Cynosarges, a school for illegitimate children of Greeks and foreigners in Athens, or from the Greek word *kyōn,* dog (the adjective form, *kunik*). The Cynics were often called the Dog Philosophers and believed that virtue, not wealth, was the highest good. They advocated indifference to material wealth, composure in the face of adversity, and the cultivation of serenity and independence of mind. They exposed the shallowness of the wealthy and powerful, and lived simply and in ways that mocked the pretensions of the rich.

Cynics

'sin-iks

n [from Greek *kyōn,* dog]

In ordinary language the word *cynic* has come to refer to a person who believes that the only thing that motivates people is self-interest. A cynic takes a suspicious attitude toward all kind acts and never trusts supposed good intentions.

Diogenes was famous for living in a tub and sleeping on his cloak. His scorn for the powerful was legendary. Alexander the Great is said to have visited him and offered him whatever he wished. Diogenes' reply is reputed to have been: "Just move out of my light." The king did as he was told and according to legend remarked, "If I were not Alexander, I'd like to be Diogenes." Diogenes and Alexander died on the same day in 323 B.C.

Diogenes is said to have walked the streets of Athens by daylight with a lit lantern looking for an honest man. Presumably the goal of his quest was never achieved.

The story of Diogenes' lantern has been used often to illustrate the hypocrisy and shallowness of the powerful and the corrupting effects of what passes for civilization.

determinism

di-'tər-mə-,niz-əm

n [from Latin *determinare,*
from *de-* + *terminare,* to
limit]

Determinism is the theory that all human behavior is determined by previous events. Determinists reject the concept of free choice. They view all actions as the result of prior causes.

Determinists differ about the nature of the determining causes of behavior. Naturalistic and scientific theories consider all causes to be physical, while deterministic theologians consider God to be the direct or indirect cause of all happenings.

There are other determinist theories of human behavior that attribute actions to specific motivations, such as self-interest or pleasure-seeking. No matter what the nature of the cause, however, a view is deterministic if it denies the possibility that the world could be other than it is.

dialectics

,di-ə-'lek-tiks

n [from Greek *dialektika,* art
of debate, from *dialektos,*
speech, discourse]

There are alternate ways of analyzing history. One is to look upon it as a chain of cause and effect, a linear series of events that proceeds in a line from action to reaction, with no underlying predetermined structure or plan. Another is to look upon it as a process, as the unfolding of a plan according to a preset pattern of development. Dialectics provides a way of looking at history as a process that proceeds according to a specified logic and unfolds a plan of development.

The first philosopher to develop an elaborate view of history as a dialectic process was Georg Wilhelm Friedrich Hegel (1770–1831). For Hegel, underlying the events of history was a playing out of the process of development of what he called the Absolute Idea. He was an **idealist** who believed that ideas which exist independently of anyone's thinking them control events in the world. People and their actions are used by the Absolute Idea; they are just play-actors on the stage of history, and play their parts even though they are often not aware of what they are doing.

According to Hegel, the Absolute realizes itself in world historical figures such as Napoleon Bonaparte (1769–1821). The history of their lives and the playing out of their destinies realize the dialectic. The history of ordinary people means nothing, and when they get in the way of the movement of the Absolute they are crushed like so many blades of grass, losses that are of no consequence to history.

For Hegel, this historical process will end with the realization of the Absolute in history. He characterizes the Absolute as total freedom, where all power struggles will end and the slave and master will willingly submit to each other's wills. The exact meaning of Hegel's notion of Absolute Freedom has been debated for over a hundred years. To get more insight into what Hegel might have meant, it is essential to understand his notion of the dialectic.

The dialectic, according to Hegel, has a logical structure that explains the way in which history unfolds. Dialectic logic is a way of reasoning from opposites or contradictions, and proceeds by what Hegel calls the triad of thesis, antithesis, and synthesis. The thesis is a statement of a condition, something that is. The antithesis is the opposite or negation of the thesis. Thus, for example, a thesis might be the condition of being a slavemaster, which is one of positive control, and the antithesis, that of being a slave, which is one of negative control (that is, of being controlled). In this condition of contradiction the master and the slave are bound to each other; neither is free. The master needs to watch and control the slave, and the slave, as slave, needs to understand what the master intends. In order to overcome this contradiction and the inevitable conflict it leads to, both master and slave have to join in a higher synthesis of both roles where each one becomes both master and slave and something more, a free self-governing person. The synthesis, in other words, joins aspects of both the thesis and antithesis, and creates something that is beyond and freer and therefore better than either of them.

The central dialectic triad for Hegel is that of Being, Not-Being, and Becoming. For Hegel, Absolute Being is a positive state, yet in and of itself, without any further specification, has no form and is essentially the same as its opposite, Not-Being. The higher synthesis where new specific Being emerges is Becoming. In other words, Becoming, the process where something that did not exist before emerges from prior being, is the central process of change and growth.

These concepts of Hegel's are hard to grasp and there are critics who say that they are incoherent. Yet it is possible to get a sense of how this dialectic triad might work in the case of the slave and the master. The master has power and positive being, yet her or his being is imperfect because it is dependent upon keeping the slave under control. The slave is a nonperson, a nonbeing. By overcoming the contradiction between the master and the slave, a new person, freer and more self-determined, becomes a player in history.

Hegel's notion of the Absolute Idea playing itself out through the trials and tribulations of history until all contradictions were overcome, and slave and master, free and determined activity, means and ends, joined in some harmonious synthesis at some future date somewhere in Germany was rejected by Karl Marx (1818–1883). However, Marx, originator of **communism** and author of *Capital,* said he turned the dialectic on its head and brought it into the material world of economics. He used the dialectical method of analysis to study history as the process by which economic relations develop toward ever-greater freedom and equality. Marx's analysis is called dialectical materialism and his political and economic theory constitute the principles of communism.

Marx's theory of history is what could be called a conflict model. For Marx, conflict between opposing economic forces leads to a synthesis of new economic forms that provide for greater freedom and equal distribution of material goods. The ultimate goal of history, the final synthesis, is the abolishment of the state, of private property, and of all political and economic distinctions. In this he has the same dream as Hegel but with his feet on the material ground. He also differs from Hegel in giving the human mind an active rather than a passive role in the development of the dialectic. The mind is able to channel and direct the world process and improve material conditions in the world. The essence of the mind is not merely to contemplate reality but to act and engage in the practice of making a more equal and just world.

Understanding the nature of the dialectic gives people insight into the process of history and enables them to understand how their actions can be most effective in changing the world. Embracing dialectical materialism involves participating in the process of change, directing it, guiding it. To adopt a philosophy, for Marx, is to adopt a way of life.

Marx rejects Hegel's notion of special individuals bearing the history of the Absolute. For him individuals cannot change the direction of history and realize the dialectic. It is groups, the collective action of working people rising up in opposition to the wealthy, that will change the world for the better. Marx begins his *Communist Manifesto* with a plea to the working class, in whom he places all of his hopes for a better world: "Workers of the world unite, you have nothing to lose but your chains." One of the most **radical** aspects of Marx's thinking was his faith in the working class and belief that workers could understand the philosophy of the dialectic and would embrace it.

(For more information about the nature of class conflict according to Marx, see the entry **class**.)

Many Marxists — that is, people who base their thinking on Marx's ideas and try to understand current political and economic struggles in dialectic terms — use the analysis of economic contradictions to seek solutions to complex social, economic, and political problems. Such dialectical arguments begin by focusing on a conflict or problem and seek out contradictions in the situation. Then they look for ways that might lead to a resolution of the conflict by eliminating its causes and developing a new synthesis of its elements. An important aspect of this Marxist analysis is that solutions are sought to problems, not just improvements, which are often the goal of social reformers. For example, in the problem of homelessness, a reformer might try to find ways to make fewer people homeless or make more services available to them; in other words, to improve the lives of homeless people without eliminating homelessness. In contrast to this, Marxists would try to analyze the conflict between the homeless and those who are responsible for their condition, and try, for example, to find a way to get both sides to agree that it would be less painful in the long run to redistribute resources and provide housing for everyone than to maintain things as they are. Reaching a synthesis might require painful, conceivably violent confrontations. And the attempt might fail. However, from a dialectical point of view, there would be no partway solution to the problem: there would either be an end to homelessness or a continuation of the struggle. In that sense Marxism is **revolutionary**: its goal is to completely change the world, by violent means if necessary, and not merely to improve things.

Recent changes in the Soviet Union and Eastern Europe have been described by some people as the failure of Marxism. The reason for this is that the governments of these nations claimed that they could meet the economic needs of all of their people by applying Marx's ideas. They failed and, though many would deny that they actually used Marxist ideas, their claims have led to the description of this as the failure of Marxism.

discourse

'dis-,kō(ə)rs, -,kȯ(ə)rs, dis-'

n [from Latin *discursus*, discussion, argument]

In ordinary language, the word *discourse* is used to describe speech or writing that expresses ideas, values, or opinions. People discourse on subjects such as authority, war, love, music, the state of politics, and other issues of social, cultural, economic, and political concern. Discourse is more formal than casual conversation and is often argumentative.

In the works of the French philosopher and critic Michel Foucault (1926–1984) the word took on a more specialized meaning, and figures in a great deal of contemporary critical analysis. Foucault, in books about discipline, mental illness, prisons, and sexuality analyzes what he calls discourses of power. A discourse in Foucault's sense is an entire vocabulary that is created and empowered to support certain forms of social dominance. This vocabulary is not simply a list of words, but a complex combination of words and associated habits, professional credentials, customs, and actions that enforce systems of social control. For example, Foucault, in *Madness and Civilization* (1961, English trans. 1965), examines the evolution of the ways people spoke about and treated the so-called insane. He writes of the creation of new professions, such as psychiatry, which are given the language and the power to declare people mad and involuntarily force them into hospitals and therapy. He also analyzes ways in which aspects of human life that were once accepted as merely eccentric came to be stigmatized and controlled by state-credentialed authorities. The power of psychiatrists was invested in their discourse — in the language invented to express their claims and pronounce their authority.

Contemporary critics of culture discuss discourses in areas as diverse as politics, sexuality, art, and literature, and analyze ways in which the language is used to legitimate the authority of some and delegitimize the authority of others. According to these critics, each discourse has its own vocabulary, rules, **contexts**, and privileged knowledge. These, taken together with institutionalized support, constitute a discourse of power. If one cannot converse in the language of the discourse, and does not have the credentials required to use that language, one is cut off from whatever power that discourse has seized. A simple example should clarify this: if one cannot speak legal language and doesn't have the credentials to practice before the bar, one is cut off from defending oneself against the claims of the law. Much of the language of the law is not required by the complexity of the issues involved. It is required in order to create a discourse that can be used in an exclusive area of power by those who have been certified to share that power, that is, by lawyers. According to a discourse analysis, in order to become a lawyer an apprenticeship is required in law school so that one can be shaped into an acceptable member of the power elite.

For Foucault and many critics influenced by him, a society is made up of many different discourse communities. An understanding of these communities and the languages they use will provide insight into the way power is distributed within that society. Some of these discourses represent the dominant **ideology** in the society — that is, the image of what is socially right and good in society as conceived of by those in power. In addition to these dominant discourses, there are dissident discourses representing other ideologies that are used by those who oppose the dominant group. Conflict and change within society can be understood by examining and analyzing conflicting discourses and the conflicting power claims they make.

Empiricism is the theory that all knowledge is derived from experience rather than reason. Empiricists claim that reality can be known only through the experience of the senses and that rationality alone has no ability to provide insight into the nature of the world.

Empiricists have the problem of showing how the complex realities that people experience can be constructed out of the samples of experience of each individual person. The leap from personal experience to a shared world of history, language, social order, and scientific insight has not been convincingly explained by empiricists, though there are still philosophers and other thinkers who believe that the true test of knowledge is its basis in experience.

Thinkers associated with empiricism are the Englishman John Locke (1632–1704), the Scotsman David Hume (1711–1776), and the Irishman George Berkeley (1685–1753). A group of thinkers in the United States, most notably C. S. Peirce (1839–1914) and William James (1842–1910), elaborated on the work of the three British empiricists. Their thinking has been given the name **pragmatism.**

empiricism

im-'pir-ə-,siz-əm, əm-

n [from Greek *empeirikos*, experienced]

The Enlightenment is the name given to an intellectual and philosophical movement that developed in eighteenth-century Europe and is characterized by its belief that reason, and not superstition or the authority of unexamined tradition, can solve all of the problems of humanity. It is used interchangeably with the phrase *Age of Reason*. Progress through reason and science is a central theme of Enlightenment thinking.

Enlightenment thinkers rejected the idea that religion can be a source of truth, and believed instead that the application of reason to the evidence of the senses is the sole source of the truth. Nature can be discovered and understood rationally, and when so understood will be seen to be good and beautiful.

God's will can be seen at work in nature without the need of supernatural intervention. This attitude toward God and religion, characteristic of much Enlightenment thought, is called **deism.**

In conjunction with their deist beliefs, Enlightenment thinkers replaced ideas of divine authority and the rights of kingship with ideas of **universal human rights** and the **natural rights** of all individuals. The ideals of the French and American revolutions were Enlightenment ideas.

Some thinkers usually associated with the Enlightenment are the philosophers John Locke (1632–1704), Immanuel Kant (1724–1804), and Jean Jacques Rousseau (1712–1778). The French *Ency-*

the Enlightenment

in-'lit-ᵊn-mənt

n [from Middle English *en,* in or put in + *lightenen,* light, to put light into, to illuminate] clopédie under the editorship of Denis Diderot (1713–1784) was an attempt to gather into one set of books all of the rational knowledge of the world then available. It was the first attempt to make a systematic study of the state of the world as seen through European eyes.

Many Enlightenment ideas were discredited by the action of so-called rational people during the purges and inquisitions that followed the French Revolution. They were also called into question by the existence of slavery in the newly formed United States. Reason has not proved to be the sole source of human wisdom, though many Enlightenment ideas are still central to ideas of democracy and human rights.

epiphenomenalism

ˌep-i-fi-ˈnäm-ən-ᵊl-ˌiz-əm

n [from Greek *epi*, besides + *phainomenon*, appearing]

Something is epiphenomenal if it is incidental to the real workings of an event or a phenomenon. For example, there are some thinkers, notably the German philosopher Georg Wilhelm Friedrich Hegel (1770–1831) and his followers, who believe that decisions and actions of the majority of people are epiphenomenal to the larger workings of history. For them, history has its own logic, and manifests itself in a few world historical figures like Napoleon (1769–1821). The rest of humanity merely witnesses or is affected by what happens but has no role in making history.

Another example of marginalizing a phenomenon and assigning it to the category of the epiphenomenal is the denial that consciousness plays any essential role in the determination of action. There are behavioral and psychological theories that claim that consciousness is merely an accompaniment of physiological processes that are the "real" causes of behavior. For them, the presence or absence of consciousness makes no difference to the way one behaves. These theories claim that consciousness is powerless to control and modify behavior, incorporate feedback, or influence action in any way whatsoever.

epistemology

i-ˌpis-tə-ˈmäl-ə-jē

n [from Greek *epistēmē*, knowledge]

Epistemology, the theory of knowledge, is the branch of philosophy concerned with how people know what they know. It studies the nature, possibilities, and limits of people's knowledge as well as the role of reason and the senses in knowing about the world.

Epistemology originated with the Greek Sophists (circa 500 to 400 B.C.), who first asked questions about the relationship between reality and appearance, the grounds for certainty in mathematics and logic, the ability to know what others are thinking, and the relationship of cultural conventions to knowledge of universal values. Some of the Sophists took their skepticism to extremes and questioned whether any aspects of reality can be directly known or whether the senses just present us with the appearance of things and not their essences.

Epistemology developed in response to the Sophists' questioning. Today, epistemologists are still reflecting on how knowledge is possible and on the role of reason and the senses in the acquisition of knowledge. Much of what is known about the Sophists comes from Plato (427–347 B.C.), who first explicitly raised the questions: What is knowledge? How is knowledge justified and how is certainty possible? What is the relationship between knowledge and belief? What knowledge comes from the senses and what comes from reason? For this reason Plato is often credited as being the earliest epistemologist.

essence

'es-ᵊn(t)s

n [from Latin *essentia,* being]

The essence of a thing consists of the characteristics and qualities that define it. For example, some thinkers claim that the essence of being human is mortality, the fact that all people die. To them, having two hands, each with a thumb and four fingers, two eyes, and skin of a certain hue are not essential characteristics. One can still be human, according to their definition, in the absence of any of those characteristics.

Though the question of defining the essence of being human may sound remote from everyday life, questions about essence can and sometimes do have serious political, social, and personal consequences. For example, debates about defining the essence of life are central to struggles over abortion rights, and questions about the essence of insanity are equally central in debates over criminal responsibility.

existence

ig-'zis-tən(t)s

n [from Latin *exsistere,* to come into being, occur, from *ex-,* out of + *sistere,* to stand]

Knowing the essence of a thing, however, does not guarantee its existence. Existence implies actually being in the world, in space and time, and not merely being a product of human imagination, the subject of a linguistic definition, or a matter of historical memory. It is possible to define the essence of unicorns, flying horses, and magical beings who have the power to transform reality. However, no good evidence has been presented to establish their existence.

Establishing the existence of past events, and of people and places that no longer exist, can also be a difficult matter requiring the development of criteria for accepting present evidence as proof of past existence. Questions about the validity of our claims to know are questions of **epistemology**.

existentialism

,eg-(,)zis-ten-chǝ-,lizǝm

n [from translations of Danish *ekisistentiel* and German *existential*]

An existential approach to experience is one that assumes that people create themselves through the choices they make. It assumes that one is not born with an essential human nature that determines how one makes major human decisions, but rather, as Jean-Paul Sartre (1905–1980), one of the central existentialist thinkers, has said, "existence precedes essence." Of course there are constraints of history and economics that narrow the range of choices one can make, but within these constraints people are, again as Sartre has said, "condemned to be free."

For existentialists, there are two overriding facts humans must face: First, freedom exists as an absolute and therefore a person is responsible for her or his actions. This is especially true of some moments in life where the choices that have to be confronted are life determining. An example of such a choice is deciding, during time of war, whether to allow oneself to be drafted or to resist the draft and choose another option. However one chooses in this case, the results of the choice will determine the kind of moral person one becomes and the way one will live. Crucial decisions such as this are called **existential choices**. Second, death is an inevitable and leads to not-being, to Nothingness, and therefore life and its choices are all one has.

Given these facts, several problems arise within human life. Life ends; it has no validation, justification, or eternal reward. There is no reason why there should be life rather than nothing, and one has to accept life as a raw, given, absurd fact. Thus action, values, feelings and relationships have to all be developed in the face of this ultimate absurdity.

Of course, a person can live without taking responsibility for choice, can even deny the need to take responsibility. If one does this, according to Sartre, one lives in bad faith with oneself and as a hypocrite in the world. However, since there is nothing beyond one's decisions and the consequences they have in the world, the need to make decisions can cause considerable anxiety of an almost philosophical nature. That anxiety, called **angst** after the German word for anxiety, is a metaphysical experience, something akin to the longing for salvation and sense of inadequacy before God often described by religious thinkers.

Existentialism is a philosophy of responsibility and of the uncertainty caused by the need to make choices. It has roots in the questionings and musings of the Danish philosopher/theologian Sören Kierkegaard (1813–1855) and the German philosopher Friedrich Nietzsche (1844–1900). In addition to Sartre, others associated with existential thinking are Albert Camus (1913–1960), Maurice

Merleau-Ponty (1908–1961), Simone Weil (1909–1943), Martin Heidegger (1889–1976), and Simone de Beauvoir (1908–1986).

In the last years of his life, Sartre tried to integrate the insights of existentialism into a Marxist framework and show how choice can play within the constraints of economic and historically determined situations.

Existential psychology is a branch of psychotherapy that deals with problems of choice and responsibility. It studies how people create their own worlds, and concentrates on helping patients clarify the choices before them in the present and the responsibilities these choices will entail.

fatalism

'fāt-ᵊl-,iz-əm

n [from Latin *fatum*, thing spoken]

Fatalism is the belief that all things are determined by fate. It is sometimes called the "doctrine of necessity" and holds that everything that happens on earth has been predetermined and therefore that human choice does not exist. In its religious form, it asserts that God has determined everything that will happen in the universe's history and that human action is futile, as it is according to God's plan.

Fatalism, as an attitude, implies a submission to everything that happens as inevitable. It can lead to an indifference to action, an attitude of resignation, and an expectation that bad things are bound to happen.

Predestination, which is a form of fatalism, denies that people have free will and claims that people are unable to change the pre-ordained course of events.

Great Chain of Being

The concept of a Great Chain of Being is meant to illustrate, through the existence of the fullest and greatest variety of creatures on Earth, the creativity and greatness of God. According to this idea, which dates back to the Greek philosopher Aristotle (384–322 B.C.) and was developed by the German thinker Gottfried Wilhelm von Leibniz (1646–1716) in the seventeenth century, the Great Chain of Being is characterized by:

- plenitude, which means that every conceivable species of being has been realized;
- continuity, which insures that each form of life merges into another form which differs only slightly from it, creating a continuity of linked life forms; and
- hierarchy, which means that life forms rise from the low-

est to the highest, all the way up to God, with people being the link between the higher animals and the angels.

According to Leibniz, because the world consists of all possible beings, it is "the best of all possible worlds" in the sense that it is the only possible world. This view of Leibniz has been called "philosophical optimism" and was mercilessly parodied as being naïve and silly in Voltaire's (1694–1778) novel *Candide*.

idealism

,īd-ē-(ə),liz-əm, 'ī-(,)dē-

n [from Latin *idealis*, from Greek *idea*, appearance]

In common usage, idealism is the belief in the perfectibility of life. Idealism is the opposite of realism, which holds that the world is a difficult place and that conflict and struggle are a necessary part of human life. In politics, realists criticize idealism as being unrealizable and naïve. Idealists respond that it is possible to make a better world and that realism is actually an attempt by people in power to discourage change for the better.

In philosophy, idealism has a more specific meaning. Systems of thought that claim that ultimate reality lies in a realm of ideas that transcend everyday reality are versions of idealism. Some forms of idealism, such as those found in Plato's (427–347 B.C.) philosophy, attribute reality to eternally existing ideas. These eternal Ideas are models of perfection, which the human world mirrors imperfectly.

Other forms of idealism, such as that found in the philosophy of Georg Wilhelm Friedrich Hegel (1770–1831), consider human history to be the stage on which the Ideas play themselves out. The Ideas are evolving forms that determine possible behavior and give meaning to the actions of people who are fundamentally not in control of their destiny.

Idealism as a philosophy is contrasted with **materialism, naturalism**, and **pragmatism**, all of which deny reality to anything that transcends the world of the senses and of material objects and individual beings.

indeterminism

in-di-'tər-mə-,niz-əm

n [from Latin *indeterminatus*, from Latin *in-*, without + *determinare*, to limit]

Indeterminism is the belief that human action is determined by a free will that is independent of all physical causes whatsoever. Theories of indeterminism attribute the action of this free will to instinct or impulse, reason, the moral sense, passion, character, and the "self." Freely willed acts cannot be described by any other causes than an undetermined power to decide and can be explained only with reference to this power.

Because freely chosen actions cannot be explained by any outside causal factors, people are responsible for their willed acts. Some people accept this responsibility and others try to avoid it by denying their free will. However, for an indeterminist, there is no avoiding personal moral responsibility.

Materialism is a view of the world that holds that all the aspects of the universe, including human life, can be reduced to and explained in terms of matter and its properties in space and time. Materialists hold that even consciousness, though it might not be fully reducible to terms of matter and physical energy, is still dependent upon matter for its existence. For materialists, the mind's processes and states can be explained only when they are correlated with physiological processes and subjected to the laws governing physical motion and energy.

materialism
mə-'tir-ē-ə-ˌliz-əm

n [from Latin *materia*, matter]

The word *naturalism* has two related meanings, one psychological and one philosophical. Psychological naturalism holds that human actions and thoughts are based on natural desires and instincts. It places the cause of human behavior with such supposedly natural desires and instincts as pleasure, dominance, love, jealousy, greed, and anger. Naturalism in this form denies that rationality is at the center of human behavior and claims that human motivation is similar to animal motivation and governed by pleasure and pain principles.

Philosophical naturalism is concerned with the relationship between people and the external world. It claims that the universe needs no supernatural explanation, but is self-explanatory or self-existent. There are no underlying metaphysical or theological reasons why things are the way they are. Human behavior can be explained as part of the natural world and has no divine purpose, and human motivations, moral ideals, and conduct are determined by the organic structure and needs characteristic of the human species. Naturalism is similar to **materialism**, though it does allow for psychological realities whereas materialism reduces everything to physical (that is, material) states.

naturalism
'nach-(ə)rə-ˌliz-əm

n [from Latin *naturalis*, of nature]

ontology

än-ˌtäl-ə-jē

n [from Latin *ontologia,* from Greek *ontos,* being + *logia,* study of]

Ontology is the study of being, of existence and its relationship to nonexistence. The word *ontology* was first used in the seventeenth century by **scholastic** writers who examined the nature of God and existence. Ontology was distinguished from the theological study of being (that is, of being in the context of religion) by the German philosopher Christian von Wolff (1679–1754).

The ontological argument for the existence of God was first proposed by the scholastic philosopher Anselm (1033–1109). It is supposed to be a proof of the existence of God based upon the nature of being and depends upon a particular logical analysis and definition of the idea of a perfect being. Anselm argued that existence has to be part of the nature of a perfect being since a being that lacked existence would not be perfect. For him, reason and logic demand that an idea, part of whose essence is existence, must be real since it can be thought.

Anselm's argument was convincingly countered by Immanuel Kant (1724–1804) in *The Critique of Pure Reason,* who argued that the idea of a perfect being does not have to be accepted. Kant wrote that we can deny that the concept of an all-perfect being can even be thought. Kant also claimed that existence is not an attribute like color or shape or size. When you say that something "is," you claim its existence and existence must always be tested by experience. It is not an intrinsic property of a thing like size or shape.

In modern philosophy, **Being** is a major category in the work of Martin Heidegger (1889–1976), who distinguishes Being from **Nothingness** and tries to explain what characteristics Being must have if human consciousness is to be what it is. For Heidegger, who disagrees with Kant and does treat existence as an attribute, Being and Nothing are opposites that form a whole. Life exists on the boundary of Being and Nothingness, and this causes people to experience **angst**, a metaphysical anxiety bound up with the fragility of human existence.

The works of Jean-Paul Sartre (1905–1980) and that of other **existentialists** and **phenomenologists** also treat Being and Not-Being or Nothingness as categories with their own properties and characteristics.

Phenomenology was founded as a philosophical movement by the German philosopher Edmund Husserl (1859–1938). Husserl's goal was to create a philosophy based on the relationship between an experiencing subject and the objects in the world. By experiencing subject, Husserl meant a person who is conscious, and who is, at the same time, conscious of being conscious. Awareness of the nature of oneself experiencing the world of objects and other people is central to a phenomenological analysis. This consciousness of being conscious enables a person to become distanced from her or his experience and to reflect on it. Husserl calls this stepping outside oneself "phenomenological reduction." Through this reduction Husserl believes it is possible to describe experience without presuppositions and to uncover the fundamental structures of consciousness and the "**life-world**" (*Lebenswelt*) of people. The idea of the "life-world" or "lived experience," which is somewhat similar to William James's (1842–1910) **stream of consciousness**, is one of the main concepts of phenomenology.

The life-world of phenomenologists involves an intimate relationship between the **subject** and the **objects** of experience. In fact, for phenomenologists, experiencing involves having values and feelings and making judgments about things in the world, thereby giving them meaning. The subject or person makes meaning; there is no raw experience separate from that meaning. This making of meaning as a natural part of experiencing the world is called by phenomenologists intentionality. To understand intentionality we have to step back from experience, use phenomenological reduction, and reflect upon the fullness of the experienced moment. Only in this way can we come close to reconstructing reality and understanding the patterns of our lives within it. One of the great contributions of phenomenology to contemporary thought is this appreciation of the density of every person's experience and the consequent refusal to simplify experience or try to fit it to some preestablished theoretical constructs.

Ludwig Binswanger (1881–1966) and other phenomenological psychologists try to make sense of the intentionality — that is, the meaning-making — of their psychotic patients. They try to do a phenomenological reconstruction of the worlds their patients live in by taking their patients' words and stories seriously and understanding them as manifestations of the meaning-making of disordered minds. By reflecting on their patients' experiences they try to extract patterns and structures that reveal the meaning the patients give to their own experience. Then they try to enter empathetically into the patients' worlds and communicate with them based on an under-

phenomenology
fi-ˌnäm-ə-ˈnäl-ə-jē

n [from German *phänomenologie*, from Greek *phänomenon*, phenomenon + *-logie*, study of] standing of their intentionality. The development of these respectful bonds of communication are used to begin a healing process.

Phenomenology has had an influence upon contemporary thinkers such as Maurice Merleau-Ponty (1908–1961), Simone de Beauvoir (1908–1986), Jean-Paul Sartre (1905–1980), and Hannah Arendt (1906–1975), all of whose work is concerned with the making and understanding of meaning in the world.

phenomenon

fi-'näm-ə-ˌnän, -nən

n [from Greek *phainomenon*, from *phainesthai*, to appear]

A phenomenon is an observable event, something that can be perceived by the senses. Phenomena are distinguished from objects of reason or intuition. Thus, the number two is an abstract idea that cannot be perceived by the senses and is therefore not a phenomenon, though two of any kind of perceptible objects are phenomena.

Another way of describing a phenomenon is as an object of consciousness. The phenomenal world is the world as we perceive it through the senses and through imagination, dreams, and other forms of consciousness. In philosophy, the phenomenal world is contrasted with the noumenal world of "things-in-themselves." According to some philosophers (most notably Immanuel Kant [1724–1804]), all that can be known of the world is phenomenal. We do not have any direct experience of noumena, of things as they exist independent of human perception. The noumenal world, including God, can be inferred from appearances — phenomena — but it is not directly accessible to human experience.

philosophy

fə-'läs-(ə-)fē

n [from Latin *philosophia*, from Greek, from *philo*, loving + *sophos*, wisdom]

The word *philosophy* is derived from the Greek *philos*, loving, and *sophos*, wisdom. Wisdom is not just simply knowing but implies reflection on experience and an ability to understand values and contemplate the nature of things in the world. Philosophy is an activity in which the mind is engaged in trying to understand the principles behind the events and actions of everyday life. It predates the sciences and seems to have originated as a separate branch of study and human activity somewhere between 800 and 400 B.C. There is no recorded history of its origins, though early fragments of writings by philosophers such as Heraclitus (circa 500 B.C.), Thales (circa 600 B.C.), and Pythagoras (circa 550 B.C.) give rough dates for its emergence. The earliest centers of philosophy were at the borders of Greek culture in Sicily and southern Italy on the west, and Turkey and parts of Asia Minor and the Middle East. It may be that philosophy rose through a meeting of Greek, Egyptian, Middle Eastern, and north Mediterranean culture. This may explain how it developed as a contemplation of principles apart from the beliefs and gods of any particular religion. Instead of relying on religious authority to explain the world, philosophy used logical argumentation, principles of reason, and the belief that the principles determining the nature of reality could be known directly by the human mind.

The traditional branches of philosophy are:

- **metaphysics**, the investigation of the ultimate nature of reality, such as matter and mind, the origins of the universe, proofs of the existence of God, and the nature of time and space;
- **ontology**, the study of existence, the nature and characteristics of being, and the different ways of being in the world;
- **epistemology**, the exploration of the nature and origin of knowledge — how we know things, how knowledge is possible, and what certainty there is in knowing;
- **aesthetics**, the investigation of the meaning and nature of beauty;
- **ethics**, the study of the meaning and nature of good and evil; and
- **logic**, the exploration of the nature of reasoning and the validity of arguments.

Philosophy is an academic discipline as well as an activity of the mind. Academic philosophers are concerned with the history of philosophy as well as with reading and rethinking historical texts within the field. In contemporary philosophy, traditional philosophical problems are reencountered and reinterpreted, to take into account modern developments in psychology, sociology, and the physical and natural sciences.

Philosophy is also a self-questioning discipline. There are ongoing attempts to define just what questions are more appropriate for philosophical debate. One of the central concerns of contemporary philosophy is the study of language usage and the way in which it can lead to conceptual confusions. This aspect of philosophical thinking is closely related to **semantics**, the branch of **linguistics** that studies the relationships between meaning and language. Philosophy is also concerned with thinking about thought itself, and speculating about the language of rights and values. Philosophy is, for the most part these days, a **meta-** discipline: that is, it focuses on how people talk and think about things, rather than talking and thinking about things. Thus it studies the *way* people talk about being, the good, or knowing rather than about being, the good, or knowing.

Plato's Cave
plə-'tōs 'kāv

The allegory of the cave appears in chapter VII of Plato's (427–347 B.C.) *Republic*. Plato uses it to illuminate the way in which the highest reality, the **Platonic** ideas, which transcend mere appearances, can be known, and to show how enlightened philosopher-kings who come to know the ideas are equipped to rule by virtue of that knowledge.

The allegory of the cave is written in the form of a dialogue between Socrates and two young men. Socrates compares the situation of unenlightened people to that of men living in a huge cave who are chained so as to be able to look only toward the back of the cave. Behind them is a fire, and in front of the fire passes a procession of people carrying all sorts of objects. The shadows of the objects are cast on the back wall of the cave. Since that is all they can see, the prisoners in the cave mistake the shadows for reality. If, however, one of the men should break free, he would turn to the fire and at first be blinded. Then, after taking time to adjust to the light, he would see that he had taken the shadows for the objects they represented: he had mistaken appearance for reality.

If then he came out into the sunlight, he would be blinded again, though little by little his eyes would adjust and he would come to see reality unveiled. The same, Plato says, happens to philosophers who, by steps, reach up to the direct perception of the universal and eternal ideas, which are only weakly reflected by knowledge gained through the senses. This hard-won knowledge of the ideas, of Platonic "reality," then impels the philosopher back to earth to wake up other "blind" people. By virtue of this knowledge of the Real, the philosopher is qualified to rule and has an obligation to return to earth and lead others.

positivism
'päz-ət-iv-ˌiz-əm

n [from French *positivisme*, from *positif*, positive + *isme*, system, theory]

Positivism is a philosophical view that claims that all true knowledge is scientific — that is, in accordance with demonstrable laws of science, established by experiment, and verifiable by the evidence of the senses. This view of the world is similar to **naturalism, materialism,** and **pragmatism.** However, it is resolutely **atheistic,** and **democratic** in that it rejects all authority that claims to be absolute or God given. The theory of positivism was first articulated by Auguste Comte (1798–1857), who also coined the word *sociology*. Comte hoped to develop a science of reform based on his positivistic philosophy and sociological science of study. He believed that one could draw up a rational, step-by-step program that, if followed rigorously, would lead to the elimination of poverty and conflict. However, all attempts at realizing Comte's program have failed.

Many conservatives and religious thinkers use the word "positivist" in a negative way, to indicate someone who believes in a godless world that has no guiding absolute principles.

Logical positivism is the name given to a variant of positivism that developed in Vienna in the early twentieth century. Logical positivists formed what was called the Vienna Circle and developed the discipline of logic into a mathematical theory of logical systems. They also attempted to develop systems of logic that could provide a framework for reasoning and proof in all of the sciences. Their goal was to develop one logical and mathematical language that would be adequate to express all of science.

Some leading logical positivists were Rudolf Carnap (1891–1970) and Moritz Schlick (1882–1936). The movement failed to produce such a language, though it lead to some very significant breakthroughs in the development of logic as a branch of modern mathematics. The work it produced in logic also became unexpectedly important when it was seen to provide the mathematical theory for the development of digital computers.

The members of the Vienna Circle were socially progressive reformers and became targets of the Nazi movement in the 1930s. Schlick, one of the leaders of the group and a Jew, was assassinated on the steps of the University of Vienna by a student said to have Nazi affiliations. Other members of the group, including Carnap, emigrated to the United States during the late 1930s and early 1940s.

In England between the two world wars, Bertrand Russell (1872–1970) and A. J. Ayer developed a version of logical positivism that tried to produce a logical reconstruction of everyday reality. Ayer's book *Language, Truth and Logic* was the central document of this short-lived movement, which was called phenomenalism (as distinct from phenomenology). Their attempts to account for the complexity of experience in a system based on mathematical logic and using only statements about immediate experience (called sense data statements) proved a failure.

pragmatism

'prag-mə-ˌtiz-əm

n [from Greek *pragma*, deed]

Pragmatism is a philosophical theory of meaning, truth, and value that was developed in the United States during the mid- and late nineteenth century by Charles S. Peirce (1839–1914) and William James (1842–1910) and elaborated upon by John Dewey (1859–1952) in the early twentieth century. Pragmatism is concerned with practical action and its consequences. It has often been described as a form of **empiricism** particularly suited to the temperament of the United States during the Industrial Revolution. Pragmatism is about doing, making, and acting. It has been identified with the goal of the **progressive** movement — to dream about a better society and world and then act to make it happen. The truth of the dream comes in its making.

It is a practical philosophy that has been said to represent the inventive genius of the United States at the turn of the twentieth century. Figures like Thomas Alva Edison (1847–1931) and Henry Ford (1863–1947) have been said to be representatives of the pragmatic spirit of the United States.

For the pragmatist philosophers, the meaning of a sentence is its use, and the truth of a statement is determined by its practical consequences in the world. Truth does not lie in some eternal realm or in abstract universals, but in action in the real world. It can be found only through experiment and validated only through evidence of the senses.

The truth of a statement like "That ax is sharp" or "The fire is very hot" can be established pragmatically by using the ax and putting something into the fire. The truth of statements like "That painting is beautiful" and "It is good to help your neighbor" cannot be established pragmatically.

Statements whose truth cannot be experientially established are left in the realm of belief, feeling, and trust. Thus, for pragmatists, religion, morality, and aesthetic values are ungrounded unless they can be formulated in ways that make them subject to the test of experience.

William James, one of the developers of pragmatism, applied pragmatic thinking to religion. He wrote that though belief in God cannot be established pragmatically, it cannot be refuted pragmatically either. People have religious experiences which, as experience, cannot be denied reality. The relationship of their experiences to the existence of God, however, cannot be established pragmatically (by virtue of experience). Thus belief in God is a matter of individual choice and a gamble. James chose to believe in God since, if there was a God, he'd be rewarded, and if there wasn't, he wouldn't lose anything. James called this choice of religious belief the will to believe.

Something is "real" if it is true, a fact, an undisputed part of nature or existence, or an essential aspect of a thing. "Realism" is the philosophy of the real or, in art, the portrayal of the real. These things being said, a problem immediately arises since over the years people have disagreed upon the nature of the real. In some philosophies, the universal or Platonic idea or ideal of a thing is real (see **Plato's Cave**), while for others the appearances of things are the only reality that can be known. The real has been called unknowable. It has been attributed to some characteristics like matter and mind, and denied to all others. In each case, some version of realism is being defended while others are rejected. Thus the conception of realism held by a person or group is dependent upon a philosophy of existence. When you read that someone is a realist, it is essential to know more about their thinking before drawing any conclusions about what they actually believe.

Here are some of the most prominent versions of realism:

Platonists (from 500 B.C. to about A.D. 400) and Scholastic thinkers of the Middle Ages (circa 800 to 1250) believed that the real consisted of universals that existed absolutely, independent of people's minds. They believed these universals were eternal and some held that they were ideas in the mind of God.

The Cartesians of the seventeenth century, following the philosophy of René Descartes (1596–1650), believed that one can be certain only of the reality of mind, matter, and the existence of God. Cartesian realists question the existence of everything but mind and extended matter. For them the Platonic universals are nothing but constructs of the mind with no independently established reality.

Another form of realism states that the physical world exists outside us and is independent of our sense experience. Physicists and other scientists as well as most other people who are not tortured by philosophical paradoxes hold to this commonsense view.

In literary studies, "realism" has a different meaning than it does in philosophy. Literary realism is a form of writing (mostly prose fiction) that avoids the idealization of character and historical events and tries to deal with the lives of ordinary people. Pioneers of this form of writing were the nineteenth-century novelists Rebecca Harding Davis (1831–1910), William Dean Howells (1837–1920), Honoré de Balzac (1799–1850), and George Eliot (1819–1880).

Realistic fiction attempts to present an accurate imitation of life as it is. However, given the complexity of everyday life and the inability

realism

'rē-ə-ˌliz-əm, 'ri-ə-

n [from Latin *realis,* relating to things (in law), from *res,* thing, fact] of even the most voluminous novel to capture all the moments of a few days, realist novelists must shape and cut the reality they portray.

One kind of literary and artistic realism, social realism, is a form of advocacy for the poor and oppressed. It is specifically intended to motivate people to struggle to make society more just. In the United States just before and during the depression of 1929–1939 there were many socialist realist novels published and paintings done. Among the novelists, John Dos Passos (1896–1970), Theodore Dreiser (1871–1945), and Meridel Le Seuer (1901–) stand out. The painter and graphic artist Ben Shahn (1898–1969) and the photographer Dorothea Lange (1895–1965) also worked in this tradition.

reason

'rēz-ᵊn

n [from Latin *ratio,* reason, computation]

The word *reason* is derived from the Latin *ratus,* which means to count, calculate, or reckon. By extension, it has come to it mean to think. Reason, the ability to think, plan, and argue on logical grounds, has often been described as a uniquely human faculty, though its exact nature is a matter of philosophical and scientific controversy.

Reason is often contrasted with faith or with feeling. Arguments based on faith appeal to the authority of God or a holy text for their validity. Those arguments based on feeling appeal to personal or group emotions. Arguments based on reason, however, use logical arguments and appeal to the test of experience or to scientific law.

Reason has played a central role in the history of human thought. It is believed to be that faculty of the mind that prohibits error and allows for universal agreement. The Greek philosopher Aristotle (384–322 B.C.), in one of the earliest discussions of reason, wrote "Man is a rational animal," implying that rationality distinguishes humans from animals. The rational soul of people, for Aristotle, goes beyond concrete things and is able to think about the essence of things. It aspires to know all the truths of the world free of distortions caused by the emotions. Pure thought, for Aristotle, exists in the realm of what he calls the Prime or Unmoved Mover, the first and primary cause of all things, which is eternal and uncaused itself. The Prime Mover stirs and inspires the human intellect by its perfection and causes it to think and aspire to the truth.

The idea that the human mind can know the truth of things through abstract reason was questioned and explored in detail by the German philosopher Immanuel Kant (1724–1804) in *The Cri-*

tique of Pure Reason (1781). In that book, Kant claimed to demonstrate that the mind cannot reason its way to any truths about the nature of things in themselves or God, and that only abstract relationships such as those in mathematics and logic can be known by reason alone.

Debate continues about the scope of the application of reason to uncover truths about reality. There is general agreement, however, that rational arguments proceed by the use of the logical principle called *modus ponens,* which is called the rule of reasoning. *Modus ponens,* which dates farther back than Aristotle, is a form of argument from given premises to conclusions that logically follow from them. Here is the usual form of *modus ponens:*

Premise: p is true
Logical connection: if p then q (if p is true,
                            then q is true)
Conclusion: therefore q is true

Here is an example of *modus ponens* reasoning:

Premise: Dictators must be removed from
                         office.
Logical connection: If dictators must be removed
                         from office, then one must be willing to
                         resort to assassination if necessary.
Conclusion: One must be willing to resort to
                         assassination.

This is a rational argument for the use of murder. In order to accept the validity of the conclusion, however, one must first accept the premise (the assumption upon which it is based). Thus the rationality of the above argument can be accepted without accepting its premise.

When it comes to agreeing upon premises, emotion and faith insinuate themselves into the situation. Unfortunately, that means that one has to have a considerable amount of prior common ground before being able to proceed with rational argumentation.

Rationality is often looked upon as positive and people who disagree with rational arguments are accused of being irrational. An argument is only as sensible and valid as its premises, however, and it is always possible to question the grounds of any argument.

reductionism

ri-'dək-shə-ˌniz-əm

n [from Latin *reductio,* reduction + *ism,* system, theory]

Reductionism is a philosophical position that holds that the properties and functions of complex wholes such as biological organisms, chemical molecules, or societies can be fully explained in terms of the units of which they are composed. Reductionists argue, for example, that the properties of protein molecules can be fully accounted for in terms of the properties of the electrons, protons, and other particles of which their atoms are composed. They also argue that the properties of a society are simply the sum of the behaviors and properties of the individuals who make up that society.

Reductionism is the opposite of **holism**, which holds that there are certain properties, such as human consciousness or group opinions, that cannot be deduced from any combinations of parts of the whole. These properties are called emergent properties because they emerge from combinations of parts of an organism but cannot be reduced to these parts.

Debates over whether or not emergent characteristics exist are ongoing in the physical, social, and biological sciences. Reductionist scientists hold that the world consists of simple elements and, if there seem to be emergent characteristics when some elements are combined, it is simply because we don't presently know enough about the resulting behavior. Holists, on the other hand, believe that no satisfactory and exhaustive account of how societies, organisms, and molecules function can ever emerge from a reductionist model. There seems to be no middle ground between these two positions.

solipsism

'sō-ləp-ˌsiz-əm, 'säl-əp-

n [from Latin *solus,* alone + *ipse,* self]

Solipsism is a philosophical theory that claims that only the self can be proved to exist. It is an extreme form of **idealism** and consists of reducing reality to only what can be proved to exist by virtue of personal experience. For a solipsist, there is no world beyond one's own experience, and other people and things are only figments of one's consciousness.

Solipsists argue that their position cannot be disproved and is the only *logical* conclusion that can be drawn from the reduction of reality to terms of consciousness and experience.

In philosophy someone who acts and initiates action (the subject) is distinguished from someone who is acted upon or merely responds to the actions of others (the object). The subject has a will and makes choices and decisions, while the object has no will or thoughts and functions in response to the will, thoughts, and actions of others.

The same people can be both subjects and objects at different times. For example, when people decide to protest against war and brutality, or decide to change jobs or professions, they are acting as subjects. When the same people follow the crowd and vote without thinking, or make purchases simply because their friends do, they are responding as objects.

People can also be treated as subjects or objects by others. When people treat each other as subjects, they respect each other's humanity and have regard for their opinions, privacy, and right to choose how and when to act. When people treat each other as objects, they dehumanize the other person and treat people as things that can be owned and sold, moved and manipulated at will.

subject

'səb-jikt, -(,)jekt

n [from Latin *subjectus,* thrown under]

object

'äb-jikt, -(,)jekt

n [from Latin *objectus,* hurled]

The contrast between opinion and personal judgment and disinterested fact forms the distinction between the subjective and the objective. An attitude, philosophy, or claim is subjective if it is based on personal experience, values, or feelings — a view from within the **subject** and based on her or his knowledge of the world. It is objective if it is independent of the individual mind and can be verified by a socially agreed-upon procedure such as those developed in science, mathematics, or history.

Subjective claims are appropriate when they state the way the world looks from a particular person's point of view. In describing the personal experience of pain, which others can witness and empathize with but not partake of, the subjective view is the fullest and most reliable. The same is true when expressing judgments about the kind of things one likes to do or the people one loves.

Subjective accounts, however, cannot be the basis for claims about reality beyond the subject. In the physical world, subjective judgments of size and shape, for example, depend upon distance from an object and conditions of viewing, and can often be incorrect. Similarly, the way a person experiences heat or cold are subjective matters, but the temperature of boiling water or ice are objective facts.

The dates of historical events are objective facts while judgments about their importance are often subjective. On a more psychological level, subjective judgments about other people's motives and intentions can easily be incorrect.

subjective

(,)səb-'jek-tiv

adj [from Latin *subjectus,* thrown under + *ive,* related to]

objective

əb-'jek-tiv, äb-

adj [from Latin *obicere,* to throw in the way, oppose, from *ob-,* in the way + *jacere,* to throw]

The distinction between subjective and objective gets a bit blurred in certain realms of experience. In the case of ethics, for example, it is possible to take the position that all moral judgments are subjective and that all people have rights to their own ethical standards. It is equally possible to hold that there are objective moral values. Strong arguments can be made for the objective immorality of the values and actions of the Nazis and the Ku Klux Klan. These arguments involve embracing objective standards and claiming that they provide legitimate grounds for objective moral claims. Even though many people agree that there might be such grounds, there is no general agreement about what they are.

substance

'səb-stən(t)s

n [from Latin *substare,* to stand under, from *sub-,* below, under + *stare,* to stand]

The word *substance* is used in a special way in philosophy, referring to an object's underlying reality. Substance is said to exist in and by itself and not as a modification or relation of anything else. Substance is contrasted with appearance. For example, the color of an object changes as the light in which it is viewed changes. Its perceived size and shape also change as the viewer moves toward and away from the object. The object itself, however, remains the same. That sameness underlying appearances is substance. Substance is believed to be permanent and identical regardless of any change in qualities. The actual nature of substance is subject to debate and some philosophers (most notably **phenomenalists**) deny the existence of substance, claiming that reality is based only upon appearances.

synchronic

sin-'krän-ik, siŋ

adj [from Greek *syn-,* together + *chronos,* time]

The root *chronos* derives from Kronos, one of the Titans in ancient Greek mythology who is reputed to have given birth to the gods. Kronos is the father of Zeus, Demeter, Hera, Poseidon, and other gods. He was identified with time, and many words, such as *chronology, chronological,* and *chronic,* are derived from the root *chronos-.*

Synchronic and *diachronic* are two words that refer to different ways of studying something in time. Language, culture, life forms, events, and even astronomical bodies can be studied diachronically and synchronically.

To study something diachronically is to study its history over time.

To study it synchronically is to ignore its history and either study the current state of its being or the state of its being at one time in its history.

Here are some examples:

To study a historical event diachronically is to study the previous events in time that led up to its occurrence. To study it synchronically is to study the structure and character of the event itself. In a study of the beginning of World War I, one can look diachronically at the events over the twenty or fifty years prior to 1914 that led to the outbreak of the war. To study this synchronically, one can look at the political, social, and economic structure of Europe at the moment the war began.

To study a star diachronically is to study its history from the big bang to its current place in the universe. To study it synchronically is to study its chemical composition, velocity, heat, density, and other properties at a given moment of its history.

To study a culture diachronically is to study its development over time, including its wanderings from some original home, its interactions over time with other peoples, and the development of its art and technology. To study it synchronically is to freeze it at some moment in time and study in detail its structure and functioning at that historical juncture.

The same event or object or organization can be studied both diachronically and synchronically. One or the other of these analytic techniques can be emphasized depending upon whether an understanding of the origins or of the structure are considered more important for the researcher.

diachronic

ˌdī-ə-ˈkrän-ik

adj [from Greek *dia-*, through + *chronos*, time]

Teleology is the attempt to explain an event by its purpose, goal, or end. Teleological explanations go against the grain of scientific explanations, which argue from cause to effect, and not from event to purpose. An example of the difference between these two forms of explanation considers the development of a child into an adult.

From a "scientific" perspective, a baby develops step by step according to her or his history, genetic makeup, and experience. Interaction with others leads to the development of language. Values are developed and modified through enculturation.

From a teleological perspective, the telic cause of an infant's growth is the model of the adult it is striving to become. Children do not grow into horses or flowers. They strive toward human adulthood. That goal of growth is the driving force in development.

A teleological explanation considers the ends and purposes of

teleology

ˌtel-ē-ˈäl-ə-jē, tēl-

n [from Greek *teleos*, end, purpose + *-logia*, study of]

things to be preexisting plans and models, which are realized through specific events. From a theological perspective, those plans are God's grand designs.

utilitarianism

(ˌ)yü-ˌtil-ə-'ter-ē-ə-ˌniz-əm

n [from Latin *utilitas*, useful]

Utilitarianism is a moral and social philosophy that holds that the value of an action is determined by its consequences. Thus a morally right act is one that has good consequences and a morally wrong act is one that has bad consequences. There are a number of versions of utilitarianism that differ in their definition of good and bad consequences.

Utilitarianism originated with the work of the British philosopher Jeremy Bentham (1748–1832). Bentham believed that goodness is determined by "the greatest happiness of the greatest number." Thus the goodness of an act, its "utilitarian value," is determined by the amount of happiness it causes and by the number of people it affects. Further, happiness for Bentham meant pleasure. For him, pleasure and pain were the driving forces in human life and it was good to seek pleasure and avoid pain. He claimed that seeking pleasure and avoiding pain were both natural and moral. In fact, for him, seeking one's own personal pleasure was the highest goal of life and therefore **self-interest** was the main motivating force of existence.

The idea that self-interest is the central or sole motivating force in life is at the base of **conservative** thinking in the United States. Conservatives reject the possibility of an ideal society in which all people's needs are satisfied. If self-interest rules and there is no collective good or genuine compassion, then conflicts between people are inevitable. The best one can have will result from a maximizing of the self-interest and pleasure of the majority of the people involved in a situation.

For Bentham, seeking pleasure is moral because it is natural: he argues that what we naturally seek to do is what we ought to do. In determining what is good or bad individuals, as well as the state, must consider what will provide the greatest pleasure to the majority of the people. By equating goodness with the pleasure of the majority, Bentham made a major contribution to the development of conservative democratic thinking.

Utilitarian thinking was developed after Bentham by John Stuart Mill (1806–1873), who, like Bentham, defined the good as the greatest happiness for the greatest number, and also defined happiness as pleasure. However, he analyzed pleasure in a more complex way than Bentham did. For Bentham, all pleasures had the same value. Mill introduced the notion that different pleasures had differing qualities and values. Some pleasures were higher than others and counted for more. For example, intellectual pleasures were higher for him than bodily pleasures. The calculus of goodness had to take this hierarchy of pleasures into account.

In addition, Mill disagreed with Bentham on the issue of self-interest. He believed that **altruism,** a genuine impulse to share and help others, was as much a factor in human life as self-interest. The balance between altruism and self-interest had to be determined according to Mill's principle of the greatest good for the greatest number. If one's own self-interest contributed to the greatest good, it should be indulged. If not, it should be disciplined and checked in order to secure the happiness of the greatest number. This reckoning required careful reasoning, and it is not surprising that Mill put a great emphasis on the use of reason in moral judgment.

There was one other central principle that guided Mill's utilitarianism, the principle of laissez-faire (loosely translated from the French it means "don't interfere" or "let it be done"). This principle, which was also central to the **free-market** economic doctrines of the Scottish thinker Adam Smith (1723–1790), held that there should be the greatest amount of individual, personal, social, and economic freedom and self-expression compatible with the greatest good for the greatest number. This implies that there should be an absolute minimum of government regulation or control, and that freedom to act as one pleases and hold and express opinions are absolute values tempered only if they impinge on similar freedoms for the majority of people.

One criticism that has been leveled at Mill's majoritarian views is that it is possible for a majority to tyrannize a minority. Mill's ideas would not provide a way to protect Jews against anti-Semitism or blacks against racism unless it could be argued that the pleasure of the majority would be served better by their elimination. The whole question of minority rights causes problems for laissez-faire philosophers.

utopia

yu-'tō-pē-ə

dystopia

(')dis-'tō-pē-ə

The world *utopia* was created by Thomas More (1478–1535) by combining the Greek words for no and place, *ou* and *topos*. Utopia is no real place — it is an ideal, perfectly good, and thoroughly imaginary society. Utopian thinking is based on the idea that a perfect society can be imagined. Thomas More published one such vision in his book entitled *Utopia* (1516). Throughout the ages there have been visions of utopia ranging from the Garden of Eden to the Big Rock Candy Mountain with its "cigarette trees and soda water fountains where a bum can stay for many a day and you don't need any money."

In the nineteenth and twentieth centuries there have been attempts in Europe, Great Britain, and the United States to create small utopian communities based on communitarian principles of sharing and equality. One of the most well known of them was Robert Owen's (1771–1858) New Lanark Community in Scotland. The names of other similar communities, such as New Hope and Bethlehem, expressed their utopian beginnings. None of these communities has managed to survive.

There have also been larger attempts to create perfect societies, and these too have not achieved the fullness of the visions that motivated them. In fact, some historians believe that much of the white settlement of America's North Atlantic coast was inspired by John Winthrop (1588–1649) and his fellow Puritan settlers' utopian visions of a perfect "New World" based on his model of Christianity. During the Industrial Revolution of the late nineteenth century, some people dreamed of creating utopias based on technology, and there are still people who write science fiction about technological utopias. There have also been socialist visions of utopia and writers such as Auguste Comte (1798–1857) and Karl Marx (1818–1883) have articulated them in such powerful ways that many attempts to create socialist societies have been made. None of them has yet achieved a decent approximation to the utopian dreams of the writings.

Utopian thinking has often been parodied and put down as childish and romantic. Books such as *Brave New World* by Aldous Huxley (1894–1963) and *1984* by George Orwell (1903–1950) provide portraits of societies that are the opposite of utopian. These dystopias are repressive, thoughtless places that manipulate and destroy people.

Logic and Reasoning

In Latin *a priori* means coming before or earlier, while *a posteriori* means coming after. An argument or statement is true a priori if it is true before or independent of all experience, while it is true a posteriori if its truth depends upon or is known through experience.

Some examples of a posteriori statements are:

- *Ms.* magazine published without advertisements in 1990.
- The Chicago Cubs won the World Series in 1990.

The truth of these two statements is neither necessary nor universal. In the case above, the first is true and the second false. However, *Ms.* magazine *could* have been published with ads or not published at all in 1990, and the Cubs *could* have won the World Series.

A priori truths differ from a posteriori ones in that they are true no matter what happens in the world of experience. Throughout the history of philosophy there have been disagreements over the nature of a priori truths. Some philosophers hold that all a priori truths are logical or mathematical. The truth of these propositions comes from their meaning, and their derivation solely from the laws of logic and/or the axioms of mathematics. Examples of propositions whose truth is due to their logical form and is therefore independent of experience are:

- All female horses are female.
- If X is a green horse, then X is a horse.

Examples of mathematical propositions whose definition or derivation supposedly makes them a priori truths are:

- 2 + 2 = 4
- Parallel lines do not meet.

It is important to note that these a priori logical and mathematical truths are dependent upon assuming the truth of the axioms of the traditional systems of which they are a part. Recently, alternative logics and mathematical systems have developed, and so it is important to understand that a priori logical and mathematical propositions are true only relative to the system of which they are part. In the case of the parallel lines axiom, there are alternative geometries, one that postulates parallel lines which meet at infinity and another that has them meeting at two points (the geometry of a sphere).

There is another view of the a priori, associated with the German philosopher Immanuel Kant (1724–1804), which holds that there are some a priori truths which are innate and fixed in the mind. These truths represent principles that we use to filter and organize

a priori

,ä-prē-'ō(ə)r-ē,
,ā-(,)prī-'ō(ə)r-,ī, ,ap-rē,
,-prē-'o(ə)r-ē

adj [Latin, the former]

a posteriori

,ä(,)pō-,stir-ē-'ō(ə)r-ē,
,ā(,pä-,stir-ē-'ō(ə)r-,ī

adj [Latin, the latter]

experience. They make it possible for us to construct a coherent view of reality from the chaos of unorganized experience. Some of these Kantian a priori truths are:

- Every event has a cause.
- Time is not reversible.

A third category of a priori truths comes from theology. In fact the terms *a priori* and *a posteriori* originated in **Scholastic** philosophy, a movement dominant within the Christian church from approximately the seventh through the seventeenth centuries. For the Scholastics, in addition to a priori logical and mathematical truths, there are truths about the existence and nature of God that are a priori — that is, necessary and independent of experience.

One a priori proof of the existence of God, usually called the **ontological proof**, argues that the concept of a perfect being involves "necessary being" as part of its perfection. It is impossible to eliminate the concept of being from the concept of perfection. Therefore, the ability to think about a perfect being implies the necessary existence of God, the only perfect being.

There are still many debates about the nature of a priori truths, and about their relationship to a posteriori truths established by experience. In fact, much of current philosophical debate consists of disagreements over the boundaries between a priori and a posteriori knowledge, and therefore over the grounds of certain knowledge.

anachronism

ə-'nak-rə-,niz-əm

n [from Greek *anachronizien,* to be late, from *ana- + chronos,* time]

An anachronism is something that is out of chronological order. It is the misplacing of an event, person, object, idea, or custom in time. Placing the U.S. Civil War before the U.S. Revolutionary War, claiming Napoleon was an ancient Mesopotamian ruler, attributing the idea of automating machinery to the Middle Ages, and challenging someone to a duel in the 1990s are all anachronistic.

A person's behavior is called anachronistic if he or she is behaving in a way that was appropriate in the past but is not ordinarily done in contemporary times.

There is a special use of the distinction between analytic and synthetic statements in the fields of philosophy and the philosophy of science. This use was introduced by the German philosopher Immanuel Kant (1724–1804) in the introduction to his *Critique of Pure Reason* (1781). The distinction applies to statements, that is, assertions that can be either true or false. An *analytic statement,* according to the usual contemporary formulation, is one that is true by the nature of the meanings of the words in it and the laws of logic. Analytic statements are formally true, that is, true independent of all possible experience. Statements such as "2 + 2 = 4" and "Red flowers are red" are analytic. Analytic truths are examples of **a priori** truths.

"4" and "2 + 2" can each be logically reduced to "1 + 1 + 1 + 1" and the statement "2 + 2 = 4" can be replaced with "1 + 1 + 1 + 1 = 1 + 1 + 1 + 1," which is a form of the logical principle of identity truth "a = a."

Red flowers, by definition, are red.

A *synthetic statement* is one that is true based on experience or observation. "Elizabeth Cady Stanton advocated women's suffrage" and "Jesse Jackson is president of the United States" are both synthetic statements. The first is true, the second false. Synthetic truths are examples of **a posteriori** truths.

Kant used the distinction between analytic and synthetic statements to characterize the nature of knowable universal truths. He claimed that only analytic statements such as the theorems of logic and mathematics were universally true.

Contemporary philosophers, beginning with W. V. O. Quine (1908–   ), have questioned whether the distinction between analytic and synthetic statements is as clear as Kant implied it was. Quine tried to show that for some statements, such as "All bachelors are unmarried men," one can only prove its logical truth if *bachelor* and *unmarried man* were taken as exact synonyms and were completely interchangeable. But in ordinary language, for example, two- and three-year-old boys are unmarried males but we wouldn't call them bachelors. Quine questions whether there is a clear logical definition of synonymity in cases like these, one that is independent of experience and practical usage. He implies that there isn't, and that the line between logical truth and experiential truth is not distinct and unambiguous. This implies that the grounds for certainty and universal truth, even when based on meaning and logic alone, are often insecure.

analytic

ˌan-ᵊl-'it-ik

adj [from Greek *analytikos,* breaking up]

synthetic

sin-'thet-ik

adj [from Greek *synthetikos,* component, from *syn-,* together with + *tithenai,* to put or place]

contingent

kən-'tin-jənt

adj [from Latin *contingere,* to have contact with, befall; from *con-,* with + *tangere,* to touch]

necessary

'nes-ə-,ser-ē

adj [from Latin *necessarius,* from *ne-,* not + *cedere,* to withdraw]

cosmology

käz-,mäl-ə-jē

n [from Greek *kosmos,* world + New Latin *-logia,* study of]

Hobson's choice

,häb-sənz 'chöis

Contingency and necessity are opposites. An event is contingent if it happens by chance, or is dependent upon another event happening; an event is necessary if it could not have happened otherwise. For example, the birth of any particular individual is contingent upon the chance encounter of one of many possible spermatozoa with an egg. Necessity is involved when you drop a heavy object and it falls to the ground. In this latter case, it is the binding nature of physical law that makes the fall necessary.

If one takes a completely deterministic position and claims that all events have necessary causes, then one would hold that there is no contingency in the world. The existence of contingent events and chance happenings has been a matter of philosophic debate for at least two thousand years, and continues to challenge philosophers.

There is a category of necessity that has nothing to do with events, called logical necessity. A proposition is logically necessary if its truth is dependent upon its logical form and not upon anything else that might happen in the world. Two logically necessary statements are: "All white horses are horses," and "If A is round, then it is not not-round."

A cosmology is an account of the structure and order of the universe. There have been many mythological attempts to provide cosmologies. There have also been philosophical and theological cosmologies that have attempted to describe and explain the universe as an ordered system. In science, cosmology is a branch of astronomy that deals with the origin and structure of the universe, as well as with space/time relationships within it.

Cosmogony is the study of the origins of the universe and is a part of cosmology. It too has mythic, philosophical, theological, and scientific modes.

Hobson's choice is no choice at all.

Tobias Hobson was born in Cambridge, England, in the middle of the sixteenth century. To supplement his income as a coachman, he rented out horses to the students at Cambridge University. Whoever rented a horse had to take the one in the stall next to the door; there was no picking or choosing of any sort. You either accepted Hobson's choice or got nothing.

Hobson's choice has come to stand for a situation in which a person has to accept something whether he or she likes it or not. For example, if a person is on a trip in a remote area and must rent a car, he or she might end up in a situation where only one type of car was available. A more dramatic example would be if someone were told that she or he had to go to war or be hanged as a traitor. Unless that person were suicidal, the only choice available would be a Hobson's choice.

Holist theories assume that there are some wholes, such as biological organisms, the human mind, and societies, that have characteristics which are not the mere sum of the characteristics that make them up. These wholes are irreducible and must be understood on their own terms.

Holistic biology, for example, claims that the organic unity of living creatures cannot be reduced to the characteristics of the chemicals that make them up, or the energy they use, or any other constituent parts. Holistic psychology holds that human thought cannot be reduced to any possible combination of physical properties or specific brain functions.

Holism is often contrasted with **reductionism** and **atomism**, both of which claim that phenomena can be completely understood once their component parts are understood.

holism

'hō-ˌliz-əm

n [from Greek *holos,* whole]

Induction and deduction are two different ways of reasoning. Inductive reasoning proceeds from experience and experimentation and draws conclusions or principles from them. Deductive reasoning proceeds from theory and develops conclusions that are logically drawn from the premises of the theory. Thus induction is experience based and deduction is logic based. Both are used in everyday life to substantiate different claims to truth, and in scientific and social scientific investigations to attempt to establish the truth or falsity of hypotheses.

A hypothesis is a proposed explanation of an event or phenomenon. Here is an example of an inductive and a deductive approach to establishing the following Hypothesis A:

Water consists of a chemical compound of the elements hydrogen and oxygen.

An inductive attempt to establish the truth of the hypothesis would be to take a sample of water and, through electrolysis, try to reduce it to hydrogen and oxygen. If this is done once, and the water breaks down into the gases, the hypothesis is established as possible. However, there is no certainty that the same thing might happen the next time one does the experiment. For example, it's possible that some

induction

in-'dək-shən

n [from Latin *inducere,* to bring in]

deduction

di-'dək-shən

n [from Latin *deducere,* to lead away]

other substance was dissolved in the water used in the experiment and that the gases resulted from that substance's interaction with electrolyzed water. If, however, after doing the experiment several hundred times with purified water the two gases still result, then there is greater reason to induce or generalize that the hypothesis is true. The more times the experiment is tried with the same results, the greater the confidence one can have in the inductive hypothesis. However, as with all inductive arguments, no absolute truth of the hypothesis can ever be established since there is no certainty that doing the experiment one more time won't produce different results.

Each time you do an experiment and get the same results as predicted, you verify the hypothesis; that is, you establish, with increasing confidence, the likelihood of its truth. The experimental verification of a general hypothesis is always partial. However, it only takes once instance to falsify a hypothesis. For example, if only one hydrolysis of a sample of water results in chlorine gas and a deposit of magnesium and no oxygen or hydrogen, Hypothesis A would have to be abandoned no matter how many times it had previously been verified.

Of course, if this actually happens with a well-established hypothesis such as A, things wouldn't be as simple as giving up A. The whole experiment would be conducted again and again for similar results, and special factors, such as atmospheric conditions or undetected contaminants, that could have caused the result would be sought. The falsification of a previously established inductive hypothesis is a serious matter in science as it causes one to question the theory that explains the experimental results and not just the hypothesis itself. Thus in the case of A, if it is falsified, the entire theory of molecular structure would come into question.

The idea that *no matter how many times a hypothesis is verified it takes only one instance to falsify it* was first put forth by Karl Popper in his book *The Logic of Scientific Method.*

Deductive reasoning is reasoning according to the rules of **logic** and proof that date as far back as Euclid and were first articulated in modern form by George Boole (1815–1864). Deductive arguments are made within the structure of a clearly articulated theory that specifies the special vocabulary used in the field of study and includes all of the **axioms** and postulates (that is, assumptions) of the subject. These assumed truths are then combined using logical concepts such as "if . . . then . . ." "or" "not" "and" "all," and "some" and **rules of inference** (that is, procedures of inferring a statement from other statements such as "if A implies B and B implies C then A implies C"), which allow one to move step-by-step from premises to logically implied conclusions. A hypothesis is then verified by deduction if it can be proved by a step-by-step chain of logical argument that begins with the axioms of the theory and ends with the hypothesis. *Deductive arguments are independent of experience and experimentation.*

In the case of Hypothesis A, a deductive proof would begin with the axioms of molecular theory and with its terminology. Fundamental undefined terms, such as *positive* and *negative,* would be introduced and used to define other terms, such as *molecule.* These terms would then be used to articulate the axioms of molecular chemistry and then, using logical principles, a step-by-step proof of A would be demonstrated. According to some scientists and philosophers of science, without such a logical proof, no inductively verified hypothesis can be considered to be fully established.

The requirement for a deductive proof of scientific hypotheses is not usually met, however. Scientific ideas and assumptions are constantly changing and theories are subject to revision based on the results of experimentation. Experimental results can bring into question even the most rigidly proved deductive argument. *Scientific theory is subject to the test of experience.* Deductive proofs and formalizations of theory are useful for getting an overall view of a scientific field, and for generating new hypotheses. They are also useful for checking the logic of thinking in general argumentation.

logic
'läj-ik

n [from Greek *logos,* reason]

Logic is a tool of argument and an instrument of **reason**. It was developed as an independent branch of philosophy in order to establish grounds for agreements on ways of deducing the truth from premises without resorting to emotion or to authority. Greek and Western European philosophers from as early as the fifth century B.C. have claimed that in analyzing the logic of arguments they are also uncovering the structure of thought.

The earliest surviving attempt to categorize logical arguments and specify ways of drawing **inferences** (conclusions) is Aristotle's (384–322 B.C.) analysis of the syllogism in his work *Prior Analytics.* Aristotle defines a syllogism as an argument in which some things not originally stated follow of necessity from given premises. The idea is that the syllogism does not just restate the premises, but adds new knowledge based on the structure of the argument.

Here are two examples of Aristotelian syllogisms:

If every M is L
and every N is M,
then every N is L.

      or

If every person is mortal
and every woman is a person,
then every woman is a mortal.

If no M is L
and every N is M,
then no N is L.

      or

If no person is mortal,
and every woman is a person,
then no woman is mortal.

The basic syllogisms of Aristotle were considered to be the underpinnings of logical argumentation by European and American philosophers until the late nineteenth century. At that time there was a great flowering of mathematics and physics, and the study of mathematically formulated systems of logic developed. There were a number of mathematicians and logicians who developed new logical terminology and created a system of logic that was intended to provide a formal basis for logical argument in all the sciences as well as the logical underpinnings of formal mathematics. Some of them were the Englishman George Boole (1815–1864), the German Georg Cantor (1845–1918), and the Italian Giuseppe Peano (1858–1932).

In his book *The Laws of Thought,* George Boole attempted to show how logic could be considered part of algebra and therefore a form of mathematics. He believed that concepts such as "mortal," "person," and "woman" (the ones used in the illustration of Aristotle's syllogism), could be considered as sets or classes. Thus the concept of "woman" would, in what is called Boolean algebra, be the set of all women. The set M, representing all mortal things, would represent the concept "mortal." Then the statement "All women are mortal" could be translated algebraically as "The set of all women is contained in the set of all mortals" or $W < M$.

The main person associated with the development of a mathematically structured logical system was the German mathematician Gottlob Frege (1848–1925). Instead of considering logic as part of mathematics, he tried to show how mathematics could be derived from logic. Frege's system of logic was completely formal, independent of any meanings that could be assigned to the signs and rules of manipulation in the system. The construction of purely formal systems has a very important role in the history of logic and the foundations of mathematics.

Frege's ultimate goal was to build a perfect system, a universal calculus in which all and only the true statements of mathematics could be proved. Such a system would function like the universal calculus imagined two hundred years before by the German philosopher Gottfried Wilhelm von Leibniz (1646–1716).

Frege ran into problems completing his system, and in 1903 received a letter from the British philosopher and mathematician Bertrand Russell (1872–1970) indicating that there was a contradiction within it. In logic, a contradiction arises when a statement and its negative can both be proved within a system. A system that is free of contradictions is called consistent, and one with a contradiction is inconsistent. When a system is inconsistent, a simple proof of any statement within the system can be constructed and the system collapses. This contradiction within Frege's system is called **Russell's paradox.**

Russell, Frege, and many other logicians tried to patch up or reconstruct Frege's system so that it would be consistent. However in 1932 the German mathematician Kurt Gödel (1906–1978) proved that it was impossible: No system could even theoretically be built that contained all and only the true statements of arithmetic.

Gödel's theorem is arguably the most important and unexpected result in the history of logic and perhaps even mathematics. It implies that no universal calculus is even theoretically possible; that no computing machine can possibly be built that will turn out all and only the true statements of arithmetic (much less the rest of mathematics). Mathematics is and will remain profoundly mysterious.

$\mathbf{A}$ method is a systematic way of accomplishing a particular task, a body of rules that provides a framework for investigation, speculation, or action in a given field of human endeavor. Methodologies provide techniques for testing scientific hypotheses, studying literary texts, analyzing environmental problems, planning towns and cities, running election campaigns, advertising products, or solving mathematical problems. Methodologies usually include testing and evaluations schemes, forms of argument and reasoning, criteria for proofs, specific techniques, tactics, and strategies, decision-making procedures, and problem-solving mechanisms.

The methods used by scientists to explore and uncover objective truths about the natural and physical world have to be scrutinized

method

'meth-əd

n [from Greek *methodos,* from *meta-,* after, behind, beyond + *hodos,* way] very carefully in order to make sure that error is not introduced by the investigators' biases or hidden assumptions in their practices. The concern for a precise and clearly articulated scientific method developed in seventeenth-century Europe. Two thinkers who were instrumental in articulating this method, which depended solely upon physical experiments and observation using the senses, as opposed to truths established by religious authority or logic, were the Englishman Francis Bacon (1561–1626) and the Frenchman René Descartes (1596–1650). The method Bacon studied was **inductive**, and consisted of drawing conclusions from tables of many instances of a phenomenon. It is based on the careful and wherever possible numerical observation and measurement of natural phenomena.

Descartes's method consisted of systematically doubting everything that could not be firmly established by logic or the immediate evidence of the senses. Memory, for example, though not denied as immediate experience, was questioned whenever it claimed to establish truths about the past.

Descartes's method was **deductive** rather than inductive and refused all appeals to higher authority, whether it be the will of God, or the general consensus of the ruling class. Descartes's doubts democratized knowledge, as everyone's senses were equally valuable in the establishment of certain knowledge.

Descartes's theories reduced the area of absolutely certain knowledge to the simple awareness of oneself as a thinking being. His reduction of certainty about experience to the statement "I think, therefore I am" represents the extreme conclusion that results in depending solely upon logic and immediate conscious awareness. Thinking that is based upon systematic doubt and the evidence of the senses is called Cartesian after Descartes.

Since the search for the perfect scientific method began in the nineteenth century, it has become clear that the best method of investigation often varies, depending on what is being studied. Some methodologies are very rigid and involve highly controlled activities, step-by-step procedures, constant feedback, and clearly defined control mechanisms. Others are more open ended and involve improvisation, ingenuity, and on-the-spot decision-making. For an experiment to be successful, it is crucial to match its methodology carefully to the theory being used or the nature of the problem being explored. For example, an improvisational method can be appropriate when exploring totally unknown territory but disastrous when experimenting with volatile chemicals.

Methodologies in different disciplines and areas of human activity vary according to the aspects of the world they investigate. Anthropology, which studies cultures and groups of people, is distinguished by its field work and observational methods; "hard" sciences, such as chemistry and microbiology, by their laboratory trial-and-error methods; sociology by statistics and data collection; and mathematics by reasoning and logic. Some political groups use a methodology of civil disobedience and nonviolent confrontation; others use methodologies that draw upon what is known about propaganda and persuasion. In the fields of engineering and large-scale planning, people use complex methodologies drawn from the fields of computer programming and budgeting analysis. In all of these cases, the choice of methodology is a crucial one. It can either facilitate the work or become a major obstacle to getting things done.

null hypothesis

The null hypothesis is used in the design of experiments in the social sciences (e.g., sociology, psychology, social psychology). It states that it is possible to choose two groups for study in such a way that there is no significant difference between them. Another way to state this is that the only differences between the selected groups are due to chance. The groups may consist of office workers, students in a school, corporate executives, or members of a particular social class or race. The groups are matched so that they have the same class, gender, educational status, cultural background, and so on. All significant features of the groups are supposedly engineered to be the same. One group is then called the **experimental group** and the other the **control group.** The experimental group is manipulated in some way and the control group is left alone. Afterward they are both tested and compared to see if the experimental manipulation has created a difference between the groups. That difference can then be attributed to the effects of the manipulation, and not to any preexisting differences between the groups.

A null hypothesis is then formulated stating that there will be no difference between the tested performance of the two groups. This zero or null difference is actually not expected. The null hypothesis is formulated in order to be **falsified,** thus establishing that a difference did indeed develop and is worth future study.

An example should be helpful here as the reasoning behind formulating null hypotheses is somewhat indirect. An educational psychologist might select two groups of third-graders that are of the same race, social class, gender, and performance on reading tests. One class, the experimental group, is then provided with individual reading tutoring while the other, the control group, continues to be taught as before. After the tutoring, the two groups are given reading tests in order to see whether differences in performance between the groups have emerged.

The null hypothesis states that no differences between the groups will emerge after the tutoring. Now, the experimenters might hope that a difference will emerge and the null hypothesis will be falsified. That will then give experimenters a reason to study in greater detail the reasons for the differences that cannot be **deduced** solely from the test scores. If the null hypothesis is proved, however, then the use of tutoring to improve reading scores will be discredited and some other techniques might have to be tried.

Thus the null hypothesis provides social scientists with an opportunity either to discover significant differences in performance caused by certain experimental techniques or to discredit these attempts to make a difference.

paradox

'par-ə-,däks

n [from Greek *paradoxos,* contrary to expectations, from *para-,* against + *doxa,* opinion]

A paradox is a puzzling statement or argument that seems, on casual examination, to be self-contradictory or absurd, yet turns out to be logical or have a valid interpretation. Paradoxes often illustrate the limits of our language and thought, the places where reality is a puzzle and logic seems to break down. There are logical, mathematical, and philosophical paradoxes. There are also paradoxes of religion as well as poetic paradoxes.

Some of the best known philosophical paradoxes are called Zeno's Paradoxes. These are a series of puzzles about motion and multiplicity posed by the Greek philosopher Zeno of Elea (circa 485 B.C.). Zeno is said to have created them as indirect support for the doctrines of his mentor Parmenides (circa 510 B.C.), who held that reality is One: indivisible, immovable, and eternal. In reply to charges from other philosophers that Parmenides' theory of Oneness was inconsistent, Zeno produced his paradoxes to show that the assumption of plurality was even more inconsistent.

Here is Zeno's most well known paradox, Achilles and the tortoise (Achilles is sometimes represented as a hare), which is meant to show that motion is impossible:

> Achilles sees a tortoise in the distance and sets out to catch up with it. But when he reaches place A, where the tortoise was when he first saw it, the tortoise will have moved ahead to spot B. When Achilles reaches B, the tortoise will have gone to C, and so on. Therefore, no matter how many times this process is repeated, the tortoise will always be ahead of Achilles who, if

the logic of the argument holds, can never catch up to the tortoise.

In religion it is not unusual to encounter paradoxes. Jesus Christ is both a person and a god, both mortal and immortal. He does and doesn't have a father. Buddha/Gautuma is a person and at the same time the godhead with no location in space or time. The God of the Old Testament is to be obeyed even though that God created all and has all power over that creation. Oppositions between metaphysical characteristics such as perfection and imperfection, innocence and sin, and immortality and mortality are usually at the root of religious paradoxes, which are accepted as part of the nature of the spiritual and the mystical.

A major category of logical paradoxes are the paradoxes of self-reference. These paradoxes turn on the contradictory claims statements sometimes make when they refer to themselves. The simplest self-referential paradox is the following statement:

THIS STATEMENT IS FALSE (A)

If statement A is false, then it is true: if it is true, then it is false. So long as we allow statements in the language to refer to themselves, paradoxes such as these cannot be avoided.

One of the most famous self-referential paradoxes is called Russell's paradox after the philosopher Bertrand Russell (1872–1970), who used a version of it to demonstrate that it was extremely difficult to create a consistent formal system of axioms that had as theorems all the true statements of arithmetic. A common nontechnical version of the paradox is the following:

Consider a barber in a small town who shaves all and only those people who do not shave themselves. Does the barber shave himself? If that barber does shave himself, then he does not shave himself. If that barber does not shave himself, then he does shave himself.

In mathematics there are a number of paradoxes of the infinite. For example, consider the following paradoxical statements about the infinite number of integers beginning with one and adding one to each term to get the next term. This order of the infinite is usually called aleph, after the first letter in the Hebrew alphabet:

aleph = {1, 2, 3, 4, 5, 6, . . . and on indefinitely}

- the number of even numbers = aleph
- the number of odd numbers = aleph

These two paradoxical statements about a part of aleph equaling the whole of aleph have to do with the nature of infinite sequences.

The number of numbers in aleph can be put in one-to-one correspondence with the number of even or odd numbers as follows:

aleph = 1, 2, 3, 4, 5, 6 . . .
even = 2, 4, 6, 8, 10, 12 . . .
odd = 1, 3, 5, 7, 9, 11 . . .

This one-to-one correspondence between two infinite sets of numbers is the meaning of equality on the level of infinite sequences.

In poetry, paradoxes are used to illuminate ironies, contradictions, and uncertainties that characterize our lives. For example, the conclusion of John Donne's sonnet "Death Be Not Proud" uses the paradox of death dying to illuminate the nature of resurrection:

One short sleep past, we wake eternally,
And death shall be no more; death, thou shalt die.

There is another poetic use of paradox in which two terms that are contraries are joined together to create a single image. Such a fusing of contraries creates an oxymoron. Some examples of oxymorons are: "painful pleasure," "the lying truth," "dumb wisdom," and "joyful tears."

parameter

pə-'ram-ət-ər

n [from Greek *para-*, alongside + *metron,* measure]

The word *parameter* has several technical meanings in addition to the one used in everyday language. In informal usage, parameters are the limiting factors of a situation, conditions that are assumed or given and have to be accepted as integral to the nature of the situation. For example, two of the parameters of life in a **liberal** democracy are freedom of speech and the right to own property. In a fascist society, absence of the right to assemble and express grievances are parameters of everyday life.

As another example, being born and dying are parameters of life.

The three most common technical uses of parameter involve physics and the natural sciences, mathematics, and social sciences.

In physics and the natural sciences, a parameter is a measurable factor or physical property whose value determines the behavior of a physical system. For example, the parameters that determine gravitational attraction are mass and distance. The greater the mass, the greater the gravitational attraction, and the greater the distance, the less the gravitational attraction.

In meteorology, the parameters that determine atmospheric conditions are temperature, pressure, and density.

A mathematical parameter is a constant, a number that does not vary in an equation. For example, 2 is a parameter of the equation

$x + 2 = y$. In mathematics the parameter is most commonly referred to in equations that represent curves.

In the social sciences, a parameter is the measure of a characteristic of a whole population. For example, the mean (or average) income or the distribution of wealth in a total population are parameters. Social scientists rarely deal with parameters, since it is very difficult to interview or measure every single person in a society or large social group. Instead, social scientists use many samples of a population and develop estimates of the actual parameters of the total populations with which they work. This is one of the reasons why estimates of error have to be built into most social scientific studies.

The word *structure* comes from the Latin verb *struere*, which means to arrange in piles, to pile up, and by extension, to build or construct. The noun form, *structura*, means that which is constructed, a building.

structure

'strək-chər

n [from Latin *structus*, pp of *struere*, to heap up, build]

Buildings stand up when they have an overall coherence or framework in which the parts are interrelated and mutually supportive. This general, essential underlying framework of an entire construction is its structure. The structure can be contrasted with inessential decorations or furnishings, which are not necessary to the coherence of the whole.

There are many seemingly different things that have the same underlying structures. For example, two autos may have totally different appearances and yet the same structure. The placement of their frames and engines, the relationship of the parts within the engine, and all of the other systems that make the car go might be exactly the same, while the shape, color, and design of their bodies might be totally different. Two such cars, which are structurally the same though superficially different, are said to be isomorphic to each other. In general, two constructions that have the same structure are said to be isomorphic structures.

Though the use of the word *structure* originated in building construction, it has been extended to refer to the overall framework of mathematical and logical systems, to works of art and literature, and to social organizations such as political parties, governmental bodies, and educational and health institutions. The study of such artistic and social structures has proved to be very useful for understanding the basic coherence of works of art and social organizations.

In mathematics and logic, the structures of systems can be formally specified in basic terms — **axioms** and **rules of reasoning.**

The study of structure and the attempt to uncover the rules that govern structural coherence of systems has been extended to linguistics, anthropology, and even literary criticism. (For some discussion of the explicit study of structures, see the entry **structuralism.**)

The word *structure* has also been applied to life forms, where the structure is the framework that holds the whole together. This is often contrasted to a life form's function, which is the way it works. Loosely, the functions of a living organism or manufactured object take place within the structure that both limits and supports them.

tautology

tȯ-'täl-ə-jē

n [from Greek *tautologos*, redundant, from *taut-*, the same + *logos*, word]

There are two basic meanings of the word *tautology*. The first comes from the field of logic, where a statement is a tautology (or tautologous) if it is true by virtue of its logical form. Illustrations of this are:

- If Sam or Roger will go to the movies, then Roger or Sam will go to the movies.
- If Alice and Sallye will go to the theater, then Sallye and Alice will go to the theater.

The first of these sentences is true because "a or b" is logically equivalent to "b or a," and the second is logically true because "a and b" is logically equivalent to "b and a."

In the second meaning, a statement is a tautology if it is true only by virtue of the definitions of the words used in it. It therefore says nothing about the world, even though it might superficially seem to. Here are two tautologies that seem to be providing information but aren't:

- That family is on the poverty level because it earns less money than needed to meet its basic needs.
- He is obviously an atheist because he doesn't believe in God.

The first statement is a tautology since being on the poverty level is defined as earning less money than needed to meet basic needs. The second is a tautology since being an atheist is defined as not believing in God. Both statements are true merely by virtue of the meaning of their words.

Critical Thinking

Something is concrete if it is particular, specific, actual, palpable, or capable of being experienced. It is abstract if it is general, ideal, conceptual, theoretical, or capable of being attributed to individuals as a quality. In philosophy, concrete terms are ones that denote particular persons or things, such as "this brown dog" and "Herb's daughters Erica and Tonia." Abstract terms are ones that denote qualities that exist only as attributes of particular persons or things, such as "redness," "goodness," and "beauty."

Some philosophers, such as the Greek Plato (427–347 B.C.), believe that abstract qualities exist in a pure realm outside everyday experience and are only imperfectly manifested in concrete individuals. These abstractions are called **Platonic Ideas** and are invoked by Platonists (that is, followers of Plato who believe in the independent existence of some version of Plato's Ideas) in arguments that infer that there is a single standard for all qualities such as "beauty" and "goodness," which can be understood only through the means prescribed by their philosophy.

Other philosophers, most prominently **pragmatists, naturalists,** and **utilitarians,** assert that there are no eternal abstract qualities, only qualities that can be generalized from concrete experience. Thus, for them the concrete is the basis for the development of abstract ideas, while for the Platonists the concrete is simply an imperfect manifestation or embodiment of the abstract.

The distinction between concrete and abstract description can be seen in these two selections of poetry. The first, from John Keats's (1795–1821) "Ode to a Nightingale," employs concrete description and involves all five senses while the second, from Keats's "Endymion," employs only abstract description:

> My heart aches, and a drowsy numbness pains
> My sense, as though of hemlock I had drunk,
> Or emptied some dull opiate to the drains. . . .

> A thing of beauty is a joy forever:
> Its loveliness increases; it will never
> Pass into nothingness. . . .

abstract

'ab-,strakt, 'ab,

adj [from Latin *abstrahere,* to draw away, from *ab,* away + *trahere,* to draw]

concrete

(')kän-'krēt, 'kän-, kən-'

adj [from Latin *concrescere,* to grow together, from *com-,* with + *crescere,* to grow]

algorithm

'al-gə-,ri<u>th</u>-əm

n [from Arabic *al-khuwārizimi*, from *al Khuwārizimi*, A.D. 825, Arab mathematician]

An algorithm is any step-by-step procedure for solving a problem or performing a task. Originally, the word applied to procedures for arithmetic computation. However, cookbook recipes, repair manuals, and route maps are also examples of algorithms.

The ninth-century Arabic mathematician Abu Jafar Muhammad ibn-Mūsa al-Khwārizimi wrote a book on how to solve arithmetic problems using the numerals 0, 1, 2, 3, 4, . . . which had entered the Arabic world from India in the eighth century. The 0 was crucial as it introduced the base 10 system in which mechanical computing can be done with ease. Al-Khwārizimi's Latin name was Algorismus, and his instructions for computation came to be called algorithms.

Computers require algorithms in order to function. Computer programs provide step-by-step instructions that control the way in which computers process data. In order for the computer to function, there cannot be any uncertainty in these programmed sequences or algorithms.

It was natural for mathematicians to look for a universal algorithm, one that would provide a step-by-step sequence that would provide either a proof or a disproof of every properly written mathematical statement and all possible computations. In the 1930s, in three independent efforts, Kurt Gödel (1906–1978), Alan Turing (1912–1954), and Emil Post provided proofs showing that no universal algorithm was even theoretically possible. This means that it is not just difficult but impossible to create a computer that will turn out all and only true mathematical statements and do all possible correct computations. The best that one can hope for is a series of partial algorithms that provide techniques for providing proofs and calculations for defined and limited areas of mathematics. This disappointed scientists who dreamed of a universal calculating machine that would mechanically solve all mathematical problems. These dreams were first articulated by the German philosopher and mathematician Gottfried Wilhelm von Leibniz (1646–1716) in the seventeenth century. Their disappointment, however, leaves plenty of work left for programmers and mathematicians.

Analysis consists of examining a complex whole and breaking it down into its component parts. The analysis of a mathematical system, for example, consists of breaking the system down to its axioms, undefined terms, and rules of inference. The analysis of a political problem consists in breaking it down into competing power interests and groups. And the analysis of a chemical compound entails discovering its component chemical elements.

An analysis sometimes results in components that have none of the characteristics of the whole. For example, analyzing salt (NaCl, sodium chloride) into its component elements, sodium and chlorine, breaks down a solid that is edible into a poisonous gas and a volatile metal that burns on contact with oxygen. Analyzing the human mind in terms of localized brain functioning turns language into electronic waves.

Synthesis consists of combining parts, elements, or components into a complex whole that has characteristics that differ from those of the components. In psychology, a synthesis would join together all of the components of behavior to provide an account of the complex whole we call a person. In sociology, a synthesis would show how all of the members of a social group function as members of the group and how that behavior differs from their behavior as individuals outside the group.

A synthesis must leap from the behavior of the parts of a group or thing to the behavior of the whole. For example, none of the parts of an automobile serves, independently, as a vehicle. When organized and assembled according to a plan, however, they take on a new character that makes the whole useful. The same should be true on a theoretical level when it comes to trying to explain human behavior. One can enumerate all of the component interests and competing power groups that are party to a political or economic struggle, yet to get a sense of how they work one has to understand the ways they interact with each other as wholes. For example, a government bureaucracy has its own rules, rituals, and procedures, and people who work within it have to conform to its demands if they want to survive. The whole controls the behavior of individuals, often with very negative results.

It is important to understand that the ability to analyze an object, event, or person into component parts, no matter how thorough the analysis, does not necessarily mean that a full explanation has been provided. The synthetic characteristics of the whole may disappear through analysis. Full understanding often requires both analysis, which provides insight into the component parts of a whole, and synthesis, which considers them in dynamic interaction.

analysis

ə-'nal-ə-səs

n [from Greek *analusis*, a releasing]

synthesis

'sin(t)-thə-səs

n [from Greek *syntithenai*, to put together, from *syn-*, together + *tithenai*, to put or place]

cybernetics

ˌsī-bər-'net-iks

n [from Greek *kybernētēs*, pilot, governor, from *kybernan*, to govern or steer]

Cybernetics is the science of self-regulating systems. A self-regulating system is one that corrects its own errors without the interference of any outside manager. A good example of a cybernetic or self-regulating system is a flush toilet. When you flush the toilet, the water runs out and then the tank starts to fill up again. There is a float inside the tank, which is attached to a shut-off valve. As the water rises in the tank, the float also rises and moves the valve to the shut position. At a certain point before the tank overflows the float is high enough to shut the valve and stop the water from coming in. No outside person is needed to regulate the refilling of the toilet tank: it is self-regulating.

A machine that is self-regulating and self-correcting is called a servomechanism.

Cyber is Greek for pilot, steersman, or governor. The word *cybernetics* was coined in the 1940s by Norbert Wiener (1894–1964) to designate the science of control and communication in living and machine systems. Concern for the nature of control mechanisms or steering devices distinguishes cybernetics from other sciences.

One of the central concepts of cybernetics is feedback. A system that guides its own behavior uses the results of its own past and present performance to determine future performance. Feedback is information provided to individuals, groups, or machines that can be used to determine the effectiveness of past actions and the nature of future actions. In cybernetics, one starts with a goal, acts to achieve the goal, gets feedback about the effectiveness of one's performance, and then modifies the next behavior according to that information. This is very difficult from a stimulus response (SR) analysis of behavior. In the stimulus response mode, a stimulus is presented, the organism or machine responds, then a new stimulus is presented and the organism or machine responds in the same way if the stimulus is the same. There is no inner processing, no mechanism that takes control of the response. Cybernetics posits processed responses rather than the automatic ones that SR psychology posits.

The science of cybernetics developed out of Wiener's work in World War II developing firing mechanisms for antiaircraft guns. The guns had to be self-adjusting, since in order to hit moving targets they had to find out where the targets were and how fast they were moving and then calculate where they would be in order to aim the gun. Information about the speed and direction of the target had to be fed back into the aiming mechanism in order to adjust the gunshell's path. Aiming directly at the plane was a guaranteed miss.

The science of cybernetics is applied in the design of robots, artificial limbs, and other machines used to move around in environments without external controllers. Cyberneticists study how animals and plants adjust to changes in their environments. They also study brain functioning, planning and strategy, and the design of active systems. The study of computer-based artificial intelligence is another area in which cybernetics is used.

A dichotomy is a division of a group into two parts, and in particular into two parts that are mutually exclusive and therefore do not have any common members. Mutually exclusive parts are those that, by definition, exclude each other. By using a negative it is easy to build mutually exclusive divisions. Thus, the group of living things can be divided into:

> birds and not-birds
> two-legged creatures and not-two-legged creatures
> flying and not-flying animals

There are also dichotomies that are positively rather than negatively defined. The division of a group of people into females and males is a dichotomy. So are the following divisions:

> of a set of checkers into black and red pieces
> of a group of objects into manufactured and natural

A digit is one of the ten numerals — 0, 1, 2, 3, 4, 5, 6, 7, 8, or 9 — in the base-ten Arabic number system. Thus the number 45 has two digits, 4 and 5.

The word *digit* also refers to the numerals in a number system of any base. Thus a number system with the base two has only two digits, 0 and 1, and a number system with the base five has five digits: 0, 1, 2, 3, 4.

To digitalize something is to represent it by a series of numbers in a digital number system. The ability to represent music and visual images as well as numerical operations by the digits of a number system (usually the base 2 system with the digits 0 and 1) is at the core of the development of electronic computers, which for that reason are often called digital computers.

In music, the frequency of a sound, which can be represented by number indicating the number of waves per second, is a digital representation of the sound.

Visual images can also be digitalized. For example, black-and-white newspaper photos are made up of black dots and blank spaces.

dichotomy

di-'kät-ə-mē, də-

n [from Greek *dikhotomia*, from *dichotomos*, divided, from *dikha*, in two + *temnein*, to cut]

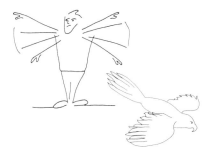

digitalize

'dij-ət-ᵊl-,īz

v [from Latin *digitus*, finger, toe]

The entire photo can be considered a grid of points running from left to right and from top to bottom. Each point that is printed can be considered a 1 and each point that is left blank, a 0. Then all the points on a photo can be represented by a list of 0's and 1's — that is, the photo can be digitalized.

In both of these cases, a list of numbers provides a numeric model that can be translated into sounds or pictures.

ecology
i-'käl-ə-jē, e-

n [from Greek *ökologie*, from *oikos*, house + *logia*, system theory]

Ecology is the study of the relations between living species and their surrounding environments. The word *ecology* comes from the Greek root *eco-*, which means household and, in an extended way, the management of the household. Ecology can be thought of as the care and management of the household Earth. The word was first used by Ernst Haekel (1834–1919) in 1873, a scientist who pioneered this field of biological study. Subdivisions of biological ecology include population ecology, evolutionary ecology, community ecology, physiological ecology, and behavioral ecology.

By the 1930s, the Chicago School of Urban Sociology developed a field of human ecology. This field of study described the movement of people through urban societies and attempted to link the structure and organization of human communities to interactions with their localized environments.

Current ecological thinking combines science with social and political action. The goal of most ecologists is to develop ways of preventing human activity from destroying the environment. The uses and development of resources are examined, in ecological thought, in relationship to their effects on the total environment rather than in terms of the short-term financial profit they might produce.

Some recent work in the field of ecology pays attention to how societies cope with environmental hazards. Major environmental disasters in the 1960s and 1970s brought a growing awareness of ecological issues and led to the formation of environmental activist groups. Many activist groups are concerned with the ecological repercussions of major disasters like the 1984 release of deadly gas from the Union Carbide Plant in Bhopal, India, the 1986 nuclear disaster in Chernobyl, and the 1988 oil spill in an Alaskan bay.

In addition to coping with human-caused disasters, ecological activism also tries to develop and implement programs to avoid them in the first place.

Friends of the Earth, Greenpeace, Earth First!, the Sierra Club, the Environmental Defense Fund, and the German Green Party are some of the major activist groups today concerned with preserving ecological balance.

An ecosystem is a system of interacting species in a particular environment. The definition of the particular boundaries of an ecosystem are often arbitrary and determined by the life forms one wants to study. For example, someone studying forests may define a whole tree-covered area as a "woodland ecosystem." But in the same woodland one may look more closely at the ecosystem of a fallen tree, including the insects that live in it, and the moss, fungi, and plants that grow on it. Thus, one would define that fallen log as an ecosystem in itself.

One of the main goals in the study of an ecosystem is to discover ways in which species become fitted to their environments. This includes how the species relates to other species, how it finds a habitat, and how that habitat relates to those of other species. This fit of a species into its ecosystem is called ecological adaptation.

The actual place and function a species has within an ecosystem is called its econiche (also called its ecological niche). If two closely related species compete for the same food or nesting place within the same territory — that is, for the same niche within that ecosystem — one of the species usually takes the upper hand and the other disappears from the environment. Thus it is rare to find two closely related species occupying the same ecological niche.

Some people argue that the whole earth is the only real ecosystem because you cannot isolate smaller environments: a dead log is still a part of a larger forest.

ecosystem

(')ē-(,)kō-'sis-təm

n [see ecology]

The word *evolution* is derived from the Latin word *evolutionem*, which means unrolling, in the sense of unrolling a scroll and preparing it to be read. In one of the word's extended meanings, *evolution* came to stand for the unrolling or unfolding, in history, of God's plan for the universe. All events, from the creation onward, are part of a divine plan that evolves, or plays itself out, over time.

In the late seventeenth and eighteenth centuries in Europe, with the development of the sciences, the word *evolution* developed the secular meaning of the unfolding or development of life forms. This meaning focused on embryology, where the fetus was said to unroll or display the evolutionary stages of the development, from lower animals to human beings, before being born. Thus, for each person,

evolution

,ev-ə-'lü-shən, ē-və-

n [from Latin *evolutio*, from *evolvere*, to unroll]

the history of the development of the human race is said to be duplicated as the fetus develops in the womb.

The development or evolution of a group or species over long periods of time is called its **phylogeny**. The historical development of an individual is called her or his **ontogeny**. The assumption that the human embryo recapitulates the evolutionary history of the species is summarized by the phrase "ontogeny recapitulates phylogeny."

In 1852 the British philosopher Herbert Spencer (1820–1903) formulated a general theory of evolution, which posited the historical development of life forms from simple to complex over the course of history. It wasn't, however, until 1859, when Charles Darwin (1809–1882) published *On the Origin of Species*, that a specific theory about the mechanism of evolutionary development was proposed. Darwin proposed the theory of natural selection. That theory states that evolution works through the competition of many species for the same place in the environment, that is, for what is now called the same **ecological** or **environmental niche**. Those species that fit best, that are fittest in their environment, survive, and the other species die out.

Darwin proposed the unheard-of idea that some species do not survive. This created a great deal of controversy, especially among religious thinkers who saw the idea of the survival of the fittest as contrary to God's will. In particular, Darwin's theory of evolution called into question the idea that God made the world in one short period of time and that it was all good. There are still religious groups that fight the idea of evolution as a scientific theory. However, though there are still some open questions about how evolution works, there is as much evidence in the fossil record and in experimental studies that proves the truth of the general concept of evolution and natural selection as there is for any other theory in any other natural science.

For Darwin, the mechanism of evolution was primarily genetic and the method competitive. He proposed that slight genetic variations took place within a species, allowing its members to be more competitive for food, shelter, and territory than other species. In the competition to survive, some species triumphed and others lost.

More recently, there have been theories of sociobiology, based on the study of social insects and their communities, that propose other mechanisms that may be at work in the evolutionary process. E. O. Wilson (1929–   ), one of the pioneers of sociobiology and a leading student of ant society, bases his theory of evolution on genetic determinism. That is the theory that evolution is governed by the genes — by inheritance — and is predictable once one knows the genetic and environmental situation of a species.

Wilson and other sociobiologists also propose that evolution takes place through **altruistic**, that is, cooperative and caring behavior as well as through competition. This type of behavior is evident in insect colonies and throughout the animal kingdom where parents often sacrifice themselves, not for personal benefit, but for the benefit of their young. The same kind of social behavior can be found in warfare, where individuals sacrifice themselves for the benefit of the survival of the whole group. For Wilson and other sociobiologists, altruism is a mechanism of evolution that subordinates the individual to the good of the group.

Though there is little disagreement with sociobiologists' claims for insect society, Wilson's attempt to extend genetic determinism to human society has roused great criticism. Wilson provides no place for the effect of any but genetic or mechanical causes, and his account of human development is said to be inadequate to describe the complex role of culture and choice in human evolution.

A fallacy is an argument that has the appearance of truth and logicality and yet is neither true nor logical. For example, consider this reasoning:

> Only elephants and whales give birth to creatures that weigh more than 100 pounds. My cousin weighs more than 100 pounds. Therefore my aunt, his mother, is either a whale or an elephant.

There are a number of common fallacies that appear in literary and art criticism, philosophy, political science, and the social sciences. It is important to be aware of these fallacies since it is easy to find arguments based upon them convincing, and to fall into the habit of using them yourself, sometimes without being aware that your conclusions rely upon false reasoning. Some common fallacies:

The inductive fallacy consists of concluding that two events have some causal or necessary relationship to each other based on a limited number of experiences of their occurrence. For example, if you hear a clock chiming twelve times at noon and then see people streaming out of office buildings, the inductive fallacy would consist of concluding that the ringing caused people to stream out of the building. Your reasoning would have ignored the fact that in our culture businesses break for lunch at noon and so the people would be streaming out whether the clock was chiming or not.

fallacy

'fal-ə-sē

n [from Latin *fallacia*, deceit, fraud]

The intentional fallacy consists of interpreting writing or other artworks according to the author's or artist's stated intentions for the work. Certainly these intentions are important but cannot be the sole criterion for judgment, as artistic intentions are often not realized and the nature and quality of a work can depend as much upon internal structures and nuances in the text, craft, social and cultural forms unconsciously embodied in the work, relationships to other works of art, and intuitions as upon articulated intentions.

"Petetio principii" fallacies either assume a premise to be true without justification or depend upon circular reasoning. An example of the first type of petetio principii is:

> Males are much better at mathematics than females. Therefore Ronald is much better at math than his sister Rhoda.

An example of hidden circular reasoning is the following:

> G is to be trusted as a presidential historian because G's accounts of events and all of the most authoritative history books are in exact agreement.

What can be hidden in this argument, and therefore make it fallacious and circular, is that all of the history books referred to use G as their source for reliable information on the presidency.

The naturalistic fallacy consists of identifying the quality "goodness" with other natural qualities such as pleasure, self-interest, or the objects of desires. This fallacy was named by G. E. Moore (1873–1958), who wrote about it in the early twentieth century as part of a critique of ethical views that identified pleasure with moral goodness. An example of the naturalistic fallacy is the argument that it is morally good for the majority of people to seek their own pleasure even if it causes pain to a minority, since the greatest pleasure to the greatest number is the same as the greatest good to the greatest number. For Moore, who disagreed with this, "goodness" is a quality that is different from all natural qualities such as pleasure and desire.

Gaia hypothesis

'gī-,ə hi-'päth-ə-səs

The Gaia hypothesis claims that the globe and all of the life on it is a superorganism actively engaged in maintaining the conditions necessary for its own survival. This theory was first formulated by the British atmospheric chemist James Lovelock, who has written extensively on it. In Greek mythology, Gaia is the goddess of the Earth. According to the Greek writer Hesiod (circa 800 to 700 B.C.), she sprung from Chaos, gave rise to Uranus (the Heavens), and then mated with him and was the mother of the Titans (one of whom was Kronos, time, the father of Zeus), the Cyclopes, and the Hundred-handed Giants.

Through Zeus, who was supposed to be the father of humankind, Gaia gave rise to all of life. In Lovelock's view, Gaia, the Earth, is being wounded by its human children. All that is done to pollute or destroy some aspect of the globe affects all of the system. The Gaia hypothesis implies that in analyzing any aspect of human functioning, the whole of the planet's living system, from chemical balance to the balance of species, must be considered.

There is considerable debate about whether the Gaia hypothesis makes sense or is true in any concrete scientific way. However, at the very least, many environmentalists find the idea of the planet as a living system a useful metaphor for thinking about ways that human injuries to the planet might be healed.

A gedanken experiment is a thought experiment. It is an exercise in imagination in which an experimental situation is called up in the mind and then an experiment is imagined. The dreamer/experimenter remains in control of the fantasy and observes the results. The point of the gedanken experiment is to develop a hypothesis that can then be tested in an actual laboratory or be used as the basis for theoretical speculations and formulations.

The idea of gedanken experimentation is difficult to grasp at first. Yet there have been a number of famous and productive gedanken experiments in physics, and it is possible that much of scientific and artistic creativity depends upon such play with the imagination preceding the formalization of a theory or hypothesis.

A simple gedanken experiment might be to imagine dropping a group of objects — lead weights of different sizes, a cork, a tennis ball, a golf ball, and a basketball — into a large bucket of water. The challenge is to imagine which would sink and which would float. This can lead to an intelligent guess about why objects sink or float in general. The results of this mind experiment could then be tested by actually doing the experiment.

One of the most famous gedanken experiments was performed by Albert Einstein (1879–1955) during the time he was developing the special theory of relativity in the early part of the twentieth century. Evidently Einstein imagined himself racing with a beam of light and as he approached the speed of the beam he got the insight that his mass was increasing to infinity and that he would not even theoretically be able to overtake the light beam. Later he formalized and

gedanken experiment
gi-ˈdän-kin ik-ˈsper-ə-mənt

n [from German *gedankan*, thinking + Latin *experimentum*, test or trial] mathematized the results of this gedanken experiment into relativity theory. The specific steps by which he translated fantasy into mathematics is not known.

genetic diversity

jə-'net-ik də-'vər-sət-ē

n [from Greek *genesis*, beginning]

There is a great diversity of plant, insect, and animal species on earth, each with a different genetic composition. These species number in the millions, and this diversity is crucial for maintaining ecological stability in an environment. Different species serve different functions and meet different challenges in the total biological environment, and when the number of species is significantly reduced it is possible that the entire environment might collapse.

Diversity ensures that the loss of a single species is unlikely to threaten the survival of the whole ecosystem. Unfortunately, this diversity is being threatened by human development, with more than a thousand species becoming extinct each year. The pace of extinction is increasing and it is possible that by the year 2050, sixty thousand plant species may be lost.

It is not clear how far the resilience of the earth can be stretched before all life forms are threatened. Care must be taken to preserve genetic diversity at the peril of creating disaster for all life forms, humans included.

heuristic

hyù-'rist-ik

n [from Greek *heuriskein*, to discover, find]

A heuristic is a problem-solving technique that proceeds by trial and error. It helps in the exploration of a problem when one does not yet have a full solution available. It is the opposite of an **algorithm**, which is a step-by-step procedure for calculating or performing a task. When there is no automatic and definite means of solving a problem available, heuristic devices such as working assumptions, principles of sampling, models, ideal types, or intelligent guesses can be tried. Here are a few examples of heuristics:

One way of approaching a maze problem is to begin at the entrance and follow all the right turns until a dead end is reached and then retrace the path until a new right turn is possible. The principle of right turns will not guarantee that the maze will be solved, but it will provide a way to begin to explore paths and eliminate ones that don't work. It is a heuristic device to help discover the correct path.

In solving a murder, one can use as a heuristic principle the assumption that the murderer is that person among all of the suspects who stands the most to gain from the victim's death. Of course this might be completely wrong and the murder might be the result of an unexpected encounter or an outburst of unplanned passion. However, the assumption is a reasonable working hypothesis and over the long run is likely to help in the solution of some cases.

In analyzing a social problem, one can set up and try to apply a model that accounts for certain behavior. For example, one can choose a model that uses class or race or gender difference to account for conflict or failure. Then, in the case of analyzing a situation where there is drastic school failure in a particular city, the model can be drawn upon to examine the situation. For example, if one adopted a race-conflict model, one would examine the racial makeup of the school and the community, and the racial attitudes of the people involved. Sometimes the model will lead to insight and suggestions on how to solve the problem. At other times it will be misleading and another hypothesis or model will have to be used — that is, another heuristic device will have to be created that fits the conditions of the problem.

Heuristic techniques are particularly important when trying to explain or work with complex social phenomena where reliable theories and algorithms are rare.

Iconoclasm is image-breaking, the destroying of icons and representations such as paintings, drawings, or sculptures. The destruction of human images that were worshipped as holy or sacred dates at least as far back as early Judaism (over five thousand years). In both Judaism and Islam, the making of holy images in human form is prohibited, and, if found, are to be broken; temples and mosques are decorated with abstract designs.

There have also been internal struggles over whether holy images should be represented in human form within Christianity. In 726 the Byzantine Emperor Leo III (680–741) placed a ban on images, and throughout his empire human representations of Christ and other holy figures were destroyed and replaced by symbols such as the cross, or by abstract or floral decorations influenced by Muslim art. This ban was opposed by the Roman Catholic pope and intensified the schism between Byzantine and Roman Christianity.

The meaning of iconoclasm has generalized beyond religion, and anyone who opposes established beliefs and breaks with established customs can be called an iconoclast. Iconoclastic art breaks with the traditions of past art, and political iconoclasts break with the political traditions, beliefs, and rituals of their society.

iconoclasm

ī-'kän-ə-klaz-əm

n [from Greek *eikonoklastēs*, literally, image destroyer, from Greek *eikono-*, image + *klastes,* breaker]

ideal

ī-'dē(-ə)l, 'ī-ˌ

n [from Greek *idea*, appearance]

An ideal is a standard of perfection or excellence. There can be ideals of mortality, intelligence, beauty, creativity, and so on. Ideals can differ from culture to culture and person to person. However, an ideal is always a positive model. There is no ideal of evil, ugliness, dishonesty, or incompetence. A person of high ideals is one who accepts standards of perfection, and an idealist is one who tries to realize these standards. Idealists are often accused of being impractical and unrealistic, which should not bother them since, by definition, they strive to meet standards that go beyond the real. The real and the ideal are in many ways opposites. As long as imperfection exists in the world, there will be a contrast between what is and what idealists believe can be.

interface

'int-ər-ˌfās

n [from Latin *inter*, between, among + *facies*, face, confront, meet]

An interface is a meeting point or means of communication between different systems. The interfacing of a garment, for example, is the stiffening material attached between the inner and outer layer of material in it (particularly in shirt collars). The boundary between two countries is their interface. The surface where oil and water, which do not mix, meet when they are in the same container is their interface. The wires connecting a computer with a printer interface the two of them. The word *interface* can be used as a noun to describe a meeting place or boundary, or as a verb, to describe the process of system-to-system communication.

The use of the word *interface* was originally restricted to mechanical and physical meeting places or modes of communication. However, it has been extended over the past fifteen years to refer to general connections or commonalties among people, academic areas of study, ideas, and feelings. The mechanical has become a **metaphor** for human interaction and activity — quite a switch from a more traditional type of metaphor, which attributes human spirit to the inanimate world.

meta-

ˌmet-ə-

prefix [from Greek *meta-*, beside, after, change]

*M*eta is a Greek prefix which, when used with the name of a discipline, designates a new but related discipline designed to deal critically with the original one. Statements made in a "meta" study are statements *about* a science or other subject area, rather than statements *within* the area. Thus, "2 + 2 = 4" is a statement within arithmetic and "2 + 2 = 4 is valid within Frege's formal system" is a metamathematical statement.

This use of "meta" developed from the early Greek use of "metaphysics" as the name for the work that followed the *Physics* in the collected works of Aristotle (384–322 B.C.). *Meta* at that time simply meant "after." The *Metaphysics* of Aristotle deals with the ultimate and underlying causes of events, the so-called higher knowledge that underlies physical knowledge. This would include God, first principles of motion, the laws governing all forms of causality, and so on.

Thus the word *metaphysics* came to mean the study of the ultimate grounds of reality, of the first principles that underlie the study of the world, and *meta* came to mean the study of an area of study. Some examples of "meta" fields of study:

Metamathematics is the critical study of the nature of mathematical systems, including the study of how proofs are made, terms defined, axioms determined, and issues such as whether given mathematical systems are free from contradiction.

Metapsychology is the critical study of psychology as a discipline. It deals with issues such as the grounds on which a psychological theory can talk about the unconscious, the mind, the ego, or the spirit. Other questions range from "How does a theory justify generalizing from a small number of people closely studied to all of humanity?" to "How do different theories account for the relationship between the mind and the body?" and "What are the grounds of proof and the methods of argument in particular psychological theories?"

Metalinguistics is the study of the way in which language is studied. It deals with questions such as "What techniques are used in a given theory to determine how language is acquired and how are they validated?" "What kind of evidence would a theory of language accept that might prove it was false?" "What distinguishes a separate language from a dialect of a given language?"

Metabiology is the study of the way in which biological theories work. It raises questions like "How does a biological theory gather evidence and what are the grounds it uses to claim the truth?" and "How are competing and contradictory conclusions about the same experimental results adjudicated?"

In a more general way, a metatheory can be developed to study the nature of any theory and to question its techniques, procedures, and claims to truth and validity. Metatheory itself is the study of the nature and characteristics of theories in all fields.

neo-

ˌnē-ō-

prefix [Greek, from *neos*, new]

The prefix *neo* is used to indicate a revival and adaptation of an older style or way of thinking. The use of *neo* implies that the new form is not an exact imitation of an older one but is based on the same or very similar basic principles as the old one. Thus **neoclassical** art is art based on the principles of balance, order, and harmony manifested in fifth-century-B.C. Greek and then Roman Empire sculpture and architecture, but transformed and adapted at three different times in different ways during the Italian **Renaissance**, in mid-seventeenth- and eighteenth-century-England, and in early-nineteenth-century France.

Neoconservatism is a late-twentieth-century adaption of conservative political and economic thinking that emphasizes anti-communism, the importance of capitalism in promoting democracy, and the need for order, stability, and allegiance to the cultural traditions of white male European culture.

Neo-Marxism is also a late-twentieth-century phenomenon. The word refers to a number of efforts to adapt traditional Marxist ideas to a late-twentieth-century, non–Soviet Russian context. Its different versions analyze the power of cultural forms, the role of individual choice, and racial and sexual oppression in ways that extend traditional Marxist thought.

Here are some other common neo's: neo-Platonism, neocolonialism, neoliberalism, neo-Nazi, neo-Fascist, neorealism, neomodernism, and neorationalism. If you know something about the word that comes after neo-, it's possible to make an intelligent guess about the general meaning of the "neo" word.

Ockham's razor

ˌäk-əmz 'rā-zər

Ockham's razor is the name given to the principle governing reasoning that holds that the best explanations are the simplest ones and those that assume the least. The principle was used extensively by the **medieval** English philosopher William of Ockham, or Occam (circa 1285–1349), and can be paraphrased as follows: Entities are not to be multiplied beyond necessity. If you can cut something out, as with a razor, do it.

This formulation was never stated in exactly those words in Ockham's works. The formulations that occur most frequently in his writings are: "What can be done with fewer [assumptions] is done in vain with more," and "Plurality is not to be assumed without necessity."

When scientists and mathematicians build a **formal system** in which the theorems and hypotheses in their field can be deduced from **axioms**, basic terms, and the rules of **logic**, Ockham's razor applies, and that system which is simplest is considered best.

A paradigm is an ideal model, pattern, or clear and good example of something. Some everyday uses of the word are:

- She was a paradigm of virtue.
- Your new car is a paradigm of elegance and speed.

In an extended sense, a paradigm is a model that is used to understand the nature of the world. For example, a religious paradigm is a model of understanding that sees life as governed by God or some principle that is the ultimate cause of everything. A purely **materialist** paradigm is a model of understanding that sees life as the interaction of physical objects with no god principle at work.

A paradigm in this larger sense is a filter or grid through which the world is understood. It is not a theory or set of rules governing thought so much as an orientation of mind that determines how one thinks about the world. For example, the paradigm that considers individual freedom the highest social value determines the way in which people in the United States think and talk about politics and economics. In judging or trying to understand other societies for example, we ask how much freedom they have and measure their freedom against ours.

The extended meaning of *paradigm* was first described by Thomas Kuhn (1922–   ) in his influential book *The Structure of Scientific Revolutions,* published in 1962. In this book he argues that at every moment of history there are certain scientific paradigms that determine the way people in a society think about the world. Kuhn says, "Paradigms may be prior to, more binding, and more complete than any set of rules or research that could be unequivocally abstracted from them."

However, according to Kuhn, "When scientists disagree about whether the fundamental problems of their field have been solved, the search for fundamental rules gains a function that it does not ordinarily possess." The world at that time is ripe for a paradigm shift, for a totally new set of grids to be adopted as determinants of the organization of experience.

Some examples of major paradigm shifts are:

- Copernicus's thinking of the earth moving around the sun instead of thinking of all of the heavenly bodies rotating around the earth;
- Benjamin Franklin's development of the concept of positive and negative electrical charges, which replaced the theory of electricity as an effluvium, or flowing gas or vapor.

These two paradigm shifts led to fundamental reconceptualizations of the world. It was because of these reconceptualizations that

paradigm

'par-ə-ˌdīm, -ˌdim

n [from Greek *paradeigma*, pattern, from *para-*, alongside + *deiknynai*, to show]

new specific scientific discoveries and social relations were made possible. For Kuhn, scientific progress takes place through such paradigm shifts.

The idea that change takes place through paradigm shifts has spread beyond the field of science. There are scholars who see social, artistic, and cultural changes as resulting from paradigm shifts in fields as diverse as mathematics, literature, music, philosophy, and anthropology. Some scholars claim that the current development of **feminist** paradigms, which shift perspective from a male-centered and **patriarchal** view of human values to a female-centered or gender-fair view, have led to the creation of new forms of social relations.

As a final note, there are scholars who strongly disagree with this paradigm shift theory. Some believe that change takes place slowly and cumulatively, and that what seems like a paradigm shift is actually the result of many small changes built upon each other. Others see development and change in science and society as a history of competing ideas. They believe that there are always alternate and opposing explanations vying to become the "accepted" explanation of reality. In this view, every paradigm has proponents who will gain from its acceptance, and opponents who will lose. The struggle over personal interest is as important as some supposedly "objective" scientific attempt to uncover "the truth." The philosopher Paul Feyerabend (1924–) is a leading exponent of this **dialectical** view of the development of science.

pedant

'ped-ᵊnt

n [from Greek *paidagogos*, from *pais*, boy + *agogos*, leader]

The word *pedant* is derived from the Latin *pedagogus*, which means teacher. This meaning has been extended to refer to a teacher who adheres to strict and formal rules in teaching, and is dry and uninteresting. More generally a pedant is a person who is unduly concerned with book learning and formal rules and regulations without an understanding or experience of practical affairs.

A pedantic argument is one that is full of quotes and references to books and authors but lacking in intelligence or wisdom.

Postmodernism grew out of disillusionment with **modernism**'s failure to produce a perfect, rational, planned, and compassionate world. The dreams of modernity were admirable but in the light of contemporary history seem naive. Loss of faith in society's perfectibility through centralized planning and technological development arose in Europe and the United States throughout the mid-twentieth century, and by 1990, with the collapse of centralized communism in the Soviet Union and Eastern Europe and the push toward deregulation and privatization in the United States and Great Britain, modernism was no longer a central force in economic planning or political thinking. According to some critics, it was replaced in the arts, design, and the media by what has been called postmodernism.

Postmodernism replaces modernism's utopian faith in technology and planning with an ironic, self-mocking, and somewhat detached attitude toward culture and progress. Instead of elevating abstract, sparse, and functional styles, as was the case with modernist architecture, postmodern architecture fuses historical styles freely and with a sense of play and humor. Postmodern office buildings are characterized by nonfunctional arches and other ornaments, small Greek or **Renaissance** buildings stuck on top or built into the facade, as well as bright colors and mosaics. These postmodern buildings mix cultural styles and are fun to look at in contrast to the sparse modernistic buildings that represent an earlier generation of skyscrapers.

Postmodernism opts for stylistic diversity in the realm of design and decentralization in the realm of organization. It produces works that mock themselves: advertisements that make fun of people who take advertisements seriously, and works of fiction that expose their own artificiality. **Irony** and self-reference are the hallmarks of the postmodern sensitivity. It is as if the postmodern artist or designer is calling attention to all of the conventions of craft and the poses of art in order to expose the pretentiousness of modern culture.

Postmodern culture is eclectic: it picks and chooses from the creative expressions of the world's peoples, though it is still based mainly upon European and American culture. It is sensitive to the biases of Eurocentrism and considers them ironically and without the excessive posturing and boasting that was common during periods of European colonial expansion. It is possible to look at postmodernism as an attempt by some European and American critics and artists, followed by the media, to question the primacy of European **canons** and reposition Europe and the United States in a more modest and egalitarian world context. It mocks linearity, rationality, and the idea that technology produces progress.

postmodernism

(')pōs(t)-'mäd-ər-niz-əm

n [from Latin *post*, behind, after + *modo*, just now, from *modus*, measure]

Some writers and critical thinkers associated with postmodernism are Jean Beaudriard, Julia Kristeva, Umberto Eco, and J. F. Lyotard. Their works mix the anecdotal and personal with the philosophical, and analyze media, the fine arts, society, politics, culture, habit, and manners in ways that break down the usual boundaries of criticism.

qua

'kwä, 'kwā

prep [Latin, as]

Qua is Latin for "as" or "who." It is used in philosophy, criticism, and other intellectual writing to pick out a certain characteristic of a person or thing and describe it in some way. Some examples should clarify this definition.

> Angela Davis, qua militant, speaks out with a strong, direct, and strident voice, whereas in private she is reserved and intellectual.

The use of *qua* in this sentence separates out Angela Davis's militant public speaking from her private and intellectual life. It makes it possible to speak about that one public aspect of her life while making it clear that she is much more complex than is indicated by a description of her public self.

Here's another example of the use of *qua*:

> He was a very fine therapist though, qua father, he was unable to apply his own professional insights.

This distinguishes an individual, as therapist, from the same man as a father, and says that he cannot put his own professional principles into practice in his personal life.

The word *qua* makes a powerful intellectual distinction between someone considered from the point of view of one characteristic or considered as a complex whole. It allows for a conscious and explicit simplification of character for the sake of argument. Of course, it is important to be careful that a use of *qua* does not oversimplify and distort a person's character or actions.

Anthropology and Linguistics

The first known inhabitants of a place are called aboriginal people. The word *aborigine* is often applied to the earliest known inhabitants of Australia, the people who lived on the continent before the coming of the Europeans.

The aboriginal inhabitants of the United States arrived from Asia over ten thousand years ago. They were called Indians by Europeans who came to the North American continent in the fifteenth century and mistook the native people they met for inhabitants of India. The aboriginal people of the Americas call themselves by many different names and encompass a wide range of cultures and societies.

The words *aborigine* and *aboriginal* were given the negative connotations of **primitive** and **savage** by Europeans and European Americans. Today, the terms *indigenous* and *first peoples* are often used instead of *aboriginal*.

aboriginal

ˌab-ə-'rij-nəl, -ən-ᵊl

adj [from Latin *aborigines,* from *ab,* from, out of + *origine,* beginning]

The word *acculturation* is used in anthropology to describe the process whereby one society is affected by another through continuous contact over a period of time. Acculturation can occur through borrowing or adapting the language, customs, government, or values of another culture through contact with its members.

Acculturation can be studied in detail if the cultures involved are fairly isolated. Technology and modern communications make such isolation rare, however, and there are so many different influences that lead to cultural change and resistance in the contemporary world that it is difficult to use a simple acculturation model. Today, there is almost no place in the world so remote that one might not come upon a radio, tape recorder, an electric guitar and portable amplifier. Music passes back and forth between cultures and nations so that it is possible to talk about international musical influences. For example, the blues form, which originated in the African continent and was nurtured and developed in North America, has passed back to Africa within the last forty years where once again it has been acculturated to contemporary and traditional African music, leading to a new fusion music. This music can now be heard in Japan, the United States, Latin America, and Europe as well as in Africa.

Electronic communication and the existence of worldwide social, political, and cultural exchanges make the study of acculturation central to an understanding of contemporary history.

acculturation

ə-ˌkəl-chə-'rā-shən, a-

n [from Latin *ad,* to move toward + *cultura,* to settle, inhabit, till the soil]

animism

'an-ə-ˌmiz-əm

n [German *animismus,* from Latin *anima,* soul]

In Latin the word for the soul, *anima,* is also the word for breath. The breath of life was identified with the soul, and for many people in ancient Greece and Rome (500 B.C. to A.D. 300) it was breathing and having a soul that distinguished living creatures from objects. Animistic belief systems go beyond identifying life with the soul, and attribute a soul, and therefore conscious life, to objects and natural phenomena as well. Thus for animists, rocks, trees, mountains, even the earth itself can have a soul. For many peoples of the world there are also sacred places and objects that are believed to have souls and special powers that can be used to help or harm people.

In some animistic systems, the soul has existence independent of living people and objects. In many African cultures, for example, the spirits of the dead survive bodily death and can have major effects on human affairs. In Christianity and some other religions, the souls of all people have independent and immortal existence.

anthropology

ˌan(t)-thrə-'päl-ə-jē

n [from Greek *anthropo,* human being + *logia,* study of]

Anthropology is the social science that deals with the culture, environment, physical nature, development, physical and biological characteristics, and technology of all the peoples on the earth. Among other subjects, anthropology studies cultural change, migrations of peoples, the relationship between culture and technology, the effect of religious belief on action, education, and the transmission of culture, the role of gender in culture, and the development of classes and groups within societies. It also studies inter- and cross-cultural relationships.

Anthropology as a scholarly discipline originated in the United States and Europe in the 1860s and initially consisted of the study of non-**Eurocentric** cultures, with an emphasis on the **primitive** cultures of the world. In effect it was the study, by European and U.S. scholars, of cultures unfamiliar to them. These cultures were said to be descendants of earlier cultures that had not changed from their original forms and therefore were primitive and simple. Built into the dual notions of primitivity and simplicity was the assumption that non-Western cultures (with the exception of some Asian cultures) were deficient in their ability to think, develop moral values, create complex art, and understand the world. Accompanying this notion of primitive culture was the idea of the **savage**: the "wild Indian" and the "native."

There were two main theories about the savage nature of the primitive. One view was that so-called savages were wild, violent, murderous, and uncontrollable. The savages' language was said to consist of no more than grunts and shouts, and their art made without skill or intelligence. Along with these thoroughly dehumanizing assumptions went the notion, which fed into and was used for justification for European **imperialist** and **colonialist** domination of the world in the second half of the nineteenth century, that savages *needed* to be tamed by higher beings. In addition, savages were subhuman, not only did they *need* to be subdued but they could be used as beasts of burden and made into slaves without worrying about moral issues. Thus the concept of the primitive was often used to justify slavery.

The second view derived from Jean Jacques Rousseau's (1712–1778) notion of the "noble savage": innocent, childlike, and pure, but not adult and incapable of the full responsibility of citizenship. This noble savage existed outside human society and, therefore, according to Rousseau, was not corrupted by it. Though this notion was more benign than the view of the wild savage, it too assumed that so-called primitive peoples were not fully intellectually developed and therefore needed to be cared for by more "civilized" people.

The focus of anthropology has changed significantly over the past thirty years. As the world has gotten smaller and Europe and the United States have become more integrated into a culturally diverse and complex world, the normative role of Eurocentric culture in anthropology has been replaced by a more respectful, objective, and cross-cultural orientation. The notion of primitivity, with its implications of inferiority and simplicity, has been abandoned as a category for the comparative study of **cultures**. Every language spoken on earth has, upon closer and more respectful scrutiny, been found to be equally complex, and sophistication, skill, wisdom, sensitivity, morality, and intelligence have been found by Europeans to know no geographic boundaries.

When studying culture and anthropology, it is essential to remember that the notions of primitivity and savagery are European constructs, created out of cultural arrogance and used to exploit people.

A number of new categories, such as preindustrial, preliterate, complex, or simple cultures are now carefully defined and applied when cultures are compared. There is no single culture that is put at the top of a hierarchy and used as an ideal model. The idea that some cultures are higher or better than others is no longer scientifically respectable.

anthropomorphism

,an(t)-thrə-pə-'mȯr-ˌfiz-əm

n [from Greek *anthrōpmorphos,* from *anthrōp-,* human being + *morphos,* shape]

connotation

ˌkän-ə-'tā-shən

n [Medieval Latin *connotare,* to mark along with, from Latin *com-* + *notare,* to mark, note]

denotation

ˌdē-nō-'tā-shən

n [from Latin *denotare,* to mark, note]

Anthropomorphism is the attribution of human characteristics, especially feelings, to nonhumans. Young children's stories are often anthropomorphic. In them it is not unusual for animals to talk, cry, play games, and eat porridge at small, medium, and large tables. In fantasy games one encounters talking dragons and all kinds of magic objects and creatures that manifest human characteristics.

Anthropomorphic thinking can also attribute human motivation to natural phenomena such as the weather or the sea. The idea that there is will and intent involved in natural disasters is very old and stems from the idea that different aspects of nature are controlled by or manifestations of the will of different gods.

In studying and thinking about animal behavior, it is important to be sensitive to ways in which anthropomorphism can sneak into the questions asked. For example, questions such as do animals laugh? or play? do they plan future activities? are they conscious of their own actions? can easily lead one to study animal life based on the way humans think and function. This can result in ignoring the special characteristics of the senses and perceptions of animals, and can provide descriptions of animal behavior and motivation that are refuted by more detailed and objective observation.

The words *denotation* and *connotation* both have to do with the meaning of words.

The denotation of a word is its exact, precise, explicit, primary meaning. It refers to the definable class of things, beings, ideas, actions, qualities, or conditions named by the word.

The connotation of a word consists of the associations that the word has accumulated, either socially or culturally, or as a result of personal experience.

The denotation of a word is the same from person to person, whereas its connotation can and usually does differ for different people. For example, the word *horse* denotes a four-legged, vegetarian, solid-hoofed mammal that has been domesticated by humans since prehistoric times. It can connote, among other things, hard work, speed, freedom, wildness, motion, and travel.

Sometimes confusion can result if a word has different denotations for people without their being aware of it. For example, it is common usage in the United States to use the word *America* to denote the United States. However, in Canada, Mexico, and other parts of Latin America, the word *America* denotes all the nations on the North and South American continents. Thus the statement "America is an advanced industrial society" might be considered true by someone from the United States and false (or meaningless) by someone from Mexico.

Without common denotations it is difficult to hold coherent conversations. Of course, sometimes it is difficult even with such agreement.

The word *culture* comes from the Latin *colere,* which has a number of meanings, the primary of which are to settle, inhabit, cultivate (crops and domestic animals), and protect or defend. The word refers to human settlements and to the ways in which people have altered the environment and developed permanent binding settlements and communities. It also refers to all those rituals, skills, crafts, technologies, arts, and other forms of expression that have been created to bind together groups of people and enable them to survive.

Culture is found everywhere in the human world and can be contrasted with nature, in the sense of the world untouched by humans. People transform the natural world into a cultural world where they can dominate and feel at home. Culture ranges from language to clothes, from ritual to technology. It encompasses all of the ways that people shape nature, relate to each other, and form their social lives. It does not refer to individual and private life so much as to shared life. It is essential to understand that all human beings live within cultures and also have the capacity to create culture.

Culture is studied by the discipline of **anthropology**. Scholars such as A. R. Radcliffe-Brown (1881–1955), Ruth Benedict (1887–1948), Bronislaw Malinowski (1884–1942), and Margaret Mead (1901–1978), whose work in the first half of the twentieth century helped establish anthropology as an academic discipline, accepted the classification of cultures into complex and primitive, and concentrated their work on so-called **primitive** cultures. These cultures were generally found in Africa, South and Latin America, the Pacific Islands, and in American Indian communities. Anthropologists entered these cultures as outsiders and studied them through the lenses of their own cultural biases, which crept into even the most careful ethnographic work — that is, work that describes the values, worldview and culture of others. Their observations should be read as part scientific observation and part traveler's diary.

In the early years of the development of anthropology, there was a general assumption in the field that the so-called primitive cultures were historically and **evolutionarily** less advanced and simpler than so-called complex cultures of twentieth-century Europe and the United States. Hidden for the most part behind these assumptions

culture

'kəl-chər

n [from Latin *cultura,* to settle, inhabit, till the soil]

was the implication that primitive people were less intellectually capable and emotionally complex than the people who were studying them. Hints of these cultural biases and racist attitudes can be found in many early anthropological texts.

Contemporary anthropologists have shifted much of their attention to the study of industrialized nations and to the analysis of cultural life in cities, the culture of work and school, and other aspects of modern living in economically developed societies. There also has been a flowering of **feminist** anthropology that studies women across cultures as well as the cultural forms of exploitation of women.

More generally, the word *culture* is used to distinguish "high" from "low" culture and to devalue the culture of ordinary people while elevating the culture of the wealthy. This is done by reserving the word *culture* for the sanctioned **classics** of art, music, and literature or for works that are sanctioned by the official outlets of upper-**class** culture.

In addition to this narrowing what is and what is not considered culture, the culture of the wealthy is separated from the rest of a society. Anything not associated with the wealthy is labeled "popular" or "folk" culture. It is important to realize that this ranking of cultural creations is itself an act of culture, one that reveals a great deal about the society that makes it.

The educator Paolo Freire, in his work *Pedagogy of the Oppressed*, analyzes how this definition of culture as the sole possession of a privileged few is used to convince peasants and other poor people to believe that they do not make culture, and that therefore they are inferior to their oppressors and subhuman. Freire's educational process consists of showing poor people how they too make culture, and therefore can remake society and transform the world to eliminate their poverty and oppression. For Freire, the ability to make culture creates the possibility of social change.

diaspora

di-'as-p(ə-)rə

n [Greek for dispersion, from *diaspeirein,* to scatter, from *dia-*, across, through + *speirein,* to sow]

Literally, diaspora means the spreading of seeds beyond the area where they originated. It is most often used to refer to the dispersion or spreading out of a group of people from an original homeland. The earliest uses of the word refer directly to the dispersion of the Jewish people dating from the year A.D. 70, when the temple at Jerusalem was destroyed by the Romans, and Jews were driven into exile in other parts of North Africa and into Europe. One major characteristic of the Jewish diaspora is that the Jews maintained their identity in exile rather than assimilated to the lands they settled in.

The word *diaspora* has come to refer to the dislodging of any large number of people from their historical homeland to other places where they continue to maintain their original identity. Thus the African diaspora refers to the dispersal of peoples of African descent through slavery, primarily to North and South America, beginning in the seventeenth century. The Armenian diaspora refers to the dispersal of the Armenian people during the eleventh and twelfth centuries when Armenia was besieged by the Seljuk Turks. Many Armenian communities were established at that time throughout Asia Minor and what is now the Soviet Union, and most of them still survive with an Armenian identity and language.

Ethnocentrism is an attitude or perspective by which one evaluates other cultures or societies in light of the values of one's own culture. The term *ethnocentric* was coined by W. G. Sumner (1840–1910) in his book *Folkways* (1906).

Ethnocentrism is a problem for anthropologists, historians, sociologists, folklorists, and others who study cultures other than their own. Anthropologists, for example, have been known to observe other cultures while believing in the superiority of Western European culture, and therefore rank these cultures according to how closely they resemble European culture. The societies that are closest in resemblance are considered sophisticated and those that differ are ranked in orders of primitivity. The notion of **primitive** is constructed from an ethnocentric perspective that is specifically **Eurocentric**, that is, centered on European values.

Ethnocentrism is not only to be found in the social sciences. Newspapers and magazines, as well as other forms of media reporting, often reveal ethnocentric biases. School social studies and history texts are some of the worst offenders in their ethnocentrism. Take this example from the American Heritage Junior Library Series volume entitled *Discoverers of the New World* (1960). The book begins with the words "America was once the biggest secret on earth." Secret for whom? The people who lived on the North American and South American continents or the Europeans? This very first sentence announces its Eurocentric bias by excluding the native population of those continents from its reference.

There are shifts in perspective that put other cultural and social traditions at the center of observing human cultures and societies. For example, it is possible to take an Afrocentric or Hispanocentric view of things. It's also possible to observe and interpret things from a **feminist**-centered position or an Asian-centered position. In these and other possible cases, the world is interpreted according to the values of the center.

ethnocentric

ˌeth-nō-'sen-trik

adj [from Greek *ethnos*, nation, people + *kentron*, a point and in particular the center point of a circle]

In a feminist-centered view, women would be put at the center of analysis and questions about how things affect women would be primary. This perspective would produce a very different view of the strengths and weaknesses of a society than one that was male-centered. In asking, as an example, about the political structure of a society, the first questions would be where the women fit into the power structure. The nature of freedom in that society would then be judged based on an answer to that question.

etymology

,et-ə-'mäl-ə-jē

n [from Latin *etymologia,* from Greek, from *etymon,* true sense of a word + *-logia,* study of]

Etymology is the study of the history and origins of words. Some etymologists study the different elements of a word (prefix, root, suffix) and try to trace them to their linguistically earliest known occurrences. Others try to study the social history of words and see how changes in the organization of human societies affect the changes in the ways certain words are used.

Thus the linguistic origins of the word *insane* can be studied as one kind of etymological investigation. As another type of etymological investigation, the social history of the changes in meaning and usage of *insane* (and related words referring to mental instability) that occurred in late-nineteenth- and early-twentieth-century Europe, as psychology and psychiatry developed as professional disciplines, can also be studied.

indigenous

in-'dij-ə-nəs

adj [from Latin *indigenus,* from *indigena,* a native, from Old Latin *indu, endo,* in, within + *gignere,* to beget]

A plant, animal, or person that is native to a particular region or environment is said to be indigenous to that area. Indigenous plants are those that, at least in recorded time, were growing in a place rather than imported by people or animals from some other place. Thus potatoes and tomatoes are indigenous to North America though not to Europe, even though they are staples of many European diets.

Indigenous peoples are people who are the earliest known human dwellers in a place. Thus the Maori are indigenous people of New Zealand and the Maya are indigenous people of Mexico and parts of Central America. With the European and Asiatic colonization of the world over the past five hundred years, many indigenous peoples have been destroyed. Today, many are still threatened with extinction. For example, the indigenous people of the Brazilian rain forests are at risk of being destroyed along with their forest environment. To counter the destruction of indigenous peoples, there is an international movement, centered at the United Nations, to support and enforce a Bill of Rights for indigenous peoples throughout the world.

Interdisciplinary studies combine several different fields of learning and academic perspectives to study a particular phenomenon, theme, or historical period. For example, a course on modern advertising could serve as an interdisciplinary course in art, history, psychology, and sociology. Many colleges have interdisciplinary majors. Women's Studies and American Studies are often interdisciplinary majors; they focus on one particular subject but require knowledge of a variety of academic perspectives. One American Studies major may focus on art and literature in American culture, while another American Studies major will be concerned with American labor history from a sociological, psychological, and historical point of view.

interdisciplinary

in-'tər-'dis-ə-plə-,ner-ē

adj [from Latin *inter*, between, among + *discipulus*, pupil, from *discere*, to learn]

The word *jargon* is derived from the Old French word *gargon*, which meant any noise in the throat such as the warbling of birds or the growling of dogs. Its primary meaning is language that is obscure, overly complex, and pretentious. A secondary meaning is technical language that is specific to a certain area of study and not found in ordinary conversation.

Many academic fields of study and professions have their own vocabularies — a jargon — which name specific concepts and ideas within that field, creating a useful shorthand.

Sometimes technical jargon can be used to make simple things sound complex and hide meanings from people. For example, in the field of medicine, disease conditions created by doctors are called *iatrogenic*. Thus if a doctor gives you the wrong pill and you break out in hives and the doctor says, "I'm sorry, but you have an iatrogenic disease," he or she would be using jargon. A nonjargon way of saying the same thing is: "I'm sorry I messed up on the prescription."

Here's another use of the primary meaning of *jargon* that a columnist writing on the state of the economy might use: "In order to rationalize business, the XYZ Corporation is down-sizing." Translated this means "In order to increase profit XYZ is firing or retiring workers and increasing the work load of the remaining employees."

jargon

'jär-gən, ,gän

n [from Middle English *jargoun*, from Old French *gargon*, gorgon]

Linguistics, one of the fastest-growing academic disciplines, is the study of the structure, history, development, and use of human language. It ranges from the detailed description of the sounds languages utilize and the rules governing their usage (**phonology**), to the abstract structure of language and the rules governing the formation of correct statements (**syntax**), to the dynamics of meaning and the relationship of meaning to the world beyond language (**semantics**).

linguistics

,lin-'gwis-tiks

n [from Latin *lingua*, language]

It also encompasses the comparative and historical study of the languages of the world; theories of linguistic universals; the study of language evolution and change; and the mechanics of speech and gesture.

Two branches of linguistics that have come to prominence within the field over the past fifty years are psycholinguistics and sociolinguistics. Both of these fields are interdisciplinary — that is, they cross the lines of traditionally defined academic fields. Psycholinguistics draws from both psychology and linguistics, while sociolinguistics draws from sociology and linguistics.

Psycholinguistics is the study of the psychological processes at work in language usage. In recent years a great deal of work has been concentrated in two areas of this field: the study of the child's acquisition of language, and learning to speak a second language.

Sociolinguistics is the study of the relationship of language to social life. It includes such topics as the relationship of language to ethnicity and social class, the special languages of institutions, the development and usages of propaganda, and the examination of the nuances of language usage in different conversational situations.

matriarchy

'mā-trē-ˌär-kē

n [from Latin *mater,* mother + Greek *archein,* to rule]

patriarchy

'pā-trē-ˌär-kē

n [from Greek *patriarchēs,* from *patēr,* father + *archein,* to rule]

A woman who leads her family, social group, or society is called a matriarch. Older women who are wise and acknowledged leaders are also called matriarchs.

In anthropology, a matriarchy is a family, social group, or society in which mothers, and by extension women, hold power and are the socially, culturally, and economically dominant figures. This dominance can be manifested by the ownership of property, by the passage of inheritance and power to daughters (matrilinear inheritance), and by husbands coming to live with the family or social group of their wives and mothers-in-law (matrilocal residence).

The "fathers" of the Hebrew people are called Patriarchs, as are the bishops of the Greek and Russian Orthodox Church. The word *patriarch* is also used to refer to older males who are deemed to be wise and in whom social and familial authority rests.

In anthropology, a patriarchy is a family, social group, or society in which fathers, and by extension men, hold power and are the dominant figures. This dominance can be manifested by the ownership of property, by the passage of inheritance to sons (patrilinear inheritance), and through wives coming to live with the family or social group of their husbands or fathers-in-law (patrilocal residence).

Matriarchy and patriarchy have figured centrally in much recent **feminist** thought. Values that have been associated with the matriarchy are empathy, nurturance, connection with the earth and growth, cooperation, **altruism**, and spirituality. Values associated with the patriarchy are self-centeredness, **self-interest**, abstract intellectuality, violence, competitiveness, conquest, and **materialism.** This represents a dichotomy of virtues, and not all feminist thinkers believe that the situation is so simple. For some, the specific qualities individuals incorporate into their personalities have as much to do with the nature of one's socialization as one's sex.

The feminist critique of society centers around the dominance or **hegemony** of the patriarchy in most contemporary **cultures.** According to this analysis, male hegemony manifests itself in all areas of life. It is economic, resulting in women receiving less pay than men for equal work, being denied job promotions, performing unpaid household labor, and being expected to take sole responsibility for child-rearing. It is cultural, as evidenced by the media turning women into sex objects and portraying them as less competent, powerful, and intelligent than men. And it is also physical and sexual. Males consider sexual relations as forms of combat and competition, and this attitude often leads to women being beaten and abused.

Feminist critiques of the patriarchy are not merely negative. They propose ways of reorganizing the mind and society so as to replace the negative values of the patriarchy with the more compassionate values of the matriarchy.

Phonology is a branch of linguistics that attempts to provide a detailed description of the sounds languages utilize and the rules governing the relationships between sounds within a given language. It also studies the difference between sounds and the rules governing their uses across languages.

phonology

fə-'näl-ə-jē, fō

n [from German *phonolith*, from Greek *phōnē*, sound, voice + *-logia*, study of]

An early example of a phonological analysis is that done by the German scholar Jacob Grimm (1785–1863), who is better known as a recorder of folk tales. Grimm investigated the patterns of sound changes that took place in Germanic languages (German, Frissian, Dutch, English, Scandinavian, and Gothic) as they separated from their Indo-European ancestor languages. One of the things he studied was the shift in consonant sounds between Latin and these languages. Two examples of shifts in English of the sort he described are the shift from *t* in Latin to *th* in English (from "tres" to "three"); and the shift from *d* in Latin to *t* in English (from "duo" to "two"). These shifts have become known as Grimm's law.

pluralism

'plur-ə-,liz-əm

n [from Latin *pluralis,* more than one]

P*lural* means more than one. Any system that explains things in terms of more than one ultimate component is a form of pluralism. Any theory of physics that posits two or more elementary particles that cannot be reduced to each other and do not have a common underlying substratum is pluralistic. Any psychological system that posits more than one basic, nonreducible motivating force or drive is also pluralistic.

Cultural pluralism consists of accepting the existence of many cultures of equal value in the same society. It is the opposite of the notion that a society needs a dominant single cultural self-definition that all members must adhere to no matter what their cultural origins.

poststructuralism

'pōst'strək-chə-rə-,liz-əm,
'strək-shrə-

n [from Latin *post,* after + *structus,* pp of *struere,* to heap up, build]

Poststructuralism encompasses a number of contemporary theories of criticism that attempt to undermine structuralist interpretations. They deny that a fixed structure underlying and determining the nature of a text or a social phenomenon exists. **Deconstructionist,** Marxist (see **dialectics**), and **feminist** theories of criticism are considered poststructuralist. They argue that texts can be shown to have internal contradictions rather than consistent structures. They provide close **hermeneutic** readings of texts that attempt to expose many hidden and inconsistent meanings in texts or social activities. The main theorists of poststructuralism are Jacques Derrida and Jacques Lacan.

It is difficult to be confident of some poststructuralist interpretations, since they rely upon hidden, symbolic, associative, and interpretative meanings imputed to texts and events by critics. In the spirit of poststructuralism, one should question the grounds for any poststructuralist analysis with the same force that poststructural analysis questions the subjects of its analysis.

race

'rās

n [French, generation, from Old Italian *razza*]

The word *race* was first introduced into the English language in the 1500s. At that time, it had three different usages. In the first, race referred to a group of animals or plants, such as the race of horses, the race of roses, and the human race. The second used race to refer to a person's direct blood descendants, as in the phrases "the race of Ruth" and "the race of Moses." In the third, groups of people and their descendants who have a common identity or affinity with each other were referred to as members of a race, as in the "Jewish race," or the "Nordic race."

These uses are clear and specific. The use of the word *race* was extended, in the context of human beings, to refer to groups within the human species that were supposedly related by more than common ancestors. In the late eighteenth century, a number of anthropologists studied different physical types of human beings and began to create a number of human groupings that they claimed were "races," or fundamentally different types of humans. These types supposedly differed in everything from beauty to intelligence to ingenuity, and in moral and spiritual quality. Going beyond the merely descriptive and neglecting any scientific standards of evidence and proof, these human groupings were ranked in order of superiority and inferiority. Not surprisingly, the groups in which the anthropologists included themselves were claimed to be the highest ones on all the scales.

One of these rankings was created by the German physical anthropologist Johann Friedrich Blumenbach (1752–1840), who is credited with being the founder of craniology, the study of brain sizes and shapes. According to Blumenbach, there are five distinct subgroups within the human species, distinguished by the form of the skull and by characteristics such as hair, color, and body structure. Blumenbach's groups are the Caucasian, the Mongolian, the Ethiopian (or Negro), the American (Indian), and the Malay. He identified these groups with both specific types of skull structure and with the skin colors white, yellow, black, red, and brown. He went beyond mere description, however, and claimed that, of these types, the Caucasian is the highest and all of the other forms are merely degenerate versions of it.

During the nineteenth century, the work of Blumenbach and others was taken up by some politicians and philosophers and used to justify Western European domination of the world. This went hand in hand with wars and colonization that attempted to realize this domination. One particularly influential work was by Joseph Arthur, comte de Gobineau (1816–1882). His *Inequality of Human Races* proposed the existence of one purest, most superior branch of the human race, the Nordic branch from Scandinavia and northern Germany, which he called the Aryan race. *Aryan* is the Sanskrit word for noble, and had until that time been used to describe the Indo-European family of related languages that were spoken from India to Iran and through most of Europe.

Gobineau introduced the idea of the inherent inequality of the races into European thinking. **Social Darwinists** expanded this notion in the later nineteenth century to include the idea that in the human struggle for survival, the fittest races survive and are inherently superior to all others. This provided a convenient justification for already existent **prejudices** held by Europeans against people they had conquered.

Over the twentieth century, notions of the superior Aryan race destined to rule the world were incorporated into the **ideology** of Adolf Hitler, with its virulent anti-Semitism, resulting in the **Holocaust**. More recently, there has been some revival of pseudo-scientific claims for the racial superiority of the white race, based on supposed genetic studies. One of the leading figures associated with this intellectual rationale for racist behavior is Arthur Jensen (1923–). Despite these claims, there is no established agreement on a scientific definition of race, much less an agreement on the relationship of the so-called races to each other.

Racism, which depends upon the false assumption that the division of the human species into subgroups called races is a clear and viable one, consists of the following notions:

- There are scientifically distinguishable races within the human species that can be ranked on a scale of inferior to superior.
- Whites from Europe (and particularly Northern Europe) are of the highest rank with respect to desired traits such as intelligence, artistic ability, and ingenuity. Other people, whose skin color differs from that of Europeans, are inferior.
- The superiority of the white race justifies its treatment of other races as inferior and even as less than fully human.

Thus in the mid- to late-nineteenth century the idea of race and racist attitudes developed in Western Europe and were taken up by whites in the United States. Though racism was not used initially to justify genocide and exploitation, it fit in quite well with the social and political development of **capitalism** and **imperialism** during the nineteenth century and became a common attitude throughout the world when Europeans and white Americans came in contact with others.

Racism has not just focused on Africans, Asians, and Latin Americans. In Europe, Nazi racism focused on the entire Jewish people, which it classified as a race and tried to exterminate.

Racism has become deeply embedded in the fabric of Western thought and action. **Discrimination** based on race can be found on a personal level where social mixing across race is stigmatized. It can also be found in the laws of some countries, where marriage of whites to peoples of different colors are prohibited, or where public facilities are segregated by skin color. It is also manifested as institutional racism where job advancement, pay, admissions to college and professional schools can be granted according to racial preferences for whites. These restrictions are sometimes enforced by custom and habit. Other times they are actually written into by-laws and charters. Often covert agreements replace explicit discriminatory laws when a society attempts to legislate racism out of existence.

Semiotics is the study of signs, sign systems, and the way meaning is derived from them. It was first proposed by the American thinker Charles Sanders Peirce (1839–1914) and many of its early ideas were developed by the Swiss linguist Ferdinand de Saussure (1857–1913). From its earliest history, semiotics was primarily interested in language; the study of other communications systems has broadened its concerns. Systems of gesture and of visual imagery as used in film, video, and photography have begun to be analyzed. In addition, style, fashion, and other aspects of popular culture that involve communication in its broadest sense (including different ways of conveying status and social roles) are also studied.

semiotics
ˌsē-mē-'ät-iks

n [from Greek *sēmeiōtikos,* observant of signs]

Semiotics, in its broad scope, overlaps with **sociology, anthropology,** and other social sciences, as well as with literary, theater, and film criticism. Semiotics is an **interdisciplinary** field that attempts to provide other disciplines with tools to use in the study of the sign systems and communication.

Semiotics utilizes several distinctions originally made by Ferdinand de Saussure. One is the distinction between the signifier and that which is signified (that is, between a sign and what it stands for). Another is the distinction between **synchronic** and **diachronic** (that is, between the study of the structure of a system at a given time and the study of the changes and development of a system over an extended time period). A third is the distinction between langue and parole (that is, between the whole system within which particular usages have meaning and utterances are made, and the particular usages and utterances that in fact are made).

Structuralist literary critics have an affinity for semiotics because of its emphasis on langue. This emphasis encourages the study of the relationships between particular literary works and the entire language systems in which they are embedded.

Poststructuralists have questioned some of semiotics' underlying assumptions, including the opposition between signifier and signified. The feminist poststructuralist philosopher Julia Kristeva has transformed the usage of the word *semiotic* to describe feminine language. This language is, according to her, metaphoric, associative, affective, and intimate as opposed to rigid, rationalistic, logical, assertive, and cold masculine language.

sex

'seks

n [from Latin *sexus*]

Sex is a biological characteristic of humans and almost all animals. In humans there are two sexes, male and female. This may seem like an obvious and trivial distinction to make in a dictionary of ideas. The apparent simplicity of the distinction disappears, however, when one probes into the question of what exactly is entailed by being a member of one sex or the other. For some people, sex characteristics go beyond the biological realm and encompass aspects of personality and intelligence. For these people, maleness and femaleness are genetically determined and therefore unchangeable. People who hold this view usually claim that males are naturally endowed with intelligence, creativity, and competitiveness and are therefore suited to be rulers and leaders. Women are supposedly naturally endowed with sensitivity, empathy, and supportive instincts and are therefore suited to take care of children and the home. This view of sex-determined characteristics has been disputed by **feminists** as well as other advocates of equality and democracy. It has also been found to be without any agreed-upon scientific validity.

Opposed to the genetic view of sexual characteristics is the belief that sexuality is culturally constructed, that sexual roles are created by groups of people and children are taught how to assume the roles that their culture has defined for them. The word *gender* is used to describe these culture-bound sex-related roles. For example, in certain cultures males hunt and females farm. Therefore boys are educated to associate with other males who will join them in hunting groups, to learn how to survive away from a settlement for long periods of time, and to be physical and aggressive in pursuing prey. Females, on the other hand, are taught to care for the settlement, to have the patience it takes to cultivate and harvest the crops, and to care for the very old and very young who must remain at the settlement. What some people would call genetically determined sex characteristics in this society are inculcated in the children by the older people. In fact there are other societies in which these roles are reversed — the men farm and the women hunt.

In our society, gender roles are reinforced by advertising, TV, music, and other forms of cultural expression. Sometimes the roles a culture reinforces create a situation of domination and there are revolts against and changes in gender roles. The feminist movement in the United States, for example, has attempted to eliminate male dominance and to equalize the power available to both sexes.

The French writer Monique Wittig goes even further and writes about the possibility of a world without gender distinctions. There would still be biological differences between males and females, but there would be no differences in access to power, work, and pleasure. In such a culture there would not be a need for pronoun distinctions such as he/she and her/him. The language would have a single pronoun that means person and there would be no cultural forms that divide people into males and females for the sake of activities or privileges.

sexual orientation

'seksh-(ə-)wəl
ˌōr-ē-ən-'tā-shən

The phrases *sexual orientation* and *sexual preference* are currently used to describe a person's sexual behavior. The difference between the terms is that *orientation* implies that a person's choice of sexual partners is either the result of genetics or behavior established at an early age and cannot be changed, while *preference* implies that the choice of partners is more casual and subject to modification. The former term is preferred by gay and lesbian groups, while the latter term is more commonly used in the media. There are basically four different types of sexual choice that exist within human society:

- HETEROSEXUAL people choose sexual partners of the opposite sex.
- HOMOSEXUAL people choose sexual partners of the same sex.
- BISEXUAL people choose sexual partners of either sex.
- ASEXUAL people do not have sexual partners

The terminology of sexual preference has been adopted in order to eliminate labeling homosexual or bisexual individuals as pathological or in any way diseased or abnormal.

Judgments about people's sexual orientation are governed by social and cultural attitudes. In some societies, homosexual, heterosexual, bisexual, and asexual orientations are all considered natural and are integrated into the social fabric. In others, such as the United States and Britain, heterosexuality is considered the only "normal" sexual orientation, and homosexuality and bisexuality are stigmatized and even at times made illegal. Homosexual and bisexual individuals in such contexts are treated with scorn, hatred, and even fear. This attitude of fear and derision toward gay, lesbian, and bisexual people is called *homophobia*. Homophobia is a social problem like sexism and racism, and is sometimes very difficult to eliminate.

Homophobia has existed throughout the history of the United States. However, in the 1970s and 1980s, when many gay and lesbian people "came out of the closet" and asserted their right to live free of harassment and stigmatization, homophobia increased in some places. In response to this, and to their growing economic power, many gays and lesbians participated in gay and lesbian rights movements as a way of asserting their civil and political rights. They organized politically and elected officials to local, state, and federal offices. Many of these officials are openly gay and lesbian themselves.

In the 1980s, gays and lesbians also organized to force medical and pharmaceutical bureaucracies to focus efforts on finding treatments and cures for AIDS and providing care for the people with AIDS. This ongoing action, sometimes quite militant, has had some effect in forcing attention and resources on the issue.

structuralism

'strək-chə-rə-,liz-əm, 'strək-shrə

n [from Latin *structus,* pp of *struere,* to heap up, build]

Structuralism is the explicit study of the underlying structures and patterns of organization of language, society, culture, mathematics, literature, and other systems. In linguistics, structuralism is an approach to the analysis of language in terms of structures and systems that originated with the work of the Swiss linguist Ferdinand de Saussure (1857–1913). Saussure argued that language is a system of interrelated signs that are themselves arbitrary and have no intrinsic relationship to the meanings they are associated with. There are systematic ways in which these signs (which are the units of language) are combined with each other within the structure of specific languages. Saussure stresses the dichotomy between **form** (the organized structure of a system) and **substance** (the world in which the system is applied, the content that the structure organizes), and considers the formal aspects of language to be the most important. He also distinguishes between the **signifier** (the sign that functions within the system) and the **signified** (the meaning arbitrarily attached to the sign), and asserts that knowing how the signifier functions tells more about the language than knowing how meaning works in a language.

Thus for Saussure and the structuralists, the rules of correct language formation **(syntax)** can be studied independently from the study of meanings **(semanticists)**. This view is not universally accepted, and the idea that signifiers are chosen arbitrarily within a language is contested by semanticists (and other linguists who call themselves **poststructuralists**). These scholars point out that the rules of language are not applied invariably by speakers and that **metaphor** and other poetic **tropes**, which often do not obey syntactic rules, are essential and not marginal parts of language usage.

In the social sciences, structuralists posit the existence of structures and rules that generate and maintain the coherence of social systems. People who function within these social systems may be unaware of these rules and underlying structures, but behave according to them nevertheless.

Structuralist thinking in the social sciences emerged through the central influence of the work of the French anthropologist Claude Lévi-Strauss (1908–   ). Lévi-Strauss believed that there are underlying oppositions, rules of exchanges, and equivalences embedded within social structures. He sees kinship, for example, as structured by a series of exchanges of women throughout a society in such a way that the family and clan structures of the society are maintained. Society-wide structured relationships underlie choices of marriage partners and individuals are rule-governed signs (in Saussure's sense) within the society. In his book *The Elementary Structures of Kinship,* Lévi-Strauss claims to provide a systematic description of the kinship structures that exist within nonindustrial human societies.

Taking the lead from Lévi-Strauss, anthropologists, other social scientists, and literary critics have searched for underlying structures that account for surface behavior. Different types of structures have been devised for each new area selected for study. But they all reflect Lévi-Strauss's idea that the development of structures to organize experience is a basic property of the human mind. Thus culture, art, and social organization are all reflections of the organizing principles that the mind uses to structure behavior and create predictability in an uncertain world in need of organization.

In general, structuralists try to discover, in any field of inquiry, the guiding logical principles or patterns that they can use to develop a systematic account of behavior or events. Structuralism is **synchronic**: Structuralists take no account of history and therefore of changes that take place over time. Rather, they attempt to articulate a system of relationships that exists at one historical moment and consider a society, language, or other system as if it were frozen in time. The ideal structuralist field is mathematics, since mathematical structures can be said to exist beyond the vagaries of temporal experience.

The project of discovering the structures that underlie human behavior has not produced many agreed-upon results. Human experience seems too irregular and subject to as yet unexplained changes and modifications to be easily captured within a logical structure that takes no account of history or circumstance. For that reason, many anthropologists, social scientists, and critics are looking beyond structuralism for an understanding of the range, variety, and variability of human experience.

syntactics

sin-'tak-tiks

n [from Greek *syntaktikos,* arranging together]

semantics

si-'mant-iks

n [from Greek *sēmantikos,* significant, from *sēma,* sign, token]

Semantics and syntactics are branches of linguistics, the study of language systems.

Syntactics, the study of syntax, is the study of the order and structure of signs and symbols in a communication system. It tries to make explicit the rules of construction of grammatically correct assertions within a system. It does not have to do with meaning but with structure.

The mastery of syntax — that is, of the rules of formation of statements within a system of communication — usually takes place unconsciously. Children do not consciously learn the syntactic rules of their native language while they learn to speak, yet they can usually apply these rules and speak grammatically by the age of four. The question of how these rules are mastered, of whether there is a genetic basis for the acquisition of language in the structure of the brain or whether language is learned through experience, is currently debated within the field of syntactics.

Noam Chomsky's (1928–) theory of universal grammar contends that the inherited structure of the brain contains a universal grammar comprising the rules of transformation that are used to create grammatical statements. This universal grammar is transformed through experience into the specific grammar of particular languages. According to Chomsky, without this built-in ability to transform words into grammatical statements, language could not be acquired. Chomsky and his associates have been working over the past thirty years to formulate the specifics of this universal grammar. Many other researchers in the field of syntactics have questioned its validity. There is at present no universally accepted theory of how people master the ability to speak grammatically.

Semantics is the study of meaning rather than the syntactic study of structure and grammar. It is currently of theoretical interest in the fields of **psycholinguistics** and **semiotics**, though no semantic theory has yet been able to capture the complexity of ordinary conversational language.

Semantics deals with the relationships of the meaning of words, signs, and symbols to the person or group that uses them; those aspects of experience or the world to which they refer; their ability to communicate meaning; their relationships to the meanings of other signs and symbols; and their role within a whole communication system.

Semantics deals with **metaphor** and other extended meanings of words and symbols, as well as with the way in which meanings change according to the context in which they are used. It is a wide-open field with many unanswered questions, including the most basic one: What is the meaning of meaning?

Sociology

Alienation is the social condition of feeling powerless, apathetic, emotionless, and estranged from society. It represents a split between a person and her or his environment, a sense of not belonging anywhere. In such a state, there are no secure values and people and things have an unreal quality. The main character in the Albert Camus (1913–1960) novel *The Stranger* is a good example of an alienated person. He is unmoved by the death of his mother and a murder he commits. One gets the feeling that, though he has not gone mad, his feeling of involvement in human life has dried up, that he is estranged from humanity.

Alienation often accompanies **anomie**, the state of having no guiding values or moral principles.

Alienation was introduced as a category into philosophical and social scientific discourse by the German philosopher Georg Wilhelm Friedrich Hegel (1770–1831). Hegel described it as a split in the individual soul. For him, alienation occurs when the soul is divided into pure thought, which has no relation to experience, and material existence, which just happens and is not given any value. This split state, with mind thinking about nothing and body experiencing without reflecting on that experience, is what Hegel means by alienation.

alienation

ˌā-lē-ə-nā-shən, āl-yə-

n [from Latin *alienus,* from *alius,* to estrange]

Altruism is the willingness to act in ways that help others without any hidden self-interest or motive. Altruistic behavior is generous and compassionate. Examples of altruistic behavior are giving food to hungry people simply because they are hungry, or rescuing someone from a fire or from drowning without regard to personal reward or even safety.

There are some thinkers who deny the existence of altruism. The earliest thinker who characterized people as aggressive, competitive, and driven solely by **self-interest** was Thomas Hobbes (1588–1679). For him all actions that seem altruistic are simply disguised and are really calculated to benefit the person acting. There are many conservative thinkers today who hold a Hobbesian view of human nature and use this to claim that capitalism is a natural form of economic behavior. They also claim that socialism and all other theories that claim that human society can be perfected and people can learn to cooperate and live without competition have, as their philosophical basis, a foolish and naive belief in altruism and the innate goodness of people.

Opposing this Hobbesian view is the view that altruistic drives are natural and that they lead to the bonds that tie people to each other.

altruism

ˈal-trü-ˌiz-əm

n [from French *altruisme,* from Latin *alter,* for others]

A variant of this view was held by Joseph Butler (1692–1752), who held that self-love and the disinterested love of others were both part of human personality. Many **socialists** and **liberals** argue that the economic organization of life should be generous and compassionate and not merely competitive. They argue for the need for social altruism and deny that self-interest is the sole force that motivates human behavior.

The prominent Russian thinker Prince Peter Kropotkin (1842–1921) wrote in his book *Mutual Aid: A Factor in Evolution* (1914) that the social evolution of animal and human society was driven by forces of cooperation and altruism. He believed that society would eventually eliminate national and cultural boundaries, and that in the future, government would no longer be necessary. Society would become one congenial, cooperative self-governing order.

Another form of altruism, biological altruism, has been discussed by a number of sociobiologists, including E. O. Wilson (1929–   ), who specializes in the study of the social world of insects. These biologists conclude from their observations of animal societies that some animals have a genetically determined altruism. This results in individuals dying but the species continuing. It is important to emphasize that according to these biologists this form of altruism is completely genetically determined and does not have any implications about the will, spirit, or consciousness of animals.

anomie

'an-ə-mē

n [from Greek *anomia,* lawlessness, from *a-,* without + *nomos,* law]

The word *anomie* was introduced into the vocabulary of sociology by Emile Durkheim (1858–1917) in his book *Suicide.* He wrote: "Anomie . . . is a regular and specific factor in suicide in our modern societies . . . [which] results from man's activities lacking regulation and his consequent sufferings."

Anomie is a sociological term that refers to the absence, in a society or individual, of any guiding moral values, norms of expected behavior, or principles for the regulation of action. A situation of anomie is often thought to be the result of mass society, where individuals or small groups can be cut off from any sources of authority, or so **alienated** from society that they reject all of its values.

In the film *Modern Times,* Charlie Chaplin portrayed a little person lost in an enormous, indifferent, alienated, and unregulated industrial society. Such people are the victims of anomie. They have no values to guide them, no people to help them navigate, and no way to become connected to a nurturing social group.

Anomie develops most easily in large cities where people find themselves treated like objects and have no social or moral center from which to draw sustenance.

Assimilation refers to the process by which an individual who is new to a society comes to take on the values, habits, language, and culture of that society and gives up old values, habits, languages, and culture. Some societies elevate assimilation to the position of national policy and legislate national customs and language.

In the United States the policy of assimilating and "Americanizing" foreigners who apply for citizenship has been called a "melting pot" policy. Recently there have been a number of ballot initiatives that advocate making English the official language of the United States. If passed, all official documents and communications would be only in English and immigrants would have to learn to use English to get by.

There are major debates these days about whether the United States should assimilate all citizens into its dominant Western European–based culture, or become a multicultural, multilingual society.

assimilation

ə-ˌsim-ə-ˈlā-shən

n [from Latin *assigmulare,* to make similar]

Caste is a form of social organization that divides a society into groups that are ranked as inferior or superior. Castes are defined by birth and, within a caste system, people cannot move from one caste to another no matter how much wealth or status they accumulate. People must marry within their own caste and caste members are often restricted to certain professions and are constrained by religious ritual and social custom.

Hinduism is a caste religion with an elite at the top of the hierarchy and "untouchables" at the bottom. It is widespread in India, though there is pressure within that nation to erase the restrictions of caste and even break them down altogether. The Sikh religion broke from Hinduism over the issue of caste, among other differences, and does not itself have a caste system.

Caste differs from economic class in its strict, lifelong divisions. Theoretically, it is possible for a lower-class person to move into the middle class through hard work; or, conversely, for a rich person to become poor. The caste system does not allow for any shift in social stature, either upward or downward. Thus a rich untouchable is still untouchable, and a poor member of a high caste is still a member of that caste.

Using the terminology of caste to describe a given social system

caste

ˈkast

n [from Portuguese *casta,* race, lineage, from feminine form of *casto,* pure, chaste] can sometimes be a matter of debate. There are some anthropologists, for example, who feel that African Americans are victims of a caste system in the United States. The fact that a person who has any part African blood is considered, within the United States, an African American and not white or mixed, is one indication of the way in which inheritance is used to determine caste.

This view is disputed by others, who argue that only class boundaries are drawn in the United States and that all racial prejudice can be interpreted in terms of class. However, given the prevalence of racism toward African Americans of all economic classes, it would seem that caste distinctions play a significant role in American society.

change

'chānj

n or v [from Latin *cambiare,* to exchange, from Greek *skambos,* crooked]

There are a number of words used to indicate the nature and direction of social, political, and economic change. These words, which also have other uses in the context of politics (see the entry **political spectrum**), form a loose continuum, at the center of which is the status quo. The status quo is the current historical situation in a particular community, state, or nation. Conservatives are, in the context of trying to describe the nature of change, people who want to maintain the status quo. Progressives are people who advocate a new social, political, or economic order that provides for more personal and group freedom, and a greater equalization of opportunity, wealth, and power. Reactionaries are people who want to return to an older order characterized by some traditional authoritarian rule such as kingship.

In the context of the Soviet Union during the late 1980s, the old-line Communists who support the status quo are conservatives; the advocates of democracy and capitalism are progressives; and the advocates of the restoration of czarist Russia are reactionaries.

If change is partial and occurs through the channels of power considered legitimate in the status quo, it is called reform. Reform adds to the current arrangements or modifies them but it does not attempt to change totally power relationships or create a new order.

Change is **radical** when it involves new power relationships that are fundamentally different from those under the status quo. Sometimes these new relationships are progressive, sometimes reactionary. Radical change goes beyond mere reform, however, in rejecting the status quo and creating a completely new power structure.

Radical change can take place over a period of time, or it can happen suddenly. When radical change takes place suddenly and power relationships change practically overnight, such change is called **revolutionary**. Sometimes, as in the Sandinista revolution in Nicaragua, revolution is violent. At other times, as in the recent Czech revolution, it occurs without violence.

In order to keep from being confused by the way these change words are used, especially in the media, it is important always to remember that change is measured from the perspective of the prior status quo. Once you discover the nature of that situation, you can begin to understand the direction of the change that is taking place.

*C*harisma is derived from the identical Greek word, *charisma,* which means divine grace, a gift from the gods. In Christianity, charisma is a divine gift of healing that God grants to some Christians. In an extended and more secular sense, charisma has come to refer to a powerful and magnetic charm some individuals have that makes it easy for them to attract followers. Martin Luther King, Jr., and Adolf Hitler were both charismatic, which shows that excessive charm can function in both beneficent and malevolent ways.

charisma

kə-'riz-mə

n [from Greek *charisma,* favor, gift, from *charizesthai,* to favor]

*T*he term *class* is used to illustrate social, economic, and cultural divisions within society. David Ricardo (1772–1823) was the first to give class a concrete economic meaning. He identified laborers as a socioeconomic class within capitalism with lives and interests that were completely different from those of the people for whom they worked. Other theorists developed Ricardo's theory into a whole schema of classes and the divisions between them in capitalist society. This economic theory of class division was then elaborated upon by Karl Marx (1818–1883).

For Marx, one's class is defined by one's relation to the means of production. In other words, one's control over the work process and relation to ownership determines one's class. Those in control of labor and capital accumulation are the **capitalist** class and those who sell their labor in the capitalist market are the working class. For Marx, these are the only two classes and they are defined in purely economic terms. At the bottom of the working class, however, comprising the poorest of the industrial and agricultural laborers, is the proletariat. At the center of the revolution that Marx predicted is a class-conscious proletariat.

Writing during the Industrial Revolution, Marx spoke primarily of the industrial laborer and the managing and owning capitalist who

class

'klas

n [from Latin *classis,* a group called to arms, class of citizens]

controls the entire labor process. He believed that the divisions between these two different classes are the principal source of social change. For him, all history is a history of the conflicts between the exploiting capitalist class and the exploited working classes. According to Marx, this class struggle is inevitable and its result will be the overthrow of the capitalist system and the development of a collective form of economic control. This struggle will be developed when laborers develop class consciousness, that is, awareness of their common enemy, the capitalist class, and their common strength and destiny.

Not all class theorists define class on purely economic grounds. One of the most prominent alternative class theorists was Max Weber (1864–1920). Weber argues that class is defined by culture, politics, and lifestyles. People who fall within the same economic class may occupy different social class positions. Weber believes that different people have different life chances, that is, different opportunities for earning money, developing skill, obtaining education, and owning property. These life chances must be taken into consideration when defining class. An industrial worker who would be categorized working class by Marx would be reevaluated using different criteria by Weber. After looking at the worker's economic position, Weber would account for the worker's "life chances" as well as her or his cultural background and life outside work. Weber does not see a society divided into a two-class system. Instead he posits a system of social stratification where there are many different classes that sometimes overlap in social, cultural, and economic areas. For example, imagine a divorced woman of color with children and a recent college graduate who happens to be the boss's son, both of whom occupy the same position in a business. Marx would claim they were in the same class. Weber, on the other hand, would acknowledge the similarity of their jobs but would also point out that they have very different chances for promotion because they are in different socioeconomic classes. The life chances of a poor person of color are very different from those of someone who inherits a million dollars.

There are other definitions of class that are used by the government and the media to define how well people are doing in the society. These distinctions usually define class according to income and distinguish the upper, middle, and lower classes on that basis. Sometimes even finer distinctions are made, defining upper, upper-middle, middle, lower-middle, upper-lower, and lower classes. The figures used to determine these classes are calculated to represent the type of lives affordable with different incomes, which can often be misleading. A family with an income of $30,000 a year, $20,000 in savings, and a fully owned house and two cars is in a very different situation from a family with the same income that has no home, no savings, and no transportation.

There is one more definition of class worth mentioning. By this definition, social class is defined by the schools you attended, the social background of your family, and the people you associate with, rather than by the amount of money you earn or have saved. For example, a person who attended private schools and an Ivy League college, has a family tree dating back to the early settlers of New England, and who associates with schoolmates and family friends, though earning only $25,000 a year and having no savings, would be considered upper class. Another person, who attended public high school but not college, has immigrant parents, and associates with people she or he grew up with in a working-class community, would be considered middle class even if she or he earns $100,000 a year and has $50,000 in savings. Under this definition, much more than income determines one's social class.

Discussions that utilize class differences have to be read very carefully, because the basis of the distinctions between classes are often unclear. It is important to uncover an author's explicit definitions of class in order to analyze the validity of his or her claims.

Diffusion is the spread of one substance throughout another. When you put vegetable dye into a glass of water, the color diffuses throughout the liquid. In anthropology, cultural diffusion consists of the spread of a phrase, style, song, or other cultural habit throughout a society. The origin of the habit can be another culture or society, a subgroup within the given society, or an individual. For example, a person with a powerful and unique presence like Elvis Presley is the source of cultural habits that diffuse widely through many cultures throughout the world.

diffusion

dif-'yü-zhən

n [from Latin *diffusus,* pp of *diffundere,* to spread out, from *dis-,* apart + *fundere,* to pour]

G*eist* is a German word that can be loosely translated as spirit. However, the English word *spirit* doesn't capture all of the nuances and tones of the German word. Geist refers to mind as well as spirit — to intellectual and cultural aspects of experience, which are thought to exist above and beyond individuals. The geist supposedly manifests itself in all aspects of human experience: in games, songs, musical and artistic forms, in literature and poetry, as well as mathematics and sciences. The deepest expressions of human thought

geist

'gi-st

n [German for spirit]

and feelings, as well as the most ordinary activities of daily life, are supposedly emanations from the geist. It is almost as if the geist is a power or influence that makes mind, culture, and ideas possible. The German philosopher Georg Wilhelm Friedrich Hegel (1770–1831) even went so far as to consider geist the underlying fundamental reality of which human history and particular experience are only the surface.

According to Hegel and other German philosophers of the late eighteenth and early nineteenth centuries, such as Johann Gottlieb Fichte (1762–1814) and Friedrich Wilhelm Joseph von Schelling (1775–1854), who are grouped as **idealist** philosophers because they believe in the reality of ideas that exist on the level of geist and not in the concrete material world, geist defines what is specifically human. Animals have mental processes, but it is human beings who use symbols, create language, and use logic because of their relationship to the spirit or geist that stands outside of and over history.

Positing the existence of an objective world of spirit beyond that of individual human beings and yet not depending upon the existence of a god or deity is one way people in nineteenth-century Europe dealt with spiritual matters in a nonreligious way.

The German idealists gave the geist a history. They claimed that each historical time period (the zeit) had its own spirit which they called the zeitgeist. Thus the **modern** period (late nineteenth and early twentieth centuries) had a zeitgeist that differed from the zeitgeist of the **Romantic** period (late eighteenth, early nineteenth centuries). The former can be partially characterized by a glorification of rationality and a belief in the perfection of humankind through the use of technology. The latter longed for a return to nature and liberation from tyranny of the rational. It glorified the irrational and the unconscious and elevated feelings over reason.

The zeitgeist was said to account for the way in which historical times determined human behavior. A great deal of simplistic, **Eurocentric** history has been written using the idea that each historical period has its characteristic geist. This idea is poetic and appealing, and allows people to make broad generalizations about the direction of history and the nature of culture. Some writing about the geist embodies the dangerous idea that the geist of some national cultures are superior to that of other nations. Hitler (1899–1945), for example, talked of the historical destiny of the Aryan geist as embodied in German character and culture.

Hegemony is the dominance of one group over another. The word was derived from the Greek word *hēgemōn*, which means a guide who seeks the way to power, decency, or some other goal. It also means leader, the one who seeks and also enforces the way. The word comes from the Greek root *heg-*, which means "to seek."

Hegemony originally referred to the dominance of one political state over another. For example, one can refer to the Roman Empire's hegemony over Europe in the first century A.D., to the Soviet Union's hegemony over Eastern Europe before 1989, or to the United States' hegemony over the Philippines for most of this century.

The meaning of *hegemony* was extended by the Italian thinker Antonio Gramsci (1891–1937) to refer to class relationships within a society as well as to the relationship between states. Gramsci, who was imprisoned by Mussolini in 1926 and died there in 1937, wrote of hegemony and revolution from prison. In his *Prison Notebooks* and other writings, he describes class hegemony as domination of one socioeconomic class over another by means of consent of the dominated, not by violence.

According to Gramsci, the dominance of the owning and ruling classes over people who work for wages is not just political, economic, and military. It extends to the dominant class projecting its way of seeing and valuing the world on the class it dominates, so that ruling-class ideas and values seem normal and part of the natural order of things. Class hegemony uses persuasion as well as force to convince people that being dominated is good for them and part of the eternal order of things. For example, in the United States, acquiring wealth is valued by working-class people, most of whom accept the idea that quality is identified with wealth. To be rich is good and to be a permanent member of the working class is a form of failure. Thus the working class accepts the values of the bourgeois and its hegemony over ideas and dreams as well as of wealth.

For many revolutionary thinkers such as Gramsci, the goal of revolution is to overthrow the hegemony of the bourgeois and replace it with the hegemony of the working class. This implies that the values of cooperation and economic equality must replace the values of competition and concentration of wealth. Thus, revolution would involve new forms of experience and consciousness as well as the reorganization of political and economic relationships.

Recently the use of the word *hegemony* has been extended even further to include gender, racial, or ethnic dominance. Feminist critiques refer to the male or **patriarchal** hegemony, and advocates of cultural diversity refer to white or **Eurocentric** hegemony. *Hegemony* in these contexts means more than mere physical or economic

hegemony

hi-ˈjem-ə-nē,
-ˈgem,ˈhej-ə-,mō-nē

n [from Greek *hēgemonia,*
from *hēgemōn,* leader]

dominance. It refers to a whole system of relationships in which the ideas and ideals and values of one group supplant those of another group. Male hegemony, for example, conceives of the world from a male perspective and as a consequence it is accepted as normal and natural that men have prerogatives and powers that women don't have. These male values pervade literature and art, and can be manifested in everyday aspects of life such as dress and language. Thus, male hegemony is expressed in many ways that people are not conscious of unless it is pointed out by critical analysis. The use of the pronoun *he* to refer to all people is just one example of how male dominance can be pervasive and unnoticed.

Struggles for gender, ethnic, and racial equality are battles over cultural and social hegemony, and for that reason, critical analyses of the nature of hegemonic relationships in democracies are central to current thinking in our society.

homogeneous

ˌhō-mə-'jē-nē-əs, -nyəs

adj [from Greek *homogenēs,* from *hom-,* same + *genos,* kind]

heterogeneous

ˌhet-ə-rə-jē-nē-əs, he-trə

adj [from Greek *heterogenēs,* from *heter-,* other + *genos,* kind]

A group is homogeneous if it consists of members who are alike. A substance is homogeneous if it has a uniform structure or composition.

The opposite of homogeneous is heterogeneous. The Greek root *heteros* means one of two and has the common meaning of not being uniform. A group is heterogeneous if it consists of members that have different characteristics. A group of people is ethnically heterogeneous if it has members of different ethnic groups.

Homogeneity and heterogeneity are not absolute characteristics. There are always differences (and similarities) among the individuals in any group of people. It is important, when talking about the homogeneity of a group, to be specific about the characteristics or properties that are used to define the sameness of members. One can say that a group is homogeneous if all of its members are of the same race, culture, occupation, or social class. The same group can be heterogeneous if other characteristics are considered. For example, a group of Jews or Puerto Ricans can be ethnically homogeneous but heterogeneous with respect to such characteristics as social class, school achievement, and gender.

Serious errors and misleading conclusions can arise from being vague about the characteristics that define the homogeneity or heterogeneity of a group, or from leaving out some important common characteristics of a group's members. For example, a number of studies of the performance of minority children in public schools in the United States conclude that poor performance is associated with membership in a minority group. However, this conclusion ignores the fact that the minority groups studied were all poor. Thus, a more appropriate conclusion of the study is that poor performance is correlated with some combination of poverty and minority status.

The words *heterogeneous* and *homogeneous* have a special use in the field of education. A class is homogeneously grouped if all of the students have similar school achievement test scores. It is heterogeneously grouped if the students have a wide range of scores. There is a considerable disagreement over whether children should be grouped hetero- or homogeneously in school. Some people claim that homogeneous grouping leads to segregating students by class and often by race. Others claim that it lets all students function at their highest level.

Homogeneous grouping is also called tracking or streaming. The struggle over tracking is central to many highly charged educational debates over how best to educate children who display the kind of heterogeneity that is characteristic of American society.

ideology

,īd-ē-'äl-ə-jē, ,id-

n [from French *idéologie,* from *idéo-,* idea + *-logia,* study of]

The word *ideology* was coined in 1796 by the French philosopher Antoine Destutt de Tracy (1754–1836). It described a new discipline he created whose goal was to study ideas and to help people analyze their own ideas. Destutt's intent was to sort out ideas that were based on experience and were therefore valid from those that had no basis in experience and were consequently groundless. For Destutt, sensory experience, including feelings and memories, was the foundation of all knowledge. As a consequence, he believed that religious ideas were groundless, as were other claims to knowledge of truths that were not based on experience, such as universal moral values or claims for absolute political power. For Destutt, each person had the capacity to determine the truth based upon what she or he experienced. No external authorities, such as the church or state, had a right to legislate moral, political, social, or religious ideas.

This lack of respect for institutional authority got Destutt and his new discipline of ideology in trouble with Napoleon Bonaparte (1769–1821), who, with his ascension to the throne of emperor, reestablished religion in France and claimed absolute political authority for himself. Napoleon suppressed the ideas of Destutt and his followers, and attacked them publicly for being responsible for "all of the misfortunes which have befallen our beautiful France." He attempted to discredit these ideas and used the word *ideology* in a pejorative and negative sense. He identified ideologists as a small group of malcontents and revolutionaries. This particular use of the word *ideology* still persists in political debate alongside its primary sociological use. When the word *ideology* is used by **conservatives** or **reactionaries**, it implies, as did Napoleon, that people who express opposition to established authority are ideologues — troublemakers and revolutionaries who hold dangerous and false ideas. Their ideas are then put down as false and mere expression of group self-interest.

Today, the word *ideology* is primarily used to refer to ideas, attitudes, and values that represent the interests of a group or class of people. These ideas are expressed in the media, through the arts, and in all of the ways in which a group within a society displays its perception of the world.

Karl Marx (1818–1883) and Friedrich Engels (1820–1895) accepted the primary use of *ideology* but gave it a new twist in their work *The German Ideology* (1845–7). For them an ideology represented the expression of the ideas of the economically dominant class in a society. Ideas do not express realities so much as the values of the people who control society. They are false in that they claim truth and universality even though they are rooted in historically based economic relationships. Analyzing an ideology consists, for them, of discovering how dominant systems of ideas relate to the actual needs, demands, and self-descriptions of the ruling class.

Thus Napoleon on the conservative side of the **political spectrum**, and Marx and Engels on the radical side, agree that ideologies express ideas and beliefs of a group or class that are influenced by self-interest.

Here are two ideological statements about the United States:

- All people in the United States are free to choose to become anything they want. There are no limits to achievement in our democracy, and if you don't succeed it is your own fault.
- Democracy is a sham in the United States.

The first statement, referring to freedom and wealth in the United States, is in the class interest of people who have considerable freedom and some wealth. However, from the point of view of a poor family trapped in an urban ghetto, or of an immigrant farm worker, who have never been able to make it no matter how hard they tried, the statement is false. This does not mean that no poor people ever become wealthy. However, the statement makes a universal claim: it is a generalization from the class self-interest of people with wealth to all members of the society. In that sense, it is ideological.

The second statement takes a stance with the poor, and expresses another partial view of the situation in the United States. It is made in the interests of working and poor people and those others who choose to work on their behalf. However, people who are poor do have some democratic freedoms. They can vote, have freedom of speech, and are protected by the law in many ways (though they may also be abused by it in other ways). As a partial truth, it also is an ideological statement.

These two statements do not stand alone, but are parts of systems of beliefs and values that often determine people's actions. The field of sociology studies the relationships of these systems of belief, that is, ideologies, to the groups that hold them and analyzes the relationship between belief, social, political, and economic structure and the process of change.

Sexism consists of a belief in the inherent superiority of one sex and the resulting discrimination against the other sex. This definition applies both to male versus female and female versus male discrimination. However, the most common use of the word *sexism* is in reference to male discrimination against females. This is because male dominance is pervasive throughout the world, and struggles against sexism are most commonly struggles for the liberation of females.

sexism

'sek-ˌsiz-əm

n [from Latin *sexus,* sex]

Sexism can be seen in the behavior of individuals as well as in the actions of social institutions. Individual sexist behavior ranges from making insulting and dehumanizing remarks to date rape and other forms of physical and sexual abuse. Threatening and menacing women on the streets or considering any woman by herself in public as a sexual object whose right to privacy does not exist are also forms of sexism.

There are other common forms of individual sexism that affect the quality of everyday life for women. Some men don't listen when women speak, and insist that women clean up after them and take sole responsibility for maintaining a household. When simple choices are made, such as choosing a film to attend, food to eat, a TV show to watch, sexism allows male preferences to override female ones.

Institutionalized sexism manifests itself in laws, rules, and behavior within institutions that discriminate on the basis of sex. It can occur in many different institutional settings, such as in government, corporations, schools and universities, or churches. Within these settings, limitations of promotion and unequal wages for equal work based on sex are examples of institutionalized sexism. Other examples are accepted habits of sexual harassment on the job, lack of access to educational opportunities, limited toilet facilities, lack of child care, and denial of paid pregnancy leave.

Sometimes institutionalized sexism is so ingrained in the laws, structures, and habits of an institution that people are not aware of them until they are explicitly pointed out. For example, the idea of women as combat pilots was, until just a few years ago, not part of the image of a fighter pilot. In the same way, for many years the idea of a female president of the United States, leader of the armed forces, or CEO of a Fortune 100 corporation was unthinkable.

socialization

ˌsōsh-(ə-)lə-ˈzā-shən

n [from Latin *socialis,* from *socius,* companion, ally, associate; akin to Latin *sequi,* to follow]

The word *socialization* was first used in the areas of psychology, sociology, and anthropology in the United States in the 1930s to describe the process by which an individual learns to adapt to a group and accept its values. One of the main processes of socialization in our society is schooling, though there are many less formal socializing forces that affect people, ranging from the family and peer groups to more general social groupings such as sports and music fan groups, social and cultural clubs, clans, and political parties. In technological cultures where watching TV is an everyday occurrence, advertising, soap operas, game programs, and sitcoms all play a socializing role.

It is a truism to say that individuals either become socialized or they don't. However, people who resist socialization develop alternative social affiliations and acquire values that can conflict with socially sanctioned values. The study of **resistance** to socialization in a particular group is as important as that of the process of socialization itself.

sociology

ˌsō-sē-ˈäl-ə-jē, ˌsō-shē-

n [from French *sociologie,* from *socio-,* from Latin *socius,* companion + *-logia,* study of]

Sociology is the study of the origin, development, organization, and functioning of human society, with a particular emphasis on late-nineteenth-century to contemporary society in Europe and the United States. One of its aims is to provide an understanding of the complexities of living in the modern social world.

Some of the aspects of modern life studied by sociology are the role of the individual within the institutions of society, the nature of authority, the development of personal and group identity, the nature of crime and deviance, ecology and the human environment, the family and marriage, health and medicine, knowledge and ideology, law, political behavior, the role of race and ethnicity, social movements, gender, and urbanization.

The word *sociology* was coined by the French philosopher Auguste Comte (1798–1857) to describe a new science of society. Comte believed that there were social laws that governed the development of society. At the base of Comte's analysis of these social laws was the idea of progress, which he claimed characterized the rise of democratic functioning from the Protestant Reformation to the French Revolution. Progress consisted of the movement of human society toward higher forms of social organization in which community order and personal freedom are maximized. Comte felt that once sociology uncovered the rational laws of social development, all people would be able to agree upon how to improve society. Throughout its history, sociology has had a dual focus: to study the nature of modern society in a scientific and statistical manner, and at the same time to contribute to the improvement of that society.

It is interesting to contrast the development of sociology with that of anthropology. Anthropology developed in Europe and the United States as a vehicle for European and American social scientists to study non-Eurocentric culture. Sociology developed as a way for European and American social scientists to study part of their own society. As sociology developed during the late nineteenth and early twentieth centuries, it concentrated on the study of the conditions of the lives of the poor in Europe and the United States. This study of the poor was accompanied by a mission to alleviate the horrors of poverty. Of all the social sciences, sociology is the one that has acknowledged a social mission in addition to the creation of a new science.

Current sociologists are divided between those who still believe that a social mission must accompany the scientific study of society, and those who believe it is necessary to divorce the science from the mission and conduct "pure" science.

Today, many sociologists concentrate on gathering statistics and doing survey research about contemporary social issues ranging from the effects of advertising on TV-watchers to the effect of draft resistance and pacifism on society's ability to make war. Sociologists are to be found working with corporations developing new marketing strategies as well as with the homeless to overcome their victimization. Comte's ideas of a single positive line of progress and the ultimate triumph of rationality are no longer central driving forces in sociological research.

symbiosis

,sim-be-,ō-səs, -bī-

n [from Greek *simbios,* to live together, from *sym-,* with, together + *bios,* life]

parasitism

'parə-sə-,tiz-əm, -,sīt-,iz

n [from Greek *parasitos,* from *para-,* beside + *sitos,* grain, food]

technology

tek-,näl-ə-jē

n [from Greek *technologia,* systematic treatment of an art, from *techno-, tekhne,* skill + *-logia,* study of]

In biology, symbiosis is the mutually advantageous relationship between two organisms that live in close association. The small fish that live on sharks' backs survive by eating the bacteria carried by the shark. The shark also benefits from this relationship by ridding itself of the harmful parasitic bacteria on its back. Another example of symbiosis is the relationship between the bee and the flower. The bee lives off of the nectar collected from various flowers, while the flowers are made fertile by the bits of pollen transferred by the bee from flower to flower.

In sociology, symbiosis is the relation of mutual dependence between different groups within a community or organization that work together to their mutual advantage.

Parasitism is, in a way, the opposite of symbiosis. Two organisms are in a parasitic relationship if one takes advantage of the other and gains nourishment, shelter, or some other advantage from it while depleting the other's resources and energy. The organism that is abused in a parasitic relationship is called the host organism.

The word *technology* is derived from the Greek *tekhne,* which means working with one's hands at a skill or craft. It has come to refer to the tools and knowledge people use to manipulate and control the natural environment in order to reach specific practical goals. Hammers, nails, pens, paper, pots and pans, looms, knives, swords, and guns, assembly lines, smelters, and bulldozers are all part of technology, as are computers, video recorders, nuclear reactors, and solar voltaic cells. So is the knowledge that enables people to read, calculate, write, run a computer, design a bridge or road, repair or build an engine.

Technology is often contrasted with pure knowledge or experimentation for its own sake. It is practical knowledge and action.

Societies differ in the level of technology they employ, the access different members have to that technology, and the ends it is used to achieve. One society might make sophisticated computer systems available to every citizen for access to health and education. Another society might have the same computer technology but social arrangements that made it available exclusively to people who can afford to pay for it and have it programmed to deal solely with financial transactions.

Recently, people throughout the world have begun to see the negative as well as the positive effects of technology. Overdevelopment, the depletion of natural resources, industrial pollution, and the problem of disposing of technologically produced waste has led to the development of new technologies designed to cure environmental problems. One strand of this new technology is called appropriate technology.

Appropriate technology concentrates on the development of tools and techniques that use renewable sources of energy and local small-scale skills and resources. Renewable resources are those that are not depleted but are replenished after their use. Solar and wind energy, and **sustainable** agriculture, which is planned around renewing the soil and harvesting no more than can be replanted, are examples of appropriate technologies. Small-scale nonpolluting industries that use recyclable materials and result in durable and recyclable products are also considered technologically appropriate.

Tolerance is the capacity to bear or endure stress or pressure. It has specific meanings in different disciplines. In biology, an organism's tolerance is its ability to thrive or grow in conditions unfavorable to most other organisms. In physiology, tolerance is the ability of the body to withstand or adapt physiologically to the effects of a drug or some other physiological stimulus (such as oxygen deprivation, heat, cold, or extreme change in elevation). In environmental science, the environment's tolerance is its capacity to adapt to the effects of pollution and abuse. In psychology, tolerance is the capacity of an organism to bear pain and psychological stress. In engineering, the tolerance of a material is a measure of the amount of weight it can bear or the stress it can be put under before it cracks.

Related to these five meanings of *tolerance* is the concept of tolerance of error. When continued stress, force, or pressure is applied to a person or object, there is almost always a limit past which a breaking point is reached and breakdown occurs. One can get closer and closer to that point without causing a rupture, but as soon as one passes over a specific **threshold** (limit point) there is a break. There is no single exact point before the breaking point, and so a safe limit of the application of pressure has to be established to avoid a break. This margin is called the tolerance of error.

There is a more ordinary usage of the word *tolerance,* one very common in our language and very central to the idea of what life in a democracy should be like. In that use, tolerance consists of not interfering with something that you might find disagreeable or unpleasant but that is legal and does not hurt you or anybody else. There is a difference, for example, between religious freedom and religious tolerance. Freedom of religion does not imply a criticism of the religions of free people, whereas religious tolerance implies that

tolerance

ˈtäl(-ə)-rən(t)s

n [from Latin *tolerare,* to endure, put up with]

religious differences exist and that groups consider each other wrong but agree for the sake of peace to coexist. For that reason there are many serious problems that cannot be solved by mere tolerance. For example, racial tolerance does not mean that racism is confronted or eliminated. It simply means that there has been a social arrangement whereby races will live with each other and not act upon attitudes they might harbor. Therefore it should be no surprise that, even when tolerance is official policy, racism sometimes emerges on occasions of stress.

However tenuous tolerance is, it has been central to binding people together in a democracy in the United States. Without religious tolerance we would never have been able to separate religious from political struggles to become a religiously diverse nation.

The question of how much tolerance should exist for racism, sexism, and other antidemocratic attitudes is one that continues to be a problem in our society. Is pure tolerance for all opinions and attitudes consistent with a society that advocates social and political justice? Shall intolerance be tolerated? These are major questions facing any democracy.

triage

trē-'äzh, 'trē-

n [from French *trier,* to sort]

In its original usage, triage refers to the medical practice, developed in the treatment of victims of wars and large-scale natural catastrophes such as plagues, floods, and earthquakes, of sorting out the injured according to the seriousness of their wounds, and deciding upon criteria for the allocation of limited medical care. During disasters, the resources available to help victims are usually not adequate to meet all of the people's medical needs, and so life-and-death decisions have to be made about who gets treated and who gets abandoned to fate. Triage is the making of such decisions.

The criteria for choosing priorities of treatment is as often moral, political, or economic as medical. Issues such as whether to save the least severely wounded and abandon the most seriously injured are measured against other questions such as whether to save leaders and the rich, or to use democratic principles and treat all the injured alike. There can also be conflicts over who makes the decisions when triage becomes a necessity because of scarcity of medical resources.

Recently the use of the word *triage* has been extended to cover situations of scarcity of jobs or resources that lead to saving some people's jobs while firing others, or funding some programs while discontinuing others. Corporate triage, for example, consists of reducing the numbers of employees in order to save money or increase profits. Referring to such reductions as triage implies that the situation is so bad that everyone is at risk and not everybody can be saved.

Triage in the public sector is said to occur when major cuts have to be made in personnel for financial reasons, and decisions have to be made about which categories of employees and which individuals within those categories should be saved and which must be abandoned.

Psychology

In Greek *andr* means male or man, and *gyne* means female or woman. By combining them we get the word *androgyne,* which means having the characteristics of both males and females. An androgynous person is one who has the physical and psychological characteristics of both males and females.

In Greek mythology there is an androgynous god named Hermaphroditus whose mother was Aphrodite and father was Hermes. Sculptures of the god had the breasts of a woman and the genitals of a man. Scholars claim that Hermaphroditus was adopted by the Greeks from an earlier Asian deity and perhaps originated as one of the Hindu divinities. A hermaphrodite is a person who has the physical characteristics of both a man and a woman. A hermaphrodite is androgynous. However, the word *androgyny* has psychological implications as well as physical ones and is used more generally to refer to psychological makeup while *hermaphrodite* is usually reserved for a physical description.

The psychologist Carl Gustav Jung (1875–1961) posited that there is a male and a female **archetype** in every person; the male one he called the **animus** and the female one the **anima**. According to Jung, these two aspects of personality are often in conflict. The animus is aggressive, competitive, and coldly rational while the anima is nurturing, altruistic, and guided by feelings. For Jung, the highest level of human psychological growth came in the marrying of these two opposites into an androgynous psyche that had incorporated the characteristics of both male and female.

Virginia Woolf (1882–1941), the British author, wrote about the need to develop an adrogynous sensibility in order to overcome the dominance of males over females. She believed that a balance between the emotional and the rational, the nurturing and the conquering, could provide a common ground upon which both men and women could thrive without hurting themselves or each other.

Some **feminists,** such as Carolyn Heilbrun in *Towards a Recognition of Androgyny* (1973), have also written on this subject. They claim that **gender** roles are determined by society and established during child-rearing. In order to overcome the dominance of men and the oppression and suppression of women, they propose that men develop more of the characteristics of women, and women develop more of the characteristics of men. The resultant androgynous personality is supposed to be egalitarian. This view has been criticized for being too individualistic, and for not taking into account the whole societal exploitation of female labor to maintain male power.

androgynous
an-'dräj-ə-nəs

adj [from Greek *androgynos,* from *andr-*, man + *gynē,* woman]

archetype

'är-ki-ˌtīp

n [from Greek *arkhetupos,* exemplary]

An archetype is an original, or model, after which other things are copied. For example, the archetypes of the light bulb and the phonograph can be found in the Thomas Alva Edison museum and the archetype of Mickey Mouse can be found in the collection of the Disney company.

In philosophy, the word *archetype* is commonly used to stand for abstract **Platonic Ideas** which represent concepts such as goodness, health, strength, and beauty. The ideas do not represent any specific good, healthy, strong, or beautiful person, but the very concepts themselves which are above and beyond any examples of them. According to the ancient Greek philosopher Plato (427–347 B.C.), these archetypes are preexisting and eternal and are the foundation of any knowledge of the qualities of things. Such ideas, according to Plato, can only be grasped abstractly by certain philosophers, and are usually understood unclearly and in a confused manner by ordinary people. According to Platonists, this accounts for the sad state of most people's knowledge and justifies allowing philosophers, who see the Ideas clearly, to rule human society.

The Irish philosopher George Berkeley (1685–1753) had a different notion of archetypes. According to him, they are the images of things that exist in the mind of God and were used to create the world.

In psychology the term *archetype* was used in a technical way by the Swiss psychologist Carl Gustav Jung (1875–1961). For Jung there were several layers to the **unconscious** mind, among which are the personal unconscious and the collective unconscious. The personal unconscious contains personal material derived from one's experience and therefore differs from person to person. The collective unconscious, however, is characterized by the archetypes of the unconscious. These archetypes, which are part of an individual's inheritance from the history of the human race, are expressed through religion, myth, and symbol. For Jung, the creation of religion and myth and the use of symbols are essential psychological functions that express deep and often inaccessible levels of human experience. Jung believes that people inherit psychological characteristics as well as physical ones, and that these psychological traits represent fundamental truths about the development of the whole person.

The archetypes of the collective unconscious represent components of the personality that, when studied and integrated into consciousness, make it possible for people to become healthy and whole. Three of the many archetypes that Jung discusses are the **anima,** the

animus, and the shadow. The anima is the female principle of Eros (love) and sensitivity; the animus, the male principle of Logos (the word) or rationality; and the shadow, the representation of the evil side of every personality. For Jung, all people have both male and female characteristics, both anima and animus. The growth of personality consists, among other things, of integrating these two facets of one's self so that one can be both rational and emotionally sensitive.

Growth, for Jung, also proceeds by acknowledging, integrating, and balancing the evil within oneself, that is, one's shadow. In that way evil can be brought to the surface whenever it appears, and can be sensitively and rationally controlled.

In the field of psychology, the contrast between affective and cognitive functioning is similar to the difference between feeling and thinking. The affective domain covers feelings, emotions, and intuitions. The cognitive domain consists of **logical** reasoning, awareness, and judgment, and the **rational** structuring of sensation and perception. Knowledge of how things work develops cognitively, as presumably do problem-solving skills.

In the 1950s, the study of cognitive functioning developed into a separate science in the United States, separate from the study of affective functioning. One of the main reasons for this shift was the interest of the government and the foundations that supported the development of psychology in the United States in creating computer-based artificial intelligence programs. This was a greater priority than understanding how humans actually functioned. The goal of cognitive psychology was to isolate aspects of human thinking that could be imitated by a computer.

Studies of the cognitive development of children, based on observing their play and questioning them, form the basis of many theories of learning. The work of the Swiss psychologist Jean Piaget (1896–1980) proposes that there are invariable stages of cognitive growth children go through as they come to understand and master the physical world by manipulating objects and thinking about this manipulation. Piaget has been very influential in preschool education in Western Europe and the United States. This work has led educators to value play and to encourage children to explore their physical environment without directed teaching.

In the Soviet Union, the work of Lev Vygotsky (1896–1934) puts an emphasis on the development of cognitive awareness through social interaction as well as physical manipulation, and plays a more

cognitive
ˈkäg-nət-iv

adj [from Latin *cognitio,* to learn, from *co-,* with + *gnoscere,* to come to know]

affective
a-ˈfek-tiv

adj [from Latin *afficere,* from *ad-,* to, toward + *facere,* to do] central role in theories of child development than does the work of Piaget.

The study of affective development — that is, of the role of feelings in the development of knowledge about the world — has lagged behind the study of cognition. Affect separated from cognition has, however, played a major role in the development of psychotherapy. There are major questions that can be raised about the reliability of information based on the artificial separation of cognition and affect. Most learning mixes the emotional with the intellectual, and thought separated from feeling is not a common experience. A number of **holist** psychologists have recently begun to bridge this separation and study both cognitive and affective functioning together.

cognitive dissonance

'käg-nət-iv 'dis-ə-nən(t)s

n [from Latin *cognoscere,* to learn]

Cognitive dissonance is a form of psychological or sociological conflict in which a person or group holds incompatible and competing ideas simultaneously. For example, if a teacher encourages cooperation among students, but at the same time believes in competition, there is cognitive dissonance, not merely in the teacher's mind, but in the classroom. This might result in students not knowing when to behave cooperatively and when to behave competitively, causing considerable stress.

As another example, believing that the United States is the number one nation in the world while at the same time realizing that we have fallen behind Japan or Germany leads to societal cognitive dissonance.

double bind

'dəb-əl 'bind

A double bind is a situation in which a person has several options, all of which are unfavorable. Double binds are no-win situations that can occur in all facets of life, from the domestic to the political. The term *double bind* was coined by Gregory Bateson, who called such situations "tangles in the rules and premises of habit" (*Steps to an Ecology of Mind*). According to Bateson, double binds can lead some people into schizophrenia and can cause many different types of dysfunctional behavior.

The psychologist R. D. Laing provides many different double-bind situations in his book *Knots.* Here is an excerpt from one example that illustrates the insidious nature of double binds:

> She has started to drink
> as a way to cope
> that makes her less able to cope.

In such a situation the person is setting up an unending cycle that leads to chronic alcoholism.

The distinction between a genotype and a phenotype hinges on the distinction between heredity and the environment. The genotype of an individual consists of the individual organism's characteristics that are inherited and therefore determined by that individual's genetic makeup. The individual's phenotype consists of characteristics that are acquired through the course of life, and involve the interaction of inherited characteristics with the environment.

There are also genotypes and phenotypes that characterize groups of individuals. As an example of the distinction, almost all human beings have, as part of their genotype, the characteristic of having five fingers on each of two hands. It is possible, after an accident or war, that someone with a normal human genotype will end up with three fingers on the left hand and with no right hand at all. These phenotypic characteristics are acquired and will not be inherited by her or his children.

The Soviet geneticist Trofim Denisovich Lysenko (1898–1976) proposed that certain acquired characteristics can cause genetic modifications and become inherited. This theory, referred to as the inheritance of acquired characteristics, has often been ridiculed by Western European and U.S. geneticists. However, it does raise the question of whether environmentally developed characteristics in a population of organisms of any sort, ranging from viruses to people, can modify the genes. On the level of viruses, the question is still an open one, though the inheritance of missing limbs and fingers can confidently be said not to happen, at least on a human level. The geneticist and geologist Stephen Jay Gould discusses this issue at length in his work.

Gestalt is a German word that means whole. In psychology, a gestalt is a collection of perceptions that are organized in such a way that they constitute a whole whose properties cannot be deduced from the properties of the parts. For example, a melody is gestalt that can be perceived as a whole that cannot be deduced merely from the properties of the notes that make it up. The perception of a landscape is another gestalt whose nature cannot be reduced to a simple collection of trees and clouds and other components. Paintings provide gestalts, and discussions of artworks, though they can deal with

genotype
'jē-nə-ˌtīp, 'jen-ə-

n [from Greek *genos,* birth, race, kind + *typos,* type]

phenotype
'fē-nə-tīp

n [from Greek *phänotypus,* from *phainein,* to show + *typos,* type]

gestalt
gə-'s(h)tält,- 's(h)'tȯlt

n [German, shape, form]

parts of the work, must capture the whole or gestalt of the work in order to provide an adequate account of its nature and effect.

Gestalt psychology, the study of psychological wholes, first developed in Germany just before World War I (circa 1910). The leading figures associated with this development are Wolfgang Kohler (1887–1967), Kurt Koffka (1886–1941), and Max Wertheimer (1880–1943), all of whom emigrated to the United States in the 1930s. Gestalt psychology is based on the idea that organisms experience organized wholes rather than collections of isolated sensations and perceptions. Therefore, it begins the analysis of experience with the gestalt or whole, and moves from there to the parts, without ever trying to reduce the whole to those parts. Thus a gestalt psychologist would study how a person responds to another person as whole rather than try to reduce that response to visual components, emotional associations, or physiological responses.

introvert

'in-trə-vərt

n [from Latin *intro,* inside, to the inside + *vertere,* to turn]

extrovert

'ek-strə-ˌvərt

n [from Latin *extra,* outside + *vertere,* to turn]

The words *introverted* and *extroverted* are opposites and describe two behavioral extremes. The words were created by the Swiss psychologist Carl Gustav Jung (1875–1961) and were first described in his book *Psychological Types* (1921). An extroverted person is extremely vivacious and sociable, to the point where others may feel threatened or uncomfortable. Extroverts socialize very easily and love to be around lots of people all the time. An introverted person is withdrawn and unsociable, preferring to keep his or her thoughts and ideas private. Introverts enjoy solitude and prefer intimate relationships with one or two other people rather than public life.

An extrovert is concerned mainly with that which is objective and external, and an introvert with things subjective and internal.

Ontogeny is the study of the life cycle of individuals from birth through maturity to death. Phylogeny is the study of the emergence of a species or a phylum and its evolutionary history, covering, at times, hundreds and even thousands of years. The distinction between ontogeny and phylogeny is the distinction between an individual's growth and development and the evolution of a type of organism over a long period of time. The terms are used in the fields of biology and psychology when discussing topics relating to the development of individuals and species.

There has been speculation about the relationship between the ontogeny of an individual and the phylogeny of the species or grouping to which it belongs. One **hypothesis** about this relationship has been summarized by the phrase "ontogeny recapitulates phylogeny." This idea argues that the growth of each individual, from infancy to death, is parallel to the evolution of the species of which it is a member. This hypothesis would hold that the states of a human embryo represent earlier stages in the evolutionary history of the species Homo sapiens. The hypothesis is no more than that: its truth has never been established.

ontogeny

än-'täj-ə-nē

n [from Latin *ontologia*, from Greek *on*, pp of *einai*, to be + *genes*, born]

phylogeny

fī-'läj-ə-nē

n [from Greek *phulon*, race, class + *genes*, born]

Psychoanalysis is the name given to the theories of mind and to the process of healing illnesses of the mind developed by Sigmund Freud (1856–1939) and his associates and students. Freud's original work in the 1880s and '90s led him to develop the process of free association and create a theory of the unconscious nature of much of human motivation. In order to describe his ideas, he created a new psychological language, one that Freudians claim is indispensable in order to describe psychological truth, and that critics of Freud claim obscures those truths. Some of the basic terms in Freudian language have become widely used in ordinary speech and will be introduced in this entry rather than in separate entries as they are best understood in relation to each other and to psychoanalytic theory.

Most of Freud's original patients were women who had varying forms of hysterical paralysis, characterized by the paralysis of some part of the body with no apparent physical cause, in response to some real or imagined psychic trauma. Instead of directing his patients to tell him directly what caused their problem, Freud asked them to say whatever came into their minds and then say what their responses reminded them of. Through this process of associating words without any goal or specific challenge, Freud claimed that his patients brought into their consciousness forgotten memories of experiences and fantasies they had when they were young children and

psychoanalysis

,sī-kō-ə-'nal-ə-səs

n [from Greek *psukhe*, spirit, life + *analyein*, to break up, from *ana-* + *lyein*, to loosen]

that were influencing their current behavior. This led him to formulate a theory of mind that supposed the existence of an unconscious which could influence behavior. According to Freud's model of the human mind, there are three basic psychic components of the human mind: the ego, the superego, and the id.

The ego is the conscious organizing part of the mind that functions according to what Freud called the reality principle. This principle is basically one of adjustment and conformity to the social and economic world. The ego sets realistic and attainable goals for a person, goals that are rational and often require planning ahead and delaying immediate gratification. Becoming an adult in the Freudian scheme involves the ego learning to put off present pleasures and develop self-discipline in order to achieve long-range economic and social benefit.

Working against the ego and its reality principle is the id. The id is the unconscious, which, according to Freud, is governed by primitive urges and desires, usually sexual in nature. This drive toward self-satisfaction is the pleasure principle, the rule governing the unconscious part of the mind. Thus for Freud, the very nature of the mind is to be in conflict with itself. The id and ego war when the pleasure principle and the reality principle clash. For example, when you want to spend all your money on a wild vacation instead of save it for college tuition you are having an id/ego conflict according to Freudians.

The third party to the Freudian mind does not make things easier. The superego is the conscience, the giver of the moral law. Freud identifies it with internalized moral demands and prohibitions taken over from one's parents during childhood. These principles of right stand in judgment of the principle of pleasure and achievement in reality. They are partly unconscious and partly conscious and can lead to value conflicts. When you worry about cheating on a test or getting insider trading information, your superego is working against your id and your ego.

When there is a balance among these three components of mind, life can go along pretty smoothly. If, however, there is an extreme imbalance among them, if they continually are at war with each other, life becomes painful and frustrating. The energy used by the mind is called the libido. It is the primal biological energy that drives life, and the flow of the libido within the mind — from id to ego, id to superego, superego to id — characterizes one's mental and emotional life. This libido energy is also projected onto the outside world and charges objects and people with sexualized energy. This projection can play either a positive or negative role in a person's development. Positively, it makes it possible for people to love one another. It also makes artistic creation possible through what Freud calls sublimation. Sublimation is the transfer of libidinal energy, which is primarily sexual, to higher areas of human creative activity, such as the arts and philosophy, as a person matures and the ego and superego develop the strength to channel the energies of the id into socialized and productive activity.

For Freudians, libido energy is originally manifested as childhood sexual energy. Adult libido conflicts almost invariably assume this sexual nature, and their origin can supposedly be traced to childhood sexual traumas. Freudian theory provides a developmental psychology which traces the development of mind and the flow of libido in stages from birth through adulthood. As with all developmental theories, these stages follow one another in an invariable order and cannot be skipped. When activity at a particular stage is interrupted, suppressed, or arrested, major personality disorders can result and development can be retarded.

The Freudian development stages begin with the oral stage, then continue on through the anal stage and the phallic stage. These are phases of infancy and early childhood. During the oral stage, psychic energy (libido) is centered about sucking and the mouth; it then becomes anus centered, with bowel control being a central challenge. Finally, the development shifts to concern with the genital areas and the pleasures to be found there.

By calling this third phase phallic, Freud reveals his male-centered perspective, something Freudians have been much and justifiably criticized for over the past fifteen years.

The phallic stage leads to the Oedipal complex stage for male children and the Electra complex stage for females. For the male child, envy of the father and the wish to be one's mother's lover becomes an early obsession. For females, the desire to be like one's father is translated into an envy of one's father (called penis envy). Female sexuality is thus defined negatively, as lacking a male sexual organ, while male identity is defined as positive and aggressive, consisting of the desire to possess one's mother.

Freud's entire treatment of female psychology has been called into question, and feminist psychologists have recently worked on creating an adequate psychology of women's lives from a female perspective.

These stages are, according to Freudian theory, outgrown by normal people. Neurotic people, however, have not lived through these stages in a healthy manner, and are paralyzed by anxiety, the inability to relate to other people on an intimate level, and constant feelings of being abandoned and unloved. They have repressed traumas and unpleasant fantasies and pushed them into their unconscious. Their libido gets stuck at that stage and their behavior under stress regresses to that early childhood stage where some real or imagined sexual trauma occurred.

The terms *regression* and *repression* are central ones for psychoanalysis. Regression consists of going back in one's mind to an earlier psychic state, and feeling or even behaving just as one would have behaved at that earlier time in one's life. Repression consists of pushing unpleasant memories and experiences out of one's consciousness and making them inaccessible to memory. A common assumption of psychoanalytic thinking is that people who have had very unpleasant sexual experiences or fantasies as children repress these fantasies. They never grow beyond the psychosexual stage where the traumas occurred. Freud describes this as the libido becoming fixated at a particular stage of psychosexual development. On the basis of this theory, a person who was abused and punished for playing with their feces at the anal stage can become fixated there and spend years trying to keep things bottled up, clean, and obsessively pure. Their lives can be so governed by cleanliness and fear of soiling things that relationships with other people become impossible.

Unconscious disturbances of development are manifested in paralysis, the inability to relate to other people, and the fear of sexual contact. According to Freud's early views, people need to regress to these earlier stages and bring their fantasies or memories into consciousness in order to be relieved of their psychic burden. Free association is one way of letting the repressed past slip into the present. Another technique Freud used for the same purpose was hypnosis.

In accounting for the development of such fixations on developmentally immature behavior, Freudian theory also prescribes a therapy designed to release the fixations and free individuals to grow and live more normally. Since the fixations are believed to be caused by events and fantasies repressed into the unconscious, the goal of therapy is to get them to rise into consciousness where they can be acknowledged, lived through, and overcome. The therapist uses dreams, free association, and sometimes drawings to discover the unconscious content of the neurotic fixation. According to Freudian doctrine, these forms of expression are ways the unconscious slips out into conscious life.

There is considerable debate over whether Freud's model of the mind is accurate, and whether the therapy that accompanies it is effective. There are many different, non-Freudian forms of **psychotherapy**, but no general agreement about the nature of human consciousness and unconsciousness currently exists.

*P*syche is Greek for breath, soul, and spirit. Psychology is the study of the mind or, by extension, the study of human and animal behavior. It studies and researches aspects of behavior such as motivation, learning, thinking, perception, emotion, intention, sensation, and development. In European and American thought, there are many different and conflicting psychological theories. One of the major conflicts in the field derives from disagreements about the roles of consciousness, the unconscious, and the so-called inner functioning of the mind in studying human behavior. There are three major orientations toward studying Western psychology: behaviorism, cognitive psychology, and introspective psychology.

Behaviorists believe that there is no place for the idea of an inner world, either conscious or unconscious, in the study of human and animal behavior. Instead, they study the responses of living beings to stimuli. The schemes they have developed with this restriction are called stimulus/response theories.

One of the pioneers of stimulus/response psychology is the Russian psychologist Ivan Pavlov (1849–1936). Pavlov was a physiologist who studied the nature of the nervous system. He analyzed the nature of nervous patterns of response to external stimuli and developed a theory of neural conditioning. He posited that within the nervous system there were conditioned responses and unconditioned responses. Unconditioned responses were automatic; one could say that they were hot-wired into the nervous system. The body responds by pulling away from fire, by feeling pain when injured, by going into shock during major trauma. One doesn't acquire these responses; they are part of our inherited neural apparatus. There are other responses, however, that *can* be conditioned. These conditioned reflexes, as Pavlov called them, can be acquired through association. In Pavlov's classic example of conditioning dogs' responses, he waited for dogs to exhibit hunger by salivating. Then, while feeding them, he rang a bell. He continued this process for several weeks, building up an association in the minds of the dogs between food and the bell. After a while Pavlov found that if he rang the bell, even without providing food, he managed to elicit salivating and other behavior that dogs naturally exhibited when they were presented with food. This artificial association conditioned the dogs'

psychology
sī-'käl-ə-jē

n [from Greek *psyche*, soul + *-logia*, study of]

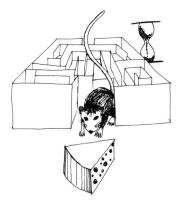

behavior and created a new reflex which put some of the dogs' behavior under the control of the psychologist.

Pavlov and his students studied many complex aspects of conditioning and behavior control. In the United States, John Broadus Watson (1878–1958) also pursued behaviorist theories. He claimed that only by restricting itself to physical behavior that can be observed objectively could psychology become a science. Accepting this restriction, he went further and claimed that human behavior can be conditioned externally as well as understood without any reference to consciousness or the unconscious. In one of his most notorious experiments, he conditioned a young boy to be afraid of his pet rat, and then deconditioned that fear. Watson put great faith in people's inability to resist conditioning and was attacked by many people who believed in free will and the importance of consciousness in determining behavior.

Another leading and influential behavioral psychologist in the United States was B. F. Skinner (1904–1990), who developed the theory of operant conditioning. Skinner conducted experiments with pigeons and rats that involved what is called positive reinforcement. This means that he never used negative reinforcement, that is, punishment, on the subjects of his experiments to get them to do what he wanted. Instead, he ignored behavior he did not want and only rewarded behavior that he was attempting to elicit from his subjects. This rewarding and reinforcing of desired behavior is called shaping. It occurred in a controlled environment or cage called a Skinner box, in which food and water were managed by the psychologist.

Shaping human behavior has been attempted, and in simple cases, such as getting young children to keep quiet or, in experimental situations, turning on certain lights or moving in certain ways, it often seems to work. In complex human activity, however, there are many different motives acting simultaneously. The desire for an instant reward is only one of them. For this reason, because behaviorism cannot account for such essential human behavior as thinking and speaking, behaviorism is currently only a minor strand in current psychological thinking.

Cognitive psychology, or the study of thinking processes and of their relationship to the nature and structure of the brain, is a central branch of current psychology. Cognitive psychology developed after World War II, when it received government and foundation support. This support was tied to the development of digital computers as well as to the study of thinking, and often focused on the similarities between the brain and the computer. This attention to artificial intelligence and its relation to human thinking is still one main strand in cognitive psychology.

Other subjects that are central to cognitive psychology are the nature of memory, perception, and learning, the development of abstract concepts, the processing of information, and the structure and acquisition of language.

Cognitive psychology has, until recently, separated the cognitive domain of thought from the affective domain of feeling and emotion, though some cognitive psychologists have begun to integrate the study of feeling into their work on cognition.

More than any other branch of psychology, cognitive psychology is interdisciplinary. It crosses boundaries between psychology, brain physiology, anthropology, computer science, sociology, and linguistics.

Several pioneers of cognitive psychology are Herbert Simon (1916–), whose work is on information processing and artificial intelligence; Jean Piaget (1896–1980), who studied the growth of thinking during childhood; and Noam Chomsky (1928–), who formulated a powerful and controversial theory about the nature of learning to speak a language and conform to its rules of usage.

Introspective psychology is the study of the conscious and unconscious contents of the mind. Introspection consists of looking within and reflecting on conscious and unconscious thoughts, and on how they affect behavior. It differs from behaviorism by accepting the existence of conscious and unconscious mental processes that affect human behavior. It differs from cognitive psychology by refusing to separate out thought and feeling and by looking at the nonrational as well as the rational functioning of mind.

Introspective psychology covers a wide field, ranging from phenomenology, existential psychology, and gestalt psychology to psychoanalysis and Jungean analytic psychology (for a more extensive account of the first four theories see their separate entries, and for Jungean psychology see the entry **archetype**). Cognitive psychologists and behaviorists have often accused introspective psychologists of not being scientific enough. They in turn have been accused of being simplistic and ignoring the major influence the mind has on behavior.

psychotherapy

,sī-kō-'ther-ə-pē

n [from Greek *psyche,* soul + *therapeia,* from *therapeuein,* to treat medically]

*P*sychotherapy is a generic term for the treatment and healing of the disorders of the mind. There are many different forms of psychotherapy, as well as a whole range and variety of psychological afflictions.

Some disorders of the mind can be tolerated or compensated for and overcome through anxiety-management strategies. Others are much more pervasive and can cause paralytic functioning, hallucinations, the inability to relate to other people, depression, and in the most extreme case, suicide. There is no common agreement among psychologists and psychiatrists about the causes or cures of mental illness, and there are as many different forms of psychotherapy as there are theories of how the mind works and how it goes wrong.

Theories range from purely mechanistic ones, which look upon psychological problems as having physical causes and physiological cures, to ones that probe for the unconscious roots of illness and use dream analysis for cures. Others look upon mental disorders as a manifestation of spiritual crises that can be cured through quasi-religious means such as meditation and spiritual enlightenment.

When examining and evaluating a psychotherapeutic theory it is important to examine how the theory answers the following questions:

- What is the theory's view of the nature of the mind and of normal functioning?
- How does the theory account for abnormal functioning? What does it propose as the cause of particular mental disorders?
- Does the theory try to fit the person to the society, no matter how troubled the society might be, or does it take into account social pathologies that lead to individual distress?
- What does healing mean within the framework of the theory? Does, for example, it mean helping a person adjust to a pathological environment? or changing a person's attitudes and values? or limiting their behavior and scaling down their ambitions?
- Who are the healers? What qualifies them to heal? What do they do? How does healing take place?
- What does getting well mean?

stream of consciousness

*S*tream of consciousness is a phrase used by William James (1842–1910) in his book *Principles of Psychology* (1890) to characterize the ebb and flow of thought, perception, imagination, and awareness that happens during people's waking hours. As an image, it is meant

to convey the sense of moving water full of fish and plant life, carrying along soil and other inorganic matter. It was James's way of incorporating the actual complexity and movement of consciousness into psychology, which had up to his time reduced experience to simple combinations of sensation and reflection.

The term has been adopted by literary critics to describe a method of narration in fiction that recreates events and thoughts exactly as characters might have experienced them on a moment-to-moment basis. The method tries to capture the full range of a character's mental processes, including remembered snatches of conversation and melodies, flights of fantasy, and imaginings.

Stream-of-consciousness narrative is sometimes used as one of a number of different narrative techniques in a novel or story, though there are some books that are entirely unbroken streams of consciousness.

Some of the most skillful users of stream-of-consciousness writing are the British novelist Virginia Woolf (1882–1941), the Irish writer James Joyce (1882–1941), and the American writer William Faulkner (1897–1962). This sample from Virginia Woolf's novel *To the Lighthouse* provides an example of stream-of-consciousness narrative:

> No, she said, she did not want a pear. Indeed she had been keeping guard over the dish of fruit (without realizing it) jealously, hoping that nobody would touch it. Her eyes had been going in and out among the curves and shadows of the fruit, among the rich purples of the lowland grapes, then over the horny ridge of the shell, putting a yellow against a purple, a curved shape against a round shape, without knowing why she did it, she felt more and more serene; until, oh what a pity they should do it — a hand reached out, took a pear, and spoilt the whole thing. In sympathy she looked at Rose sitting between Jasper and Prue. How odd that one's child should do that!

Messages and symbols are subliminal if they exist or function below the threshold of conscious awareness. Subliminal messages are hidden and are absorbed without one's being aware of their existence. Some subliminal messages can be conveyed through motion pictures. The human eye consciously recognizes a film image at the speed of four or five frames per second. If a single frame of an image is added to a film at regular intervals, the viewer will not consciously recognize that image. However, the image will register physiologically and the mind will be affected subliminally by that image. Thus

subliminal

(ˌ)səb-'lim-ən-əl, 'səb-

adj [from Latin *sub-*, under + *limen,* threshold]

if, in a comedy, an image of a terrible tragedy is slipped in subliminally, the viewer will likely have complex feelings of sadness and
depression that invade the humor of the film. If that image is not
present, the viewer is free to laugh unfettered. The unconscious
image has somehow been recognized by the mind.

Many advertisers use intriguing subliminal messages to influence
the consumer's unconscious mind. Alcohol and cigarette advertisements often use hidden symbols of power and sexual prowess in
films, tapes, and records just below the threshold of conscious recognition. These images only register subconsciously, but some claim
they are effective in creating a desire for specific products. The existence of subliminal advertising raises ethical questions relating to
the invasion of privacy and thought control. However, since these
messages are subliminal, it is hard to prove how they actually function.

Economics

A boycott is an organized action that involves refusing to do business with a company or group until it changes its way of operating. The word *boycott* originated in Ireland in the 1880s. During that time there was a major struggle to gain Home Rule for Ireland from the English. There was also a movement to protect peasants who were unjustly evicted by absentee English landlords. These struggles were led by Charles Parnell (1846–1891), an Irish member of Parliament and president of the Irish National Land League. Parnell's strategy was one of ostracism. If a landlord refused to accept a reduced rent decided upon by the tenants themselves, or if a tenant tried to buy land from another tenant who had been evicted, he or she would be subject to complete ostracism by other members of the community. Parnell described the tactic this way:

> Now what are you to do to a tenant who bids for a farm from which his neighbor has been evicted? You must show him on the roadside when you meet him, you must show him in the streets of the town, you must show him at the shop counter, you must show him in the fair and the marketplace, and even in the house of worship, by leaving him severely alone!

The strategy was first tested on Captain Charles Boycott, whose duty was to enforce the wishes of the Earl of Erne on his estates at Connaught in County Mayo. The earl refused to accept the tenants' new rents and Boycott tried to enforce the earl's decision. As a consequence, Boycott was left "severely alone." It took fifty men imported from Northern Ireland and guarded by British soldiers to harvest Lord Erne's crops. Boycott left Ireland soon after that and Parnell succeeded in getting a land reform act passed in Parliament in 1881.

Since that time, any action which consists of refusing to buy from a company or deal with it in any way as a protest against its policies and actions, or as a means of coercing it to change, is called a boycott.

boycott

'bȯi-ˌkät

n, v [after Charles C. *Boycott,* English land agent]

The word *capitalism* is used to describe an economic system that can function under any of a number of different political systems, from democracies to dictatorships. In a capitalist system, most of the property, raw material, means of production (including people's labor), and the goods produced are controlled by individuals or groups of individuals. These people, called capitalists, can buy and sell what they own or produce with minimal restrictions, and are therefore often able to sell at prices higher than their cost, which

capitalism

'kap-ət-ᵊl-ˌiz-əm

n [from Latin *capitellum,* small head]

produces profit. Buying and selling takes place in a market where values fluctuate according to the supply available and the demand of purchasers. The market is characterized by competition, whereby several producers or suppliers of the same goods vie with each other for advantage. Some markets are regulated by governments in order to protect against hoarding and artificial pricing. In an idealized free market, however, there would be no regulations other than those developed through competitive trading.

Profit is the difference between the cost of production and marketing, and the amount received from sales. One of the main goals of capitalism is to maximize profit. Profit can be used for the personal enrichment of the capitalists. It can also be used as capital, or to purchase and develop additional enterprises and increase the wealth and control of production by successful capitalists. This concentration of wealth through the accumulation of capital can, in an unrestricted economy, lead to monopoly — control of the market by single producers or suppliers. Many government restrictions on free markets are made with the intent of keeping competition alive and preventing monopoly conditions from developing.

A major criticism of capitalism, made by people ranging from **liberals** to **communists**, is that it treats human labor as a commodity to be manipulated for profit. According to its critics, it is in the interest of capitalists to keep wages low, have a supply of unemployed workers available to prevent strikes, and move industry around the world according to where labor is the cheapest. This can result in poverty, substandard living arrangements, and the kind of decline and decay found in cities and towns where industry has abandoned communities in order to relocate in places where more profit can be made.

Workers do not usually benefit from the profit made by the companies that employ them. In addition, overall social conditions can decline despite increases in profit. There is no overall social responsibility built into capitalist economics, and people who are concerned with social welfare often attack capitalism as unfair, immoral, and dehumanizing. Some critics of unrestrained capitalism are capitalists themselves. Among the modifications of capitalism they advocate are profit sharing for workers, worker ownership of corporate stock, the creation of safe and humane work environments, and the provision of generous health, pension, education, and childcare benefits for workers. They also advocate government-supported worker-benefit programs to supplement or substitute for corporate ones. There are corporations who have developed these sorts of programs and, in some nations, like Sweden, a combination of government and corporate effort provides most of them for its workers.

Radical critics of capitalism, such as socialists and communists, want to replace capitalism and its emphasis on private ownership with some form of collective ownership. They argue that workers should control their workplaces and profit from the wealth they produce. In addition, they believe that all people should be guaranteed decent work and living conditions.

Ergonomics is a branch of design that deals with the fit between people and the machines they work with, their workplaces and homes, and the goods they use. Ergonomic design takes the human factor into consideration, and tries to reduce stress caused by the objects we use and the physical environments that surround us. Some ergonomic problems are: to control noise at the workplace so that it doesn't cause hearing loss and continual nervous strain; to discover the healthiest and most comfortable position for a video-display screen in an office work station; to design a truck steering wheel and driver's seat to avoid back and upper-chest problems for truck drivers.

The word *ergonomics* was coined in 1949 by combining the Greek roots *erg,* which means work, *eco,* home or hearth, and *nomos,* which means natural law. The field was developed during World War II when the design of planes, ships, and other weapons, as well as of defense factories, had to minimize stress and fatigue and keep people functioning efficiently and alertly under extreme conditions. The design of a fighter plane cockpit, for example, had to provide as much comfort as possible for the fliers within a cramped space; it had to make sure instruments were designed so they could be read with ease; and it had to store emergency equipment such as oxygen masks and parachutes out of the way and at the same time make them easily accessible. This led to the collaboration of industrial psychologists, engineers, designers, biologists, and other professionals in the service of making machines that were designed to minimize effort and maximize ease of human use.

Ergonomics is a collaborative profession that draws insight and information from a wide range of fields, all of which bring their various intelligences to bear on the problem of making work as comfortable and human-scale as possible. Human-scale design begins with understanding the person and analyzing her or his physical and psychological characteristics, and then designing an environment that will create a comfortable fit between person and work.

ergonomics

ˌər-gə-ˈnäm-iks

n [from Greek *ergon,* work + *nomos,* natural law]

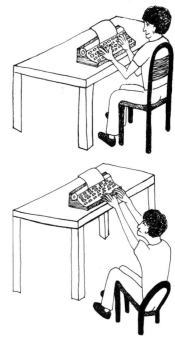

With the increasing presence of computers in the workplace and robots in the factory, ergonomic design has become essential for successful performance. Fatigue, stress, and discomfort lead to error and inattention, and in the case of technological work environments, small errors can easily lead to large disasters.

imperialism

im-'pir-ē-ə-,liz-əm

n [from Latin *imperium,* command, empire]

colonialism

kə-'lō-nē-əl-,iz-əm, -nyəl

n [from Latin *colonus,* farmer, colonist, from *colere,* to cultivate]

Until the nineteenth century, the word *imperialism* was used to refer to the reign of an emperor, or to the form of government in which all of the power was invested in a king, queen, or emperor and their descendants. During the 1800s the word took on a new meaning that was related to the expansion of European control of land and nations in other parts of the world. This expansion, beginning in the late fifteenth century with the conquest of native peoples by the Spanish in North America, led to the development of European empires abroad. The lands that were conquered became colonies of the conquering power rather than integral parts of it. A clear distinction was drawn between the land and citizens of the imperial power and the land and peoples conquered. This is distinctly different from some other forms of conquest where the boundaries of the conquering nation are expanded and the citizens of the conquered land incorporated into the new nation.

From the sixteenth century on, colonized lands were politically or militarily governed by Europeans or their appointed representatives, and their resources and labor were exploited for economic gain. In many cases Europeans tried to "civilize" these colonies by discrediting and destroying, when possible, the **indigenous** languages and cultures of the lands they conquered. Often this was done forcibly by destroying ancient temples and cities, and building new European-controlled trading centers. Traditional religions were also replaced by Christianity. This total domination of a nation's culture, politics, and economy was called colonialism. The primary colonialist powers during the late nineteenth and early twentieth centuries were Great Britain, France, Spain, the Netherlands, and Portugal. Germany, Belgium, and Italy also had foreign colonies. The United States became a colonial power after the Spanish American War of 1898.

In the early twentieth century, imperialism was studied and criticized by European writers who were attacking European imperial rule as well as its colonialist policies. Among these writers were V. I. Lenin (1870–1924), Karl Johann Kautsky (1854–1938), and John A. Hobson (1858–1940). These writers were all influenced by the works of Karl Marx (1818–1883), and viewed imperialism as a stage in the development of **capitalism.** However, they disagreed politically: Lenin was a communist, Kautsky a social democrat, and Hobson a capitalist reformer. The word *imperialism* has been used by different critics with different emphases. Imperialism has been analyzed, especially by theoretical Marxists, as an economic system in which the imperial power controls and exploits the economic productivity and resources of its colonies. It has also been analyzed, by some social democrats and other radical reformers, as a political system of control from a foreign imperial center, often by military means, for cultural and economic reasons, as well as for emigration. This latter definition is close to the nineteenth-century usage of the word.

According to this second definition, the recent political and cultural independence of almost all European colonies throughout the world would seem to signal an end to imperialism. However, if one uses the economic definition of imperialism, and considers control of the economic resources of a formerly colonized nation by the former imperial power, there is a major question about whether imperialism has ended. The economic dominance of the markets, labor, and resources of much of Africa, Asia, and Latin and South America by the United States and Western European powers can be seen as a continuation of imperialism that does not entail political or military control. This continuation of economic domination of much of the world by a few nations is called neo-imperialism or neo-colonialism.

reification

,rā-ə-fə-'kā-shan

n [from Latin *res,* thing]

The Latin *res* means thing. To regard something abstract as a concrete or material thing is to reify it. For example, one might say that a work of art is beauty reified, meaning that it is a concrete instance of the abstract concept of beauty.

In political science, the word *reification* is used to indicate the way in which human beings are objectified by societal forces. The transformation of a person into a social security number, a test score, or a statistical casualty of war are all forms of reification.

Reification is a particularly debilitating form of **alienation,** according to the writings of Karl Marx (1818–1883). For Marx, capitalist society reifies human existence and alienates people from the work they do. The alienation of labor takes place when the sole reward of work is the money that it brings in. According to Marx, an entire part of the self is destroyed when people are alienated from the process and products of their labor by working for others instead of for themselves. In Marxist thought, the only way for workers to overcome the damage done by their reification is to organize and seize control of the methods of production. Working for oneself with one's peers is, for Marx, a way to reconnect people to their work and to abolish the dehumanizing effects of reification.

safety net

A safety net is a net used to catch people who jump or fall from high places. It is used to protect tightrope walkers and trapeze artists, as well as to catch people jumping from burning buildings and other precarious and dangerous perches. Recently the meaning of safety net has been extended to economic affairs. An economic safety net is a guaranteed level of economic security provided by a state or nation to all of its citizens. Safety nets differ throughout the world. There are some nations, such as West Germany, that have a broad safety net, which includes a national health service, senior citizen pensions, free universities, unemployment benefits, paid maternity leave, and housing subsidies. Other poorer nations have no safety net at all. The United States provides a modest safety net, which includes unemployment insurance and Social Security benefits, but no national health service or maternity benefits.

There is a major debate over what kind of safety net should exist in a free-market society. This debate centers around the level of responsibility a society as a whole should assume for its least strong members.

sector

'sek-tər, -,tȯ(ə)r

n [from Latin *sectio,* act of cutting]

A sector is a segment or part of a whole. In economic discussions it is common to divide the economy into two main "sectors": the private sector and the public sector. The private sector is the part of the economy free of direct state control. In terms of output, this sector includes the economic activity of private firms, corporations, charities, and nonprofit organizations. Some argue that nonprofit organizations and charity foundations compose a sector of their own, the nonprofit sector. The industries providing services rather than tangible goods are sometimes separated out and considered a sector worth studying by itself, the service sector.

The public sector is the part of the economy controlled by state agencies and organizations. This control can be centralized or local. Nationalized industries, public corporations, firms owned by the government but not directly controlled by the government, and services providing both goods and services such as education and health are all a part of the public sector.

These economic sectors are distinguished from each other because their interests often compete. For example, organizations in the private or corporate sector often find it in their economic interest to lobby for cutting funding for the public sector and for the elimination of public-sector regulations on private-sector enterprise. Similarly, public-sector organizations oppose many actions of the private sector, fearing that private spending or tax cutting would decrease the amount of money available for spending on public services.

The word *socialism* has a fairly short but complicated history. Toward the beginning of the nineteenth century, it was used to indicate movements and **ideologies** that were committed to creating greater social and economic justice and equality in Western Europe and the United States. Socialist ideas ranged from eliminating poverty to creating cooperative businesses to distributing free land to small farmers. All of these movements had in common a concern for social well-being and opposed the individualistic struggle for power that characterizes capitalism. They advocated society based on mutual assistance rather than competition, and emphasized the need to develop political and economic forms that allowed all people to benefit from the resources available. In opposing capitalism, they advocated the social or collective ownership of the means of production rather than private ownership. There were many variants on this theme of social ownership, ranging from small nongovernmental industrial cooperative societies and farm cooperatives to state ownership of all industry. Socialist groups during the first half of the nineteenth century went by many different labels, such as cooperative, mutualist, agrarianist, associationist, or radical. Two of the most common names for socialist political groups were social democrats and democratic socialists.

Toward the middle of the nineteenth century, socialism began to be contrasted with **communism.** Communist parties inspired by the work of Karl Marx (1818–1883) and Friedrich Engels (1820–1895) developed and advocated the violent overthrow of the capitalist system as well as the establishment of a socialist society as a step toward "true communism." True communism would be a condition of total equality where political states and national boundaries would disappear and all distinctions of class and manifestations of economic inequality would be overcome.

Since the Russian Revolution of 1917, there has been a major distinction between advocates of socialism and advocates of communism of the Soviet variety. Socialists (and some independent communist non-Soviet parties) are often more gradualist than Soviet communists and do not advocate violent revolution. They participate in multiparty democracies and enter into coalitions with nonsocialist parties. Many of them advocate mixed systems of private and col-

socialism

'sō-shə-ˌliz-əm

n [from Latin *socialis,* from *socius,* companion, ally, associate; akin to Latin *sequi,* to follow + *-ism,* system, theory] lective ownership, and all of them oppose centralized state ownership on the Russian model. In fact, many socialists argue that the communist state, as developed in the Soviet Union, could more aptly be called state capitalism than communism, since the leaders, not the people as a whole, control society and benefit from state ownership.

Despite these clear differences between socialists and communists, socialists have often been linked to communism, especially in the United States. This was particularly true during the 1950s McCarthy era (named after Senator Joseph McCarthy [1908–1957] whose Senate investigating committee was ruthless in its attempt to "root out subversives"), when people who held various socialist ideas were "red-baited" — accused of being communists and often made unemployable if not actually imprisoned.

Today there are strong noncommunist socialist parties throughout Europe. During the 1980s, there were socialist governments in Greece, Spain, Portugal, Italy, and France. The Labour Party in Great Britain, which is socialist, has held office a number of times since World War II, and the socialists have controlled governments and had a strong influence on the structure of the economy in Scandinavia throughout this century. In Japan, the upper house of the Diet has recently been controlled by the Japanese Socialist Party.

The United States is the only Western democracy without a strong Socialist Party. This is true partially because of the prosperity of the nation, and partially because of the success of past government, media, and corporate efforts to identify socialism with Soviet communism and capitalism with democracy. This implied that anticapitalists of any sort are traitors to democracy.

There was a fairly strong Socialist Party in the United States during the last half of the nineteenth century and until World War I. In fact, during that war, Eugene V. Debs (1855–1926), the Socialist Party candidate for president, got over a million votes, even though he was in prison at the time for refusing to fight in the war.

After World War I, the U.S. government, in response to the Russian Revolution and fearing worldwide revolution based on the Soviet model, tried to repress communists and socialists throughout the United States. These actions were called the Palmer Raids. The Socialist Party in the United States never recovered its strength after that period.

Some socialist ideas, such as government support for a national health service, free childcare, public housing, and guaranteed jobs are advocated by members of the left wing of the Democratic party in the United States.

A sustainable economic effort is one that is self-renewing and does not exhaust the resources it depends upon. Sustainable agriculture is agriculture that does not use up the soil it depends upon, such as crop rotation. A nonsustainable use of cropland would be to graze cattle or sheep on it. Cattle and sheep tear up the land, root out plants, and over a long period of time deplete its nutrients and lead to soil erosion. Another nonsustainable use would be to grow one crop that depletes the soil year after year. This is often done because a particular crop produces a large short-term profit for the farmer.

Sustainable-yield timber harvesting is logging that is accompanied by replanting of trees in such a way that the number of trees taken and the number of trees growing back balance out. Ideally, sustainable timber harvesting can provide timber on a continuous basis so long as the amount of cutting is determined by the amount of timber that will be coming to maturity.

On a world scale, sustainable development is development that does not interfere with the functioning of ecological processes and life support systems. In particular it means that crops are managed ecologically, watershed forest protected, and **genetic diversity** preserved.

sustainable

,səs-'stā-nə-bəl

adj [from Latin *sustinēre,* to hold up, from *sub-, sus-,* up + *tenēre,* to hold]

The word *synergy* is derived from the Greek word *synergos,* which means working together (derived from *syn,* together, and *ergon,* work). Synergy is the cooperative activity of two physical agents, such as drugs or muscles, which, when working together, produce a combined result greater than they would have if working alone. A relationship is synergistic if it involves cooperative activity that produces a greater effect than either of the cooperating parties could provide individually.

The use of *synergy* has been extended to describe cooperative ventures that result in people enriching each other's lives and accomplishing more than they could merely as a collection of individuals. The concept of human synergistic functioning is part of the philosophy of **holism,** a view of life that holds that separations and divisions and reductions of things to their component parts destroys harmonious wholes and leads to dehumanization. Holists believe that people should work and live synergistically instead of competitively, and that within a person, all of the aspects of living — physical, spiritual, emotional, and intellectual — should function synergistically.

The word *synergy* is also used in the business world to describe the

synergy

'sin-ər-jē

n [from Greek *synergos,* working together]

benefits that sometimes accrue to a company through collaborative effort with other corporations or institutions of society. For example, there are synergistic relationships between university-based research departments, the federal government, and corporations. Basic research is carried out at the university and funded by federal funds. The results of the research are then made available to corporations that create and market products based on the research. This synergy makes it easier for the results of basic research to be turned into consumer products.

Another form of corporate synergy develops through mergers and acquisitions, which may or may not produce benefits to the merging corporations or the consuming public.

Political Science

To abolish something is to do away with it in such a thorough manner that it is unlikely ever to return. The word *abolish* and the related words *abolitionist* and *abolitionism* usually refer to institutions, customs, or ways of exercising power rather than to people or things. In the case of people and things, the word *annihilate* is usually considered more appropriate. Thus one can abolish royalty and annihilate the members of the royal family.

Abolition is often used in the special sense of referring to the influential movement, in the early to mid-nineteenth-century United States, that advocated complete elimination of slavery in the entire nation. Members of that movement were called abolitionists. Some of the most prominent abolitionists were the African-Americans Frederick Douglass (1817–1895), Harriet Tubman (1820–1913), David Walker (1785–1830), and Sojourner Truth (1797–1883). European Americans Harriet Beecher Stowe (1811–1896), Angelina (1805–1879) and Sarah Grimke (1792–1873), William Lloyd Garrison (1805–1879), and Henry Ward Beecher (1813–1887) were also strong proponents of the movement.

The abolitionists were very influential in mobilizing public opinion against slavery in the northern United States before the Civil War and exerted pressure on President Abraham Lincoln (1809–1865), who decreed the abolition of slavery in a preliminary Emancipation Proclamation in 1862 and a final one in 1863.

abolition

,ab-ə-'lish-ən

n [from Latin *abolēre,* to disappear]

Affirmative action is taken to correct or compensate for past or present discrimination. Its ultimate goal is to create a situation where the historical effects of discrimination no longer influence present activities and where present practices are nondiscriminatory. Most debates about affirmative action center around discrimination according to race, gender, or ethnicity.

For example, an affirmative-action program might be created to compensate victims, as a class, for the effects of past racism on current educational opportunity. Consider a private college that has had a history of refusing admission to African Americans in spite of their qualifications. That institution, because of a change in the social and moral climate or a change in the rules for receiving federal research moneys, may decide that it has to admit a considerable number of qualified African Americans (say 12 percent of the new freshman class) despite the fact that it has received applications from twice as many qualified white applicants as it has places. Reserving those 12 percent of the places in order to compensate for the fact that the school currently has no

affirmative action

ə-'fər-mət-iv 'ak-shən

n [from Latin *affirmare,* from *ad-,* to + *firmare,* make firm]

African-American students would be a form of affirmative action.

Setting aside a particular number of places for members of a group that has been a victim of discrimination (12 percent in the above case) creates a **quota**, a number of reserved places for that group.

Most affirmative-action programs in the United States result in positions that would ordinarily be filled by European-American males being reserved for people of color and women. This has been called affirmative discrimination by opponents of affirmative action. They take the position that the creation of quotas and the development of affirmative-action programs is both discriminatory and unconstitutional. Other people less charitably call this reverse racism, believing that this policy discriminates against the dominant group, usually white males.

Many debates about affirmative action suggest that its goal is to replace qualified white males by unqualified or less-qualified females and minorities through the use of quotas that are not tied to qualification. However, most arguments about affirmative action are over giving preference to equally qualified members of groups that have been victimized by discrimination over members of the discriminating group, to redress previous wrongs and bring the situation to a level of equity.

The constitutionality of the use of different forms of affirmative action to compensate for prior discrimination is currently being argued before the Supreme Court. The Court has declared some forms of affirmative action unconstitutional and has upheld other forms as constitutional. The specific characteristics of constitutional affirmative-action programs have not yet been unambiguously established.

anarchism

'an-ər-,kiz-əm, -är-

n [from Greek *anarchos,* having no ruler, from *an-,* no + *archos,* ruler]

Anarchy is the social state where people have no rulers or government, and where organizations develop on the basis of voluntary cooperation and the freely chosen association of individuals.

Anarchists call for the abolition of the state, and of all governmental authority. For them, people are essentially good and social life is corrupted by governments, national boundaries, and other imposed mechanisms of control.

There is no single anarchist philosophy. A major distinction must be made between those anarchists who believe in a stateless cooperative society, and those, usually called *libertarians,* who base their hostility to the state on its interference with the individual's right to own property and accumulate wealth. Cooperative anarchists who believe in the goodness of human beings are usually placed on the extreme left of the political spectrum. In fact, Karl Marx (1818–1883) predicted that the final **utopian** state of humanity would consist of a classless, stateless, self-governing anarchic world. A major philosophical anarchist who believed in altruism and the goodness of humanity was the Russian Peter Kropotkin (1842–1921). A contemporary U.S. anarchist thinker was Paul Goodman (1911–1972).

On the other hand, libertarians are usually placed on the extreme right of the political spectrum, believing as they do in totally unregulated free enterprise. These anarchists, concerned mostly with the protection of individual property and profit rights, share much in common with extreme laissez-faire capitalists. They do not believe in the perfectibility of humanity, and do believe that inequality in the distribution of wealth and resources reflects an essential inequality built into human nature. One of the most respected libertarian theorists is Ludwig von Mises (1881–1973).

Among anarchists there are different theories about how to achieve a stateless society. Some believe in separating themselves out of mainstream society and developing utopian communities. Others believe that communities can vote and deregulate themselves into an essentially stateless existence. Some believe in nonviolent action, and some few believe in violent insurrection.

Most political states, whatever their philosophy, are opposed to the anarchists in their midst and try to repress or eliminate them. This is purely a strategy for the state's own survival and applies particularly to anarchists of the left. One method used to discredit anarchists is to identify all of them with the few that are violent. Another method is to set agent provocateurs loose in the community and blame their actions on anarchists. These state police agents, whose job is to incite violence, are disguised as anarchists, and have been known, particularly in pre–World War I Europe, to set bombs, burn buildings, and in other violent ways give the authorities cause to deport or jail suspected anarchists.

A third method of discrediting anarchism is linguistic. The word *anarchy* is used in the media and in political rhetoric to mean chaos, and anarchists are portrayed as advocating philosophical, economic, and every other kind of disorder. However, it is important to understand that anarchist thinkers do not equate anarchism with chaos. On the contrary, they believe that people would thrive in a self-governing and self-regulating voluntary society.

apartheid

ə-'pär-ˌtāt, -ˌtīt

n [Afrikaans, from Dutch
apart, separate + *heid,* -hood,
the state of being]

The word *apartheid* means *separateness* in Afrikaans, the language of the Dutch-descended whites in the Union of South Africa. Apartheid is the social, economic, and political system engineered by the all-white Nationalist Party in the Union of South Africa after its victory in the 1948 elections to consolidate complete white control over nonwhites. Apartheid is a relatively recent development in South Africa's history, one that has been enforced by the use of state violence at the cost of many thousands of African, Asian, and colored lives. It extends from prohibiting mixed marriages and mixed housing areas to requiring people to be classified by race at birth and to carry passbooks that define their racial status. These race classifications are: white, African, mixed-race or "colored," and Asian. It has led to the removal of Africans to segregated reserves and has resulted in setting aside 13 percent of the least productive land in the nation for Africans and keeping 87 percent of the land for whites.

In the Union of South Africa, 14.3 percent of the people are white, 2.6 percent are Asian, 8.6 percent colored, and 74.5 percent African. In other words, apartheid legalizes the economic, social, and political dominance of 14.3 percent of the people over the other 85 percent.

The African National Congress, the United Democratic Front, and many church groups have opposed apartheid. In 1990, with the release of African National Congress leader Nelson Mandela and other nonwhite leaders from prison, and the beginning of discussions between whites and nonwhites on the dismantling of apartheid, there is hope for a future nonracist society in South Africa.

authoritarian

ȯ-ˌthär-ə-'ter-ē-ən, ə-, -ˌthȯr-

adj [from Latin *auctor,* promoter, originator, writer]

An authoritarian group, institution, or society is one that has all of its power concentrated in a single person or a small group. In such a group, the people in power are not responsible to anyone outside of the group. Authoritarianism is the opposite of democracy, where every individual is supposed to have an equal voice in governance.

Authoritarian groups can range from Boy and Girl Scout troops, social clubs, and families, to nations and corporations.

Surprisingly, some people submit willingly to authoritarian rule. Such people are said to have authoritarian personalities.

When an authoritarian group assumes power over all aspects of public and private life, it is said to be totalitarian. In a totalitarian state, personal life, marriage choice, work, speech, and politics are all controlled by the small group of people who hold power and their agents.

Totalitarianism is manifested within different types of political systems. For example, under the leadership of Joseph Stalin (1879–

1953), the Soviet Union was a totalitarian state that professed a communist ideology. Individual rights were not recognized, and millions of people were imprisoned and killed at the whim of the ruling party.

Fascism is another type of totalitarianism that is characterized by overriding national and racial pride, and extreme intolerance for outsiders. Usually at the head of a fascist state is a single dictator who is in control of a very strong repressive apparatus that is used to coerce cooperation and suppress dissent. Nazi fascism under Adolf Hitler (1889–1945) involved extreme German **nationalism**, which exalted Germany above all other nations in the world, and in addition identified Germans as members of a fictitious superior race of "Aryans." It went beyond this positive self-exaltation and set out upon a genocidal policy of eliminating so-called impurities that corrupted the race. This led to the genocidal attempt to kill all Jews that is called the **Holocaust**.

autonomy
ȯ-'tan-ə-mē

n [from Greek *autonomos*, self-ruling, from *autos*, self + *nomos*, law]

To be autonomous is to be self-governing. A person is autonomous if she or he is free to select her or his own values, resist pressures for conformity, and live according to those values.

A community or nation is autonomous if it is able to govern itself free from external social, economic, religious, and military pressure and control.

There are many struggles in the world today for both personal and national autonomy.

bias
'bī-əs

n [from Middle French *biais*, oblique]

There is a spectrum of words that indicate different degrees of antagonism people feel toward other people or groups of people. The same spectrum contains words that describe different degrees of control people exert over each other. Though there may be other words that fit into the spectrum, basic levels consist of the following seven words in order of increasing intensity: bias, prejudice, discrimination, exploitation, oppression, enslavement, and genocide.

Bias is strong dislike of a person, group of people, thing, or category of things. The word *bias* originally referred to a diagonal cut across the grain of a fabric. A bias cuts across the grain, disrupting the normal flow of life. Bias is an attitude that does not require any action or elaborate rationale. It is often based on feelings of discomfort and not on a theory or an **ideology**. Some biases are ingrained and difficult to overcome, while others can easily be given up. It is easy to pick up biases from one's family, friends, or the media. One of the most common causes of bias is fear of the unfamiliar.

Prejudice consists of prejudging a group of people or category of things to be negative or inferior. Though it may not lead to any hostile action, it is a closed-minded attitude that does not allow for a consideration of reasons and facts. It is a rigid, closed, rejecting attitude that is generalized toward all members of a group, whether one knows them or not. Thus prejudice against some ethnic groups by other ethnic groups cuts off communication between them. Ethnic prejudices such as the prejudice of the English against the Irish, or of Jews and Muslims against each other, can give rise to ethnic jokes and insults, avoidance, and, in extreme cases, physical violence. When an individual goes against the prejudices of a group to which she or he belongs, it is not uncommon to find that other members of that group become hostile toward the dissenter.

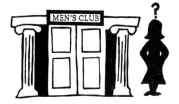

Discrimination is prejudice that exists in a situation where one group of people has the power to dominate another. When that dominant group turns its prejudice into actual, and often institutionalized, forms of depriving the oppressed group of rights or opportunities, discrimination takes place. Thus, in South Africa, when the dominant white minority deprived blacks of land, of access to education, and of the vote, racial prejudice became actual discrimination. In the United States, racial prejudice is a matter of personal opinion and not illegal, whereas job discrimination, in which a group of people is given inferior treatment, is illegal.

Exploitation consists of taking unfair advantage of a person, group of people, or natural resource for financial or other gain. For example, when industries in the United States employ illegal aliens at less than minimum wages because the aliens have no recourse to law, they are exploiting their labor for profit. Another example of exploitation is when women in a society are deprived of employment or the right to vote and are forced to raise children and labor in their homes without being paid.

It is possible to exploit people without being prejudiced against them. Scrooge, for example, had the reputation of exploiting everybody equally, that is, without prejudice. However, exploitation and prejudice are often to be found together.

Oppression consists of unreasonably harsh and cruel treatment of a person or group by another. Often oppression is added on top of exploitation, discrimination, and prejudice. It is used to force people to put up with being exploited. There is internal oppression in some nations where ethnic minorities are oppressed by majority populations. People have also been oppressed on the basis of their caste, religion, or class. In the case of many **colonialist** situations, the conquering power uses physical violence to intimidate people into working for free or for starvation wages. Oppression is often used to instill fear into a people as an attempt to control potential resistance and rebellion.

Enslavement consists of taking possession of a person and turning her or him into a slave, a thing, no longer a human being, fully owned and under the complete control of another. The only way for a slave to regain her or his humanity is by breaking the hold of slavery completely. There is no such thing as partial slavery, for though some slaves might be well treated, they still have no control of their own lives and destinies. Slavery ends with a manumission, that is, with complete release from slavery by a slaveowner, or with escape or rebellion.

Genocide is the deliberate, planned, and systematic attempt to kill an entire race, culture, religion, or other large group of people. The word was created by American attorney Raphael Lemkin during the war crimes trials held at Nuremberg after World War II as part of the indictment against Germans who were accused of participating in the Nazi attempt to commit genocide against Jews, homosexuals, and Gypsies.

Genocidal actions were perpetrated by Spanish and Portuguese invaders of the North and South American continents against native peoples. Countries such as Chile and Argentina, for example, have practically no surviving full-blood native peoples. Many other European settlers of the United States and Canada also carried out genocidal wars against native peoples. The Khmer Rouge attempted genocide against groups of Cambodian people during the 1970s and 1980s, resulting in more than a million and a half deaths.

Genocide was made a crime under international law by a United Nations Resolution of December 11, 1946, and by a United Nations Convention of December 9, 1948.

black consciousness movement

The black consciousness movement developed in South Africa in the 1970s. At that time the leading anti-apartheid organization, the African National Congress, was illegal, and its leaders (including Nelson Mandela [1918–]) were jailed. The central figure in the black consciousness movement was Steve Biko (1947–1977), who was murdered while being held in detention by the South African police.

The black consciousness movement, whose leaders tend to be much younger than those of the ANC, has a number of things in common with the **négritude** movement of the 1930s. It is centered around African cultural pride and the affirmation of the beauty and power of blackness. It advocates a thorough rejection of European values, the total and unambiguous elimination of apartheid, and the development of black majority power.

chauvinism

'shō-və-,niz-əm

n [from French *chauvinisme,* after Nicolas *Chauvin,* French soldier]

Chauvinism is excessive patriotism. Nicolas Chauvin was a soldier in Napoleon's army (circa 1815). He was wounded in battle and received a medal and a life pension. His outspoken and excessive enthusiasm for everything Napoleonic led people to call any over-riding glorification of one's country and army chauvinism. Chauvinism is fanatical patriotism.

The meaning of chauvinism has been extended to include excessive attachment and loyalty to any cause, place, or idea. Male chauvinism therefore is excessive glorification of men and advocacy of male dominance of women.

coalition

,kō-ə-'lish-ən

n [from Latin *coalescere,* to grow together]

A coalition is a group of people, organizations, clubs, or other groups that join together to accomplish a specific goal. Coalitions are temporary alliances, and members of a coalition do not usually agree on all issues, often agreeing to join together only for mutual convenience.

In parliamentary democracies like those found in Europe, there is no strong chief executive like the president in the United States. These governments are formed by a majority group in parliament. When no single party has a majority, many small parties can make the difference between a larger party being able to form a government or not. It is common to have coalition governments in parliamentary democracies. If a coalition falls apart, other groupings of parties are given a chance to form a majority coalition. If this fails, an election is called. It is possible to have yearly nationwide elections in parliamentary governments.

Coalitions usually have a general political and social orientation, being conservative, liberal, or progressive. Within that orientation, however, members of the coalition may have major differences.

In the United States, many local environmental, peace, and anti-war groups form national coalitions.

Many social scientists study political coalitions by looking at the formation of electorate groups, legislatures, the military, and large governmental and nongovernmental political groups.

Critical theory is the name given to a **radical** sociological theory that originated in Frankfurt, Germany, in the 1920s. According to critical theorists, a critical view of society, one that looks behind society's claims and articulates values and measures them against society's actual functioning, is necessary for the development of true democracy. Critical theorists reject the idea that it is possible to have a neutral social science that just studies social phenomena without criticizing them. They believe that social scientists should criticize society when it does not function democratically. For example, they analyzed the claims made by Western European societies and the United States that their societies were politically free and based on principles of free-market economics. Their analyses showed how so-called free markets are supported by government controls, banking and currency regulations, and the concentration of power in an increasingly small number of wealthy individuals. In the case of political democracies, they analyzed voting patterns, the social routes to political power, and the control of political processes by a small elite, in order to demonstrate the antidemocratic nature of supposedly democratic institutions.

The critiques developed by the Frankfurt School, as the critical theorists are usually called, were meant to lead to a critical awareness of those points in society where social change needed to be made in order for democracy to live up to its ideal images. Critical analysis was meant to lead to action that would transform society. The idea of social transformation is central to critical theory.

The transformation theory of the Frankfurt School has influenced many contemporary progressive thinkers. In this theory, social transformation is contrasted with social reproduction. A society, according to critical thinkers, tends to reproduce itself through education, culture, and other forms of initiation. Thus the powerful in a stratified society develop ways of reproducing economic and social inequalities while avoiding threats to their own power. One way of doing this, for example, is to propagate myths in schools and in the media, that those people who are rich deserve to be, and that everyone reaches the place in society that is appropriate to his or her skills and quality. If all people, poor as well as rich, come to believe that they are entitled to what they have and no more, forces for greater equality and justice will be resisted. According to critical theorists, the way to change this compliance with inequality is through the awareness of the inconsistencies and contradictions between what a society claims to be and what it really is. By seeing how the rich reproduce their power from generation to generation, for example, the poor can see how they have been duped and plan social action for the transformation of society.

Some of the main figures associated with the Frankfurt School are Herbert Marcuse (1898–1979), Theodor Adorno (1903–1969), and Walter Benjamin (1892–1940).

democracy

di-'mäk-rə-sē

n [from Greek *dēmokratia,* from *dēmos,* people + *kratos,* power]

The words *democracy* and *democratic* (with a small *d*) are derived from the Greek root *dēmos,* which means a township and, by extension, refers to the populace of a town or nation. A democracy is a society in which the population rules, not royalty, a small number of families, or the military. This apparently simple definition has some complex implications. Within every society that claims to be democratic there is some definition of membership or full citizenship that qualifies the nature of that particular democracy. For example, no known democracies give full voting rights to infants and young children, and many societies that call themselves democracies prohibit some classes of people from full participation. The United States Constitution as originally drafted and adopted in 1789, for example, did not provide for voting rights for people under the age of twenty-one, women, and slaves, though it proclaimed a democratic society. And fifth-century-B.C. Greek Athenian democracy also did not allow for children, slaves, or women to participate in major decision-making bodies.

It is very important to examine the specific meanings of the words *democracy* and *democratic* used in any discussion that claims that some group is democratic and another isn't, or that claims that one society is more democratic than another. For example, many articles and debates in the United States confuse political democracy (that is, the right to vote for leaders in the sphere of government) with free-enterprise capitalism, which is an economic system of unregulated competition. It is possible to have a socialist or communist economy in a democratic society, and the Scandinavian countries provide examples of political democracies that have an economic system that is a mixture of socialism and capitalism. The United States has an economic system that mixes free-enterprise capitalism with governmentally supported guarantees and insurance for financial institutions (such as banks and savings and loans) and some corporations (such as the automobile and computer industries in the recent past), as well as with some economic guarantees for individuals, such as Social Security and Medicare. It is very important when discussing democracy to be careful not to confuse economics and politics and to determine the specific nature of the democratic society that is being discussed.

There are several different kinds of democracy that one ought to be familiar with and take into account whenever writing or speaking about democracy. First there is the distinction between representative democracy and participatory democracy, both of which are forms of political democracy. In representative democracy, each citizen votes for representatives, who in turn run the government. The citizens do not have any direct control over the government and participate in decision-making and making laws only through elected representatives. Representative democracies have multiparty systems in which parties as well as candidates run against each other.

There are two common types of representative democracies: parliamentary democracy, as in the United Kingdom; and systems that have independently elected legislative and executive branches, as in the United States and the Soviet Union. In parliamentary democracies there is no elected president or head of state. Instead, the party or coalition of parties with a majority of seats in the parliament chooses a leader, called the prime minister. The prime minister represents the party that chooses her or him and can be replaced by that party without a popular vote. The president in a nonparliamentary democracy is chosen directly by the people and cannot be replaced by his or her political party.

Participatory or direct democracy differs from representative democracy in that people on a local level take part in making decisions about issues that affect their lives. The town meeting system in New England is an example of participatory or direct democracy. People get together regularly and discuss and vote on issues affecting their lives. Some powers are delegated to government employees subject to the will of the people. On a larger scale, local groups elect representatives to larger regional or national bodies. These representatives are expected to report to these local assemblies and receive their instructions from them. Direct democracies usually have one or no party systems and are designed to have decision-making located as close as possible to the people whose lives are affected by the decisions. Before recent reforms in the Soviet Union, the system of government was supposed to be based on a participatory democratic model, with the one party being the Communist Party. However, instead of ruling from the bottom up, the Communist system ruled from the top down, thereby cutting off direct democracy.

Democracy can function in different areas of life. When *democracy* is used to refer to the governance of a society (in terms of order, law enforcement, the maintenance of roads, national defense, etc.), one is talking about political democracy. In other words, in a political democracy the citizens choose through their votes the people who govern their political lives.

Economic democracy is quite different. An economic democracy is a society in which the people who control and distribute the economic resources of the society are chosen by the people. In other words, it is democratically elected representatives and not private citizens who control businesses and other economic resources. Advocates of economic democracy believe that electoral control of economic resources will produce a more equitable and just distribution of wealth throughout society. Most Western European societies have elements of both economic and political democracy. For example, there are many nationally controlled airlines, medical services, and industries throughout Europe that are subject to the control of elected political representatives or people appointed by them. However, in Europe there is also a substantial private industrial and business sector that is not subject to control (though it is subject to limitation and regulation). There is considerably less economic democracy in the United States than there is in Europe.

When the entire economic structure of a society is under the control of elected officials, a socialist democracy exists. In that case there is no private economic sector. When there is a mixture of elected and private control, with a strong emphasis on a welfare state and a support for unions and other workers' organizations, it is called a social democracy. Social democratic parties advocate a mixed public and private economy, government support for a minimum of security for all citizens, including health, employment, and living standards guarantees (called a **safety net**). There are many social democratic parties throughout Eastern and Western Europe.

It is very important, when writing or talking about democracy, to use the word carefully and thoughtfully. Sentences like the following lead to misunderstandings and insensitivity to the social and political structure in societies other than our own:

"That is the most democratic society in the region," when applied to a society in which the vote is restricted to landowners and the government has no economic control, and meant to be contrasted with another social democratic society, not centered in free enterprise, that has economic democracy but has a one-party direct democratic system. In this case, the comparison has to be spelled out and economic, social, and political democracies have to be compared.

"In a democracy everybody has an equal chance to be wealthy." This confuses economics with politics. In some economic democracies that may be true, but there are political democracies where the boundary between the rich and poor is clear and uncrossable.

Feminism consists of viewing all aspects of experience — from economics and ideology, to culture, politics, the media, and the arts — from the perspective of how they affect women's lives. It is based on the principle that women and men are entitled to and must have the same rights, and advocates action to eliminate any inequities based on gender or **sex.**

Central to a feminist perspective is a critique of male dominance in culture and society in the United States and Western Europe. This critique extends to gender roles and male dominance in other cultures throughout the world. A word commonly used by feminists to describe male dominated culture is **patriarchy,** the system of personal and institutionalized rules, customs, and behaviors that lead to and enforce male dominance.

Feminists within a given society often call into question the grounds of many aspects of culture and behavior within that society. This can lead to major confrontations and sometimes to major social, cultural, economic, and political changes. Within the United States, feminists have questioned the patriarchal ideas that "the woman's place is in the home," that women and not men have the obligation to raise children, that men should control the money and inheritance of the family, and that women should not be politically enfranchised or have the right to vote (to have suffrage). All of these ideas manifest the central premise that women should be dependent upon men.

American feminists have struggled to abolish these restrictions on women's freedom since the 1848 Seneca Falls Woman's Rights Convention in Seneca Falls, New York. Led by Elizabeth Cady Stanton (1815–1902), Susan B. Anthony (1820–1906), and Lucretia Coffin Mott (1793–1880), the three hundred women attending that convention declared in a women's Declaration of Independence: "We hold these truths self evident, that all men and women are created equal," and demanded, in addition to the vote, that the government "abolish all laws which hold married women less accountable for their acts than *infants, idiots,* and *lunatics.*"

Many of the demands of the Seneca Falls Convention are still being fought for. However, there has been a feminist strand in politics and social struggle in the United States throughout the nineteenth and twentieth centuries. Over that time there have been periods of greater and of lesser feminist activity. The second period of great activist feminism was from the turn of the twentieth century

feminism

'fem-ə-,niz-əm

n [from Latin *femininus,* from *femina,* woman; *fecundus,* fruitful, *felare,* to suck] until around 1920, when the women's suffrage movement triumphed and women won the right to vote. Under the leadership of Carrie Chapman Catt (1859–1947), Jane Addams (1860–1935), Elizabeth Gurley Flynn (1890–1964), Emma Goldman (1869–1940), and Margaret Sanger (1883–1966), women led a peace movement that opposed American entry in World War I, supported women's choice in childbearing and the right to contraception, and demanded the right to work and live independently outside the control of men, and the right of women to vote. Many members of the women's movement also joined **socialists, communists**, and other political **progressives** in struggles to eliminate poverty, **racism**, and **colonialism**. In 1916 Jeanette Rankin (1880–1973) of Montana became the first woman elected to the U.S. House of Representatives. Once seated, she led a congressional struggle for women's suffrage.

A third period of considerable feminist activism began in the 1960s and continues to the present. This incarnation began with an attack on the so-called "Feminine mystique" in the 1963 book of that title by Betty Freidan (1921–   ). This mystique consisted of glorifying the prosperous, white woman who was homemaker, mother, and sex symbol at the same time. This "new woman," though supposedly sexually liberated, stylish, and perpetually young, did not work outside the home, was economically dependent upon a husband, and had no independent political beliefs. In *The Feminine Mystique,* Freidan advocated that women work outside the home and control their own money as a way of negating passivity and dependence.

This post–Second World War image of prosperity and passivity was also rudely confronted by the civil rights struggle of the 1960s and the emergence of leadership from women of color such as Fannie Lou Hamer (1917–1977) and Ella Baker (1903–1986). In 1964 Freidan was instrumental in creating the National Organization of Women, which continues to be a major center of feminist activism. New leaders emerged in the 1970s in what was called the Women's Liberation movement (simplified in the popular press as "women's lib"). This movement fights for economic and social equality, and has had a powerful effect on electoral politics in the United States. Though there have been attacks on women's liberation by male (and a few female) journalists and politicians, the struggle for women's rights, linked once again to the struggle to eliminate poverty and racism, continues to be a formidable force on the American political scene.

Since the 1970s, an academic feminist movement has developed, creating what is called feminist criticism. Feminist criticism consists of a reexamination of literature, the arts, and society to study the ways in which women have been represented. Books have been examined from the point of view of the female characters; female authors' lives and struggles have been scrutinized in detail; out-of-print women's writing has been rediscovered and published; and the **canons** or criteria by which classics are judged by experts have been questioned and accused of sexist bias. New canons have been proposed. Feminist criticism has also reexamined the visual arts, and there have been many books and articles written about the representation of the female body and of sexuality in Western painting and sculpture. Critics such as Julia Kristeva, Toril Moi, and Luce Irigaray have written extensively on feminist linguistics, psychology, and philosophy.

Within the environmental movement, ecofeminism has begun to develop. Ecofeminism holds that the patriarchal values of conquest, competition, self-interest, abstraction, and repressed emotionality led to the exploitation of the earth and a callous indifference to pollution, crowding, and other forms of environmental degradation. It also holds that the matriarchal values of nurturing, compassion, generosity, and altruism are called for to heal the earth. Vandana Shiva has written extensively about ecofeminism.

In the 1970s and 1980s feminist scholars extended their critique to all areas of academic learning. An extensive feminist literature has developed within anthropology, the social sciences, philosophy, history, and other areas of the humanities.

Holocaust

'hō-lə-ˌkȯst, 'häl-ə-ˌkäst, 'hȯ-le-kȯst

n [from Greek *holokaustos*, burnt whole, from *holo-*, whole + *kaustos*, burnt]

In ancient times, a holocaust was a burnt sacrifice of a person or animal to the gods. By extension, a holocaust has come to mean a large-scale loss of life, especially one caused by fire.

The Holocaust is the name given by Jewish historians to the systematically planned attempt by Nazi Germany, from 1942 to the end of World War II in 1945, to physically exterminate all of European Jewry. This **genocidal** action was euphemistically called the "Final Solution" to the "Jewish Problem" by the Nazis.

The Nazis used mass gas chambers and assassination squads, and murdered between four and one-half and six million Jews in their attempted genocide.

In addition to the Jews, the Nazis attempted to murder all of the homosexuals and Gypsies in Europe. All of these murders were committed in an attempt by Hitler to "purify" the Aryan race. The notion of a blond-haired, blue-eyed superior race of northern Aryan peoples that needed to be kept pure was a fiction that Hitler used to justify this mass murder.

Intifada

ən-ti-fâ-'dâ

n [from the Arabic root *na-fada,* to shake, shake off]

The Intifada is the name of the current uprising of the Palestinian inhabitants of the West Bank and the Gaza Strip against the occupation by Israel. *Intifada* is Arabic for upheaval, or shaking off, and the goal of the Intifada is to shake off Israeli domination, and to create a separate Palestinian state in the land occupied by Israel since 1967.

The Intifada is also dedicated to building Palestinian national institutions and an independent economy. The basic idea behind the Intifada is for the Palestinian people to determine their own destiny, end dependency, and shake off external control.

The beginning of the Intifada, which is also called the Popular Uprising, is dated to an anti-occupation eruption in the Jabalya refugee camp in the Gaza Strip on December 8 and 9, 1987. During the Intifada, Palestinian adults and children have gone on strike, demonstrated, and thrown stones, primarily at armed Israeli troops and police, in an attempt to force Israel to give up occupied land and acknowledge an independent Palestinian state. Over eight hundred Palestinians have been killed in the course of the Intifada as of 1991.

liberalism

'lib(-ə)-rə-ˌliz-əm

n [from Latin *liberalis,* suitable for a freeman, generous, from *liber,* free]

Liberalism is the **ideology** of the free individual. People who hold this view believe that society is composed of distinct individuals rather than of different economic and social classes. Dorothy Thompson (1894–1961), an American liberal who actively urged the United States government to fight German fascism in the 1930s and Soviet communism in the 1950s, described the liberal position in this way:

> To be liberal means to believe in human freedom. It means to champion that social order which releases the greatest amount of human energy; permits greatest liberty for individuals and groups, in planning and living their lives; cherishes freedom of speech, freedom of conscience, and freedom of action, limited by only one thing: the protection of the freedom of others.

Liberal thinkers believe that the government's power to inhibit the social, economic, and political freedoms of the people should be limited. They do not believe in the government's right to interfere in the private affairs of individuals or limit freedom of speech or the right to privacy. Therefore, they tend to oppose making abortion illegal, legislating morality, and censoring the contents of books, art, and films. Most liberals, however, do believe that the state has a role in providing free public education for all people and in fighting poverty.

For the liberal, economic inequalities are considered to be natural.

The role of government is to prevent the worst inequalities while protecting the rights of people to keep what they have. A liberal economy includes the right to free trade, the existence of a free market, and the protection of property. Liberalism is associated with the free-enterprise system, but it differs from **conservatism** in advocating that the government provide a **safety net** for the poorest people and enforce minimum trade regulations in order to insure fair trading.

It is in this institutionalization of inequality and advocacy of capitalism that liberalism is directly opposed to **socialism, communism,** and all other forms of equalizing wealth and resources.

Many liberals in the United States are identified with the Democratic party, though there are a few Republicans who also identify themselves as liberals.

Nationalism consists of loyalty to a country or nation. In extreme forms it consists of exalting one nation above all others in the world. It is a potent force in determining the political and social behavior of many peoples. It is not necessarily tied to authoritarian rule; it can be found in democracies and dictatorships, in capitalist countries and socialist ones.

Nationalism emerges from people who share common territory, language, history, culture, and at times religion. In the course of history, however, some people who share such common bonds become divided through conquests and migrations. Many Armenians, for example, live in enclaves outside of Armenia but still are Armenian nationalists. Their primary loyalty is to Armenia rather than to the nation in which they currently live.

Nationalist sentiment can survive over hundreds of years despite changing political boundaries. Conflicts emerge within current countries based on old nationalist loyalties. One can see this happening throughout the world today. Yugoslavia is being split apart by nationalist struggles between Serbs, Croatians, Bosnians, and Slovenians. There are attempts by French-speaking Canadians to secede from Canada. In Nigeria there is an uneasy truce between Ibo and Yoruba peoples. And in the Soviet Union, Ukrainians, Russians, and other national groupings are claiming independence.

nationalism

'nash-nəl-,iz-əm, -ən-ᵊl-

n [from Latin *nation, natio,* birth, race, from *nasci,* to be born]

oligarchy

'äl-ə-ˌgär-kē, 'ō-lə-

n [from Greek *oligarchēs,* from *oligos,* few + *arkhein,* to rule]

An oligarchy is a government or organization in which the ruling power is in the hands of a small elite group. The word is often used negatively, with the implication that the elite rules for its own benefit and not for the benefit of the people ruled.

One modern argument for oligarchy states that large institutions cannot be run by "the people" but need a full-time corps of professional bureaucrats and managers to insure effective functioning. Management oligarchies of this sort exist in political parties, trade unions, and large corporations. These officials control the organization and sometimes ignore the interests and needs of its members, constituencies, or stockholders.

Another contemporary use of the word *oligarchy* refers to a small wealthy elite that makes major decisions in a democratic society even though its members are neither elected nor subject to public scrutiny. Members of the oligarchy are the people behind the political parties and government whose wealth gives them privileged access to power.

pacifism

'pas-ə-ˌfiz-əm

n [from French *pasifisme,* pacific, from Latin *pacificus,* peace]

Pacifism is a way of life that consists of refusing to use and actively opposing the use of war or any form of violence to solve conflicts. Some pacifists refuse any resort to violence on religious grounds or on moral principle, which they believe to be higher than human-made law. Four of the leading pacifists of the last hundred years were the Russian writer Leo Tolstoi (1828–1910), the South African/ Indian leader Mohandas Gandhi (1869–1948), the American social activist Jane Addams (1860–1935), and the American religious and social leader Martin Luther King, Jr. (1929–1968). The Society of Friends, also known as the Quakers, is a Christian church that incorporates pacifism into its religious doctrine.

Because of their adherence to principles of nonviolence, many pacifists have been jailed and persecuted during times of war. Pacifist refusal to fight in a war is called conscientious objection, as it is based on moral belief and conscience. Conscience is an awareness of the moral qualities of one's actions combined with a desire to do good. It leads to action based on principle that can even go against laws, if these laws are considered immoral.

In the United States during World War I, Eugene B. Debs (1855– 1926), the head of the U.S. Socialist Party, was jailed for his pacifist opposition to that war and received almost a million votes for president while he was in prison. In Great Britain, the philosopher, mathematician, and social activist Bertrand Russell (1872–1970) was fired from his position at Cambridge University in 1916 for opposition to the same war.

Pacifism is not the only form of nonviolent response to conflict. Nonviolence can also be used as a political and social strategy by people who believe that there are times when the use of violence is justified as a basis for moral action. For example, during the civil rights movement of the 1960s in the United States, there were members of the Student Nonviolent Coordinating Committee (SNCC) who were committed to nonviolence as a strategy for eliminating legalized racism in the South, but who were also willing to, and eventually did, abandon that strategy when they believed it wasn't working. They replaced the strategy of nonviolence with a strategy of violent self-defense — that is, with the strategy of carrying guns and being willing to protect themselves violently against violent attack. These members of SNCC were never pacifists. They chose nonviolence during the early civil rights movement because they felt that by using violence they would all be killed and none of their goals would be achieved.

To be nonviolent does not mean to be inactive. There are forms of nonviolent action that can be used to bring about social and political change. Some of these are **boycotting** a business that is supporting violence or exploitation (e.g., the United Farm Workers' grape boycott); sitting-in to demonstrate opposition (e.g., sit-ins at American draft board offices to oppose the Vietnam war, and lunch counter sit-ins to oppose segregation in the American South during the 1960s); and marching and holding prohibited public demonstrations. Such demonstrations of nonviolent opposition are called direct actions.

Direct actions can involve breaking laws even though they do not involve violence. Actions that consist of the nonviolent breaking of civil laws on the moral grounds that they are protests against immoral public policies or activities are instances of civil disobedience. The philosophy of civil disobedience as a moral protest against immoral laws was articulated by both the American writer and thinker Henry David Thoreau (1817–1862) in his "Essay on Civil Disobedience" and by Mohandas Gandhi, whose theory of nonviolent action was called Satyagraha. *Satyagraha* is a Sanskrit word that means truth force.

polarize

'pō-lə-ˌrīz

v [from Latin *polaris*, polar, from *polus*, pole]

political spectrum

pə-'lit-i-kəl 'spek-trəm

In the context of a conflict between people, groups of people, or nations, a situation of polarization exists when there are two opposite views or positions with no apparent possibility of reconciliation. It is as if one group were at the North Pole and the other at the South Pole, or as if one were at the positive and the other at the negative pole of a battery. Just as magnetic poles repel each other, the groups in a polarized situation repel each other.

When polarization takes place, violence can result unless some common ground between opposing forces can be found and some compromises made.

The political spectrum is the range of common political orientations represented within multiparty democratic societies. The **metaphor** of political views as a spectrum, with a centrist middle ground and left-wing (liberal to socialist) and right-wing (conservative) proponents on either side, originated in France in the years before the French Revolution. In the Estates General, a parliamentary body formed in 1789, the king sat in the center with moderates who favored compromise between the conservatives and radicals and preservation of the monarchy based on concessions to the people. The conservative nobility and clergy, who advocated maintaining the **status quo** — retaining the monarchy and the privileges of nobility — sat on the king's right. On his left were the liberal and radical representatives of the common people, who advocated the abolishment of the monarchy and the nobility.

Today, the makeup of parliaments in multiparty political democracies are described in terms of left, center, and right. The left wing represents the parties advocating greater equality and wider distribution of resources, often with an emphasis on placing responsibility for these actions on a centralized government. The right represents parties advocating freedom from economic regulation by the central government through a free-market economy. The center tries to moderate between the left and right, and tends to describe itself as a force that wants to protect stability above all.

This definition of political orientations encompasses both the political and economic views of the parties represented in government. Within the left and right there are also variations, as can be seen in the diagram of the political spectrum as it is usually constituted. Note that the center is a compromise position and its characteristics vary according to the distribution of parties in a parliament. For example, if the majority in a parliament were conservative, the center would be moderately conservative; but if the majority of the parliament were communist and socialist, the center would likely be liberal or social democrat.

Political Orientations Represented in Multiparty Democracies

LEFT WING
anarchist — communist — socialist — democratic socialist

CENTER
social democrat — liberal — moderate

RIGHT WING
conservative — neoconservative — reactionary — fascist — libertarian

The number of political parties within multiparty democracies varies widely. In the United States, for example, there is essentially a two-party system. A few small minority parties do exist, but none has any representation on a national level and few have representation on a state or local level. In other countries, such as Italy, France, Nicaragua, and Israel, representation in national governments ranges across the entire political spectrum, with members ranging from communist to conservative.

The three major meanings of the word *right* derive from the Latin *rex,* ruler or king. These meanings can be best understood through considering the oppositions right/left, right/wrong, and right/privilege.

The opposition right/left originally referred to different sides of a front-facing human body. An imaginary line running from the top of the head to the floor splits the body in two, dividing the body into left and right. The side containing the dominant hand, or the one that most people use to write, throw, handle a sword, shake, raise in order to show allegiance, and salute with, is the right or royal side. The right hand was used to hold the royal scepter. The other side, which is considered to be weaker, is the left side.

The opposition right/left is also used in a relative sense. Something is to the right of another thing if, when you face it, it is more in the direction of the right side of your body than the left side. Something is to the left of another thing if, when you face it, it is more in the direction of the left side of your body than the right side.

The opposition right/wrong refers to moral principles. The morally right is what is just, good, or proper. "Right" behavior, thinking, and action are defined according to some moral code, and when one considers arguments about what is right or wrong, it is essential to uncover the grounds upon which these claims are made.

Consider the statement "Capital punishment is wrong." It requires

rights

'rīts

n [from Latin *regere,* to lead straight, direct, rule, from Greek *oregein,* to stretch out] a justification, grounded in some code of moral behavior that defines and accounts for good and bad. Often claims like this one are unexamined and taken as absolutes. Once the grounds for making the statement are uncovered, it is possible to debate the validity of those principles and then of the original claim. In the case of disagreements over capital punishment, for example, it may turn out that people have fundamental disagreements on the value of human life.

The opposition right/privilege refers to the distinction between those freedoms which people are entitled to simply by being human, and those which can be earned or otherwise acquired. In **medieval** times, working people did not have rights but instead had duties they owed to their lord, the king, and the Church. Some special trading rights were reserved for merchants, tradespeople, and others who were necessary for the maintenance of the economy.

During the European Renaissance of the 1400s and 1500s, merchants and small-business people began to claim certain basic human, natural, or inalienable rights that they believed were owed them in return for service and loyalty to their rulers. These people denied that lords, princes, and priests had any special divine rights bestowed upon them directly by God. In fact, they shifted the claim for rights from the area of religion to the area of nature, and claimed that it is in the nature of humanity to have certain freedoms. This began a debate over what rights people can claim, which continues even today.

The United Nations developed a Universal Declaration of Human Rights in 1948. This declaration was an attempt to enumerate the rights to which the founders of the U.N. believed all people were entitled, and affirmed people's rights to be able to perform those fundamental activities necessary for the maintenance of human life. These rights are divided into the following categories:

- Political rights, which concern the relationship of individual citizens to their government. The right to take part in public affairs gives citizens the opportunity to affect their government. The right to assemble, vote, and move about freely are other protections provided by political rights.
- Economic rights, which govern access to economic resources and the protection against poverty. The right to a job, a home, to form trade unions, and to be protected from hunger are economic rights protecting the individual's health and security. There are many disagreements over these rights, and many nations, such as the United States, hold that economic rights do not exist.
- Civil rights, which support the individual against the

government and other individuals. The right to a fair trial by jury protects the individual from a corrupt court system. Freedom of speech and religion are civil rights that protect one's own judgment and thought.

The distinction between **equity** and **equality** is a very important one in discussions of rights. Equality refers to an amount or quantity, while equity adds to equality the element of fairness. An example will illustrate the major, and often neglected, distinction between these two ideas:

Consider two groups of people, one extremely wealthy and the other extremely poor. Suppose that, in their society, both groups have equal rights to shop in any store, eat in any restaurant, and ride on any form of transport they can afford. Equality of opportunity exists in all areas of life for these people. However, it is possible to argue that the arrangement, though it provides for equality, is unfair. The poor simply can't take advantage of their equality and the arrangement is not equitable.

Some people argue that the only responsibility a society has to its citizens is to provide for equality. Others claim that equality is meaningless in the life of the poor without equity.-

How This Guide Was Made

In deciding upon the words to be included in this guide, I called upon a number of high-school and college teachers and students. I wanted to know the concepts and ideas that the teachers felt were essential for the mastery of an understanding of their subjects. I also wanted to find out the ideas and concepts students found most useful in helping understand texts and write about issues in their classes. The subjects I concentrated upon were literature, the humanities, and the social and political sciences, including economics and anthropology.

I sent a questionnaire asking for a list of primary words and concepts in their areas of specialization to the entire humanities and social sciences faculty of Hamline University in St. Paul, Minnesota, where I taught during the academic year 1989/90. I also sent another questionnaire to the students at Hamline. The more than fifty faculty responses and one hundred fifty student responses led to a preliminary list of words, most of which I eventually included in the dictionary.

In addition to Hamline students and faculty, twenty high-school teachers I have worked with (and their more than four hundred students) helped formulate additional lists of ideas and concepts, which were then merged with the Hamline lists.

I also pursued the list formation with friends and students, adding words and concepts that seemed useful and powerful but had not appeared on the other lists.

In order to test out the importance of mastering central ideas and concepts, I taught a freshman seminar at Hamline called "Words as Definitions of Experience." The subject of the class was the study of words that represented powerful concepts and ideas. It centered on several clusters of words representing styles, political and social orientations, and the language of philosophy and criticism. I have since spoken to many of the students in the class and they tell me that it helped them navigate their other classes and provided a conceptual and critical groundwork for their subsequent studies. As a consequence, I believe that classes devoted to enriching students' conceptual armory are worth pursuing in high school and college. Recently I have taught several teacher-education classes based on that premise. Since young people in our society are too often linguistically and conceptually impoverished, classes devoted specifically to learning how to read, write, and speak intelligently and master intellectual concepts make sense and are urgently needed.

The final list of words defined in this guide appeared on more than one of the lists I gathered. I also included words that have been recommended as central to current intellectual debate. Naturally, there are many words that I did not include, several volumes of them perhaps.

Before writing an entry, I checked at least four standard dictionaries and several specialty dictionaries that included that word. In addition, other books on word origins and the history of discourse in academic fields were consulted. A partial list of my sources is included in the bibliography.

I also read books and articles in professional journals where the entry was commonly used, sat in on high-school and college classes that used the vocabularies included in the dictionary, and listened to taped panels and speeches by experts in the humanities. If I had any question about the entry, I then consulted specialists in the field.

The first draft of every entry was read by recent high-school and college graduates as well as teachers and professors, and their comments were incorporated in revised drafts. In addition, my editors at Little, Brown provided several close readings of the text with hundreds of insightful and useful comments, and I have responded to all of them.

The major guiding principle I used in writing was to avoid defining words in terms of other words that might not be known by students. This was not always possible, so I have cross referenced words that require additional conceptual understanding. The entries have not sacrificed complexity for ease of reading, and for that reason some of them are longer and more detailed than others.

This first effort at producing a guide of powerful ideas, if successful, will hopefully lead to additional volumes. The two years I've spent putting this book together have given me an enhanced sense of the power and importance of thinking clearly and speaking well. I have learned to speak all over again with the wonder and freshness about words I sense in five- and six-year-olds and find too often lost in fifteen- and twenty-year-olds. It has been an exhilarating adventure, one I hope the reader shares.

Bibliography

General Resources

Ayto, John. *The Longman Register of New Words*. Essex, England: Longman, 1989.

Bullock, Alan, and Stephen Trombley. *The Harper Dictionary of Modern Thought*. New York: Harper and Row, 1977.

Bullock, Alan, and R. B. Woodings. *20th Century Culture: A Biographical Companion*. New York: Harper and Row, 1983.

Ciardi, John. *A Browser's Dictionary*. New York: Harper and Row, 1980.

Comrie, Bernard, ed. *The World's Major Languages*. New York: Oxford University Press, 1987.

Cooke, Jean, Ann Kramer, and Theodore Rowland-Entwistle. *History's Timeline*. New York: Crescent Books, 1981.

Cowie, A. P., R. Mackin, and I. R. McCaig. *Oxford Dictionary of Current Idiomatic English*. 2 vols. Oxford: Oxford University Press, 1983.

Editorial Staff of the Longman Group Ltd. *Longman Dictionary of the English Language*. London: Longman, 1984.

McAdam, E. L., Jr., and George Milne. *Johnson's Dictionary*. New York: Pantheon Books, 1963.

Mencken, H. L. *The American Language*. New York: Alfred Knopf, 1977.

Onions, C. T. *The Shorter Oxford English Dictionary*. 2 vols. Oxford: Clarendon Press, 1959.

Partridge, Eric. *Origins*. New York: Macmillan, 1959.

Shipley, Joseph T. *Dictionary of Early English*. Totowa, NJ: Littlefield, Adams, 1968.

————. *Dictionary of Word Origins*. New York: Philosophical Library, 1945.

Soukhanov, Anne H., executive ed. *Roget's II, The New Thesaurus*. Boston: Houghton Mifflin, 1988.

Trager, James. *The People's Chronology*. New York: Holt, Rinehart and Winston, 1979.

Watkins, Calvert, ed. *The American Heritage Dictionary of Indo-European Roots*. Boston: Houghton Mifflin, 1985.

Van Doren, Charles, ed. *Webster's American Biographies*. Springfield, MA: G. and C. Merriam, 1975.

Vernoff, Edward, and Rima Shore. *The International Dictionary of 20th Century Biography*. New York: NAL Books, 1987.

Subject Area Resources

A Dictionary for Believers and Nonbelievers. Moscow: Progress Publishers, 1985.

Abrams, M. H. *A Glossary of Literary Terms*. 3rd ed. New York: Holt, Rinehart and Winston, 1971.

Barnhart, Robert K. *Dictionary of Science*. Boston: Houghton Mifflin, 1986.

Bottomore, Tom, ed. *A Dictionary of Marxist Thought*. Cambridge, MA: Harvard University Press, 1983.

Conn, Peter. *Literature in America: An Illustrated History*. Cambridge: Cambridge University Press, 1989.

Considine, Douglas M., and Glenn D. Considine, eds. *Van Nostrand's Scientific Encyclopedia*. New York: Van Nostrand Reinhold, 1983.

Dantzig, Tobias. *The Language of Science*. London: George Allen and Unwin, 1954.

Deane, Phyllis, and Jessica Kuper, eds. *A Lexicon of Economics*. New York: Routledge, 1988.

Dixon, Richard R., ed. *Dictionary of Philosophy*. New York: International Publishers, 1984.

Editorial Staff of H. S. Stuttman Co. Inc. *The Illustrated Science and Invention*. New York: H. S. Stuttman, 1977.

Elliott, Emory, ed. *Columbia Literary History of the United States*. New York: Columbia University Press, 1988.

Evans, Sara M. *Born for Liberty: A History of Women in America*. New York: Free Press, 1989.

Flexner, Stuart Berg, editor-in-chief. *The Random House Dictionary of the English Language*. Second edition, unabridged. New York: Random House, 1987.

Fuller, B. A. G. *A History of Philosophy*. 2 vols. New York: Henry Holt, 1945.

Gellert, W., and H. Kustner, M. Hellwich, H. Kastner, eds. *The VNR Concise Encyclopedia of Mathematics*. New York: Van Nostrand Reinhold, 1977.

Goldsmith, Edward, and Nicholas Hildyard. *The Earth Report*. London: Price Stern Sloan, 1988.

Gould, Julius, and William L. Kolb. *A Dictionary of the Social Sciences*. New York: The Free Press, 1964.

Harvey, Paul. *The Oxford Companion to Classical Literature*. Oxford: Clarendon, 1951.

Helms, Harry L., Jr. *Computer Language Reference Guide*. Indianapolis: Howard W. Sams, 1980.

Huyghe, Rene, ed. *Larousse Encyclopedia of Prehistoric and Ancient Art*. New York: Prometheus Press, 1957.

James, Glenn, and Robert C. James. *Mathematics Dictionary*. New York: Van Nostrand Reinhold, 1976.

Kline, Morris. *Mathematical Thought from Ancient to Modern Times*. New York: Oxford University Press, 1972.

Kneale, William, and Martha Kneale. *The Development of Logic*. Oxford: Clarendon Press, 1962.

Kramer, Edna E. *The Nature and Growth of Modern Mathematics*. New York: Hawthorne Books, 1951.

Kuper, Adam, and Jessica Kuper. *The Social Science Encyclopedia*. New York: Routledge, 1985.

Meadows, A. J., M. Gorden, and A. Singleton. *Dictionary of New Information Technology*. New York: Kogan Page, 1982.

Medawar, P. B., and J. S. Medawar. *Aristotle to Zoos*. Cambridge, MA: Harvard University Press, 1983.

Myers, Bernard S., ed. *McGraw-Hill Dictionary of Art*. 4 vols. New York: McGraw-Hill, 1969.

Myers, Jack, and Michael Simms. *The Dictionary of Poetic Terms*. New York: Longman, 1989.

Preminger, Alex, Frank J. Warnke, and O. B. Hardison, Jr., eds. *Princeton Encyclopedia of Poetry and Poetics*. Princeton: Princeton University Press, 1974.

Quine, W. V. *Quiddities*. Cambridge, MA: The Belknap Press, 1987.

Ralston, Anthony, ed. *Encyclopedia of Computer Science and Engineering*. New York: Van Nostrand Reinhold, 1976.

Randel, Don Michael. *The New Harvard Dictionary of Music*. Cambridge, MA: The Belknap Press, 1986.

Stockley, Corinne, and Lisa Watts. *Usborne Guide to Computer Jargon*. London: Usborne Publishing, 1983.

Theodorson, George A., and G. Achilles Theodorson. *A Modern Dictionary of Sociology*. New York: Harper and Row, 1969.

Uvarov, E. B., and Alan Isaacs. *Dictionary of Science*. New York: Penguin Books, 1986.

Miscellaneous Other Resources

Barltrop, Robert, and Jim Wolveridge. *The Muvver Tongue*. London: Journeyman Press, 1980.

Bartlett's Familiar Quotations. 16th ed. Boston: Little, Brown, 1992.

Bierce, Ambrose. *The Devil's Dictionary*. New York: Dover Publications, 1958.

Bernal, Martin. *Black Athena: The Afro-Asiatic Roots of Classical Civilization*. Vol 1. New Brunswick, NJ: Rutgers University Press, 1987.

Blumberg, Dorothy Rose. *Whose What?* New York: Holt, Rinehart and Winston, 1969.

Boatner, Maxine Tull, and John Edward Gates, with Adam Makkai, eds. *A Dictionary of American Idioms*. Woodbury, NY: Barron's Educational Series, 1975.

Briggs, Katharine. *An Encyclopedia of Fairies*. New York: Pantheon Books, 1976.

Byrne, Josefa Heifetz. *Mrs. Byrne's Dictionary*. New York: University Books and Citadel Press, 1974.

Chase, Stewart. *The Tyranny of Words*. New York: Harcourt Brace, 1938.

Davidson, Gustav. *A Dictionary of Angels*. London: Free Press, 1967.

Dennon, Lester E., ed. *Bertrand Russell's Dictionary of Mind, Matter, and Morals*. New York: Philosophical Library, 1952.

Funk, Charles Earle. *Thereby Hangs a Tale*. New York: Warner Paperback, 1950.

Funk, Wilfred. *Word Origins and Their Romantic Origins*. New York: Funk and Wagnalls, 1950.

Hirsch, E. D., Jr. *Cultural Literacy*. Boston: Houghton Mifflin, 1987.

Kohl, Herbert. *A Book of Puzzlements*. New York: Schocken, 1981.

Levinson, Leonard Louis. *The Left Handed Dictionary*. New York: Collier Books, 1963.

Lipton, James. *An Exaultation of Larks*. New York: Penguin Books, 1968.

Maire, Albert. *Materials Used to Write Upon Before the Invention of Printing*. Seattle: Facsimile Reproduction, 1967.

Pepper, John. *Ulster-English Dictionary*. Belfast: Appletree Press, 1981.

Room, Adrian. *Dictionary of Confusing Words and Meanings*. New York: Dorset Press, 1985.

Sorel, Nancy Caldwell. *Word People*. New York: American Heritage Press, 1970.

Walsh, Jill Paton, and Kevin Crossley-Holland. *Word Hoard Anglo-Saxon Stories*. Farrar, Straus and Giroux, 1965.

Wentworth, Harold, and Stewart Berg Flexner. *Dictionary of American Slang*. New York: Thomas Y. Crowell, 1967.

Williams, Raymond, ed. *Key Words*. New York: Oxford University Press, 1983.

Handbooks and Guides

Hornby, A. S. *A Guide to Patterns and Usage in English*. London: Oxford University Press, 1957.

Epstein, Carol. *The Doubleday Manual of Indexing*. New York: Doubleday, 1983.

Follet, Wilson. *Modern American Usage*. New York: Hill and Wang, 1966.

Fowler, Ramsey H. *The Little, Brown Handbook*. 3rd ed. Boston: Little, Brown, 1980.

Frank, Francine Wattman, and Paula A. Treichler. *Language, Gender, and Professional Writing*. New York: Modern Language Association of America, 1989.

Strunk, William, Jr., and E. B. White. *The Elements of Style*. New York: Macmillan, 1979.

Complete Word List

[The words in the **boldface** type have listings of their own. The words in text type are used or defined in the listings next to them. They do not have independent listings of their own.]

empiricism 65
enlightenment/nirvana 51
Enlightenment, the 65
enslavement, see bias
epic, see genre
epiphenomenalism 66
epistemology 66
epitaph, see genre
equality, see rights
equity/equality, see rights
ergonomics 197
eschatology 51
essence/existence 67
ethnocentric 137
ethnographic, see culture
etymology 138
Eurocentric, see anthropology; ethnocentric; geist; hegemony
evolution 115
evolutionary, see culture; evolution
existence, see essence/existence
existential choice, see Buridan's ass; existentialism
existential psychology, see existentialism
existentialism 68
existentialist, see angst; Buridan's ass; existentialism; ontology
experiencing subject, see phenomenology
experimental group, see psychology
exploitation, see bias
expressionism 9
extrovert, see introvert/extrovert
fallacy 117
falsification theory, see induction/deduction
falsify, see induction/deduction
fascism, see authoritarian; political spectrum
fascist, see political spectrum
fatalism 69
feedback, see cybernetics
feminine language, see semiotics
feminism 219
feminist criticism, see feminism
figures, see logic
first peoples, see aboriginal
fixated, see psychoanalysis

form, see classical; structuralism
formal system, see logic
formal, see logic
found poems, see genre
Frankfurt School, see critical theory
free association, see psychoanalysis
free market, see political spectrum; utilitarianism
free, see critical theory
function, see structure
futurism, see modern
Gaia hypothesis 118
gay, see sexual orientation
gedanken experiment 119
geist 161
gender, see sex
genetic determinism, see evolution 120
genetic diversity
genocide, see bias
genotype/phenotype 181
genre 31
gestalt 181
gestalt psychology, see gestalt
Godel's theorem, see logic
Gothic, see medieval
grand style, see stylistics
Great Chain of Being 69
Grimm's law, see phonology
hegemony 163
hermaphrodite, see androgyous
hermeneutic, see hermeneutics; poststructuralism
hermeneutics 32
heterogeneous, see homogeneous/heterogeneous
heterogeneously grouped, see homogeneous/heterogeneous
heterosexual, see sexual orientation
heuristic 120
hieratic style, see stylistics
high style, see stylistics
Hispanocentric, see ethnocentric
Hobson's choice 94
holism 95
holist, see cognitive/affective; holism
holistic, see holism; atomism

Holocaust 221
homogeneous/heterogeneous 164
homogeneously grouped, see homogeneous/heterogeneous
homophobia, see sexual orientation
homosexual, see sexual orientation
human ecology, see ecology
humanism, see renaissance
humanities, the, see renaissance
human-scale, see ergonomics
hyperbole 33
hypothesis, see inductive/deductive; ontogeny/phylogeny
hysterical paralysis, see psychoanalysis
iatrogenic, see jargon
iconoclasm 121
iconography/iconology 11
id, see psychoanalysis
ideal 122
idealism 70
idealist, see ideal
ideologues, see ideology
ideology 165
imperialism/colonialism 198
imperialist, see anthropology; imperialism/colonialism
impressionism 11
inalienable rights, see rights
incomplete, see logic
incunabula 34
indeterminism 70
indigenous 138
induction/deduction 95
inductive, see induction/deduction; method
inductive fallacy, see fallacy
industrialization, see Sturm und Drang
inequities, see feminism
institutionalized sexism, see sexism
inferences, see logic
inheritance of acquired characteristics, see genotype/phenotype
institutional racism, see race
institutionalized sexism, see sexism
intentionality, see phenomenology

scholastic, see **ontology**
scientific method, see **method**
sector 200
secular, see **evolution**
self-interest, see **altruism;
matriarchy/patriarchy; utilitarianism**
self-reference, see **paradox**
self-regulating system, see **cybernetics**
semantics, see **linguistics; structuralism; syntactics/semantics**
semiotics 145
service sector, see **sector**
servomechanism, see **cybernetics**
sex 146
sexism 167
sexual orientation 147
sexuality, see **sex**
sexual preference, see **sexual orientation**
shadow, see **archetype**
shaping, see **psychology**
signified, see **semiotics**
signifier, see **semiotics**
simile 40
Skinner box, see **psychology**
social altruism, see **altruism**
social class, see **class**
social Darwinists, see **altruism;
race**
social democracy, see **democracy**
social democrat, see **political spectrum**
social realism, see **realism**
socialism 201
socialist democracy, see **democracy; political spectrum**
socialists, see **altruism; political spectrum; socialism**
socialization 168
sociobiologists, see **altruism**
sociobiology, see **evolution**
socioeconomic classes, see **class**
sociolingustics, see **linguistics**
sociology 168
Socratic irony, see **irony**
solipsism 82

sovereignty, see **authoritarian**
spectrum, see **political spectrum**
status quo, see **change; political spectrum**
stimulus, see **cybernetics; psychology**
stratification, see **class**
stream of consciousness 190
streaming, see **homogeneous/heterogeneous**
structuralism 148
structuralist, see **poststructuralism; semiotics; structuralism**
structure 105
Sturm und Drang 20
style 21
stylistics 41
subject/object 83
subjective/objective 83
sublimation, see **psychoanalysis**
subliminal 191
substance 84
suffrage, see **feminism**
superego, see **psychoanalysis**
surrealism 21
sustainable 203
sustainable development, see **sustainable**
sustainable yield, see **sustainable**
syllogism, see **logic**
syllogistic logic, see **dialectics**
symbiosis/parasitism 170
symbol 42
synchronic/diachronic 84
synecdoche 43
synergy 203
syntactics/semantics 150
syntax, see **linguistics; structuralism; syntactics/semantics**
synthesis, see **analysis/synthesis**
synthetic, see **analytic/synthetic**
tautology 106
technology 170
teleology 85
text 43
theism, see **agnosticism**
theorems, see **logic**

theory of natural selection, see **evolution**
theory, see **criticism; method**
thesis, see **dialectics**
Third Estate, see **political spectrum**
threshold, see **tolerance**
tolerance 171
tolerance of error, see **tolerance**
totalitarian, see **authoritarian**
tracking, see **homogeneous/heterogeneous**
tragedy, see **genre**
transformation theory, see **critical theory**
triage 172
trope 45
unconscious, see **archetype; mandala; psychoanalysis; psychotherapy**
undefined terms, see **analysis/synthesis; logic**
universal algorithm, see **algorithm**
universal calculating machine, see **algorithm**
universal calculus, see **logic**
universal grammar, see **syntactics/semantics**
universal human rights, see **Enlightenment, the; rights**
utilitarianism 86
utilitarians, see **abstract/concrete**
utopia/dystopia 88
utopian, see **anarchism; utopia/dystopia**
verification theory, see **induction/deduction**
verify, see **induction/deduction**
wave, see **atomism**
will to believe, the, see **pragmatism**
Women's Lib, see **feminism**
Women's Liberation, see **feminism**
working class, see **class**
zeitgeist, see **geist**
Zeno's paradoxes, see **paradox**